It is a paradox, that at a time when religiously motivated ~~~~ lence to achieve perverse objectives, the potential of the world's diverse religious traditions and institutions to contribute to peace and development is largely ignored. With this book, Katherine Marshall, one of the first international development specialists who has emphasized the critical importance of religion in global development, provides anyone working in international affairs with an outstanding introduction to and analysis of a topic that is far too important to ignore.

Michel Camdessus, Former Managing Director, International Monetary Fund

Faith and globalisation are two of the world's most powerful contemporary forces; the dynamics and contours of religion form today an integral part of international relations. Yet how much do we understand about how religions work as global institutions? And when you ring up Global Catholicism and Global Islam who is at the switchboard and to whom should you talk? This is a clear, helpful and deeply informed guidebook for those wise enough to recognise the transformative power of the world faiths in the 21st Century.

Ian Linden, Policy Director of the Tony Blair Faith Foundation and Associate Professor in the study of religion at the School of Oriental and African Studies, London.

This book provides a welcome corrective to the religious illiteracy that has for too long marked the study and conduct of policy-making in relation to the world's poorer countries. Katherine Marshall has provided a superb mapping and analysis of the world's main religions, religious movements, and myriad faith-inspired organizations, and the part they have played in recent times in advancing human development (or in some cases not). She also analyses succinctly the unresolved issues which prevent religious organizations from working more productively alongside non-religious actors, especially governments and international institutions such as the World Bank. Her book should be required reading for all students and practitioners of development.

Sir Tim Lankester, Honorary fellow at School of African and Oriental Studies, UK.

Goaded by events like the HIV and AIDS pandemic and terrorist attacks, there is mounting interest in religion among international relations specialists. However, the world of religious institutions is so complex that for many it is difficult to know where to start in making sense of different entities. Katherine Marshall's book is a carefully researched and readable introduction to how many religious and interfaith institutions work, informed by practical experience. It highlights the critical roles that they play in global affairs and, still more, their potential to work for peace, social justice, and the welfare of humankind.

Gunnar Stålset, former Bishop of Oslo, Norway.

Global Institutions of Religion

This work fills a significant gap in the current literature by providing a concise introduction to religious institutions and an insightful analysis of their role in world affairs.

Focusing on formal institutions specifically dedicated to governing religious communities, the work examines the intersections between religious and other global institutions, set against the fundamental question: why and how do these intersections matter?

The work explores the role of religion within key issues including:

- Human rights
- Human security
- International development and humanitarian relief
- Climate change
- Moral responsibilities

The new forms that religious institutions are taking, their fit with human rights and democratic ideals, and their changing nature in plural societies, are a highly relevant part of the global institutional picture and this book is essential reading for all students and scholars of global institutions, international relations, and religion.

Katherine Marshall is a senior fellow at the Berkley Center for Religion, Peace, and World Affairs at Georgetown University and Visiting Professor in the School of Foreign Service. As a long time development specialist focused on the world's poorest countries, she worked for over 35 years with the World Bank.

Routledge Global Institutions Series

Edited by Thomas G. Weiss
The CUNY Graduate Center, New York, USA
and Rorden Wilkinson
University of Manchester, UK

About the series

The Global Institutions Series has two "streams." Those with blue covers offer comprehensive, accessible, and informative guides to the history, structure, and activities of key international organizations, and introductions to topics of key importance in contemporary global governance. Recognized experts use a similar structure to address the general purpose and rationale for specific organizations along with historical developments, membership, structure, decision-making procedures, key functions, and an annotated bibliography and guide to electronic sources. Those with red covers consist of research monographs and edited collections that advance knowledge about one aspect of global governance; they reflect a wide variety of intellectual orientations, theoretical persuasions, and methodological approaches. Together the two streams provide a coherent and complementary portrait of the problems, prospects, and possibilities confronting global institutions today.

The most recent titles in the series are:

Crisis of Global Sustainability (2013)
by Tapio Kanninen

The Group of Twenty (2013)
by Andrew F. Cooper and Ramesh Thakur

Peacebuilding (2013)
by Rob Jenkins

Human Rights and Humanitarian Norms, Strategic Framing, and Intervention (2013)
by Melissa Labonte

Feminist Strategies in International Governance (2012)
edited by Gülay Caglar, Elisabeth Prügl, and Susanne Zwingel

Global Institutions of Religion

Ancient movers, modern shakers

Katherine Marshall

Routledge
Taylor & Francis Group

LONDON AND NEW YORK

First published 2013
by Routledge
2 Park Square, Milton Park, Abingdon, Oxon OX14 4RN

Simultaneously published in the USA and Canada
by Routledge
711 Third Avenue, New York, NY 10017

Routledge is an imprint of the Taylor & Francis Group, an informa business

British Library Cataloguing in Publication Data
A catalogue record for this book is available from the British Library

Library of Congress Cataloging in Publication Data
Marshall, Katherine, 1947–
  Global institutions of religion : ancient movers, modern shakers /
Katherine Marshall.
     p. cm. – (Routledge global institutions series; 75)
  Includes bibliographical references (p.) and index.
  1. Religion and politics. 2. Religion. 3. Religions. 4. World politics. 5.
Globalization–Religious aspects. I. Title.
  BL65.P7M346 2013
  206'.5–dc23
                    2012035253

ISBN: 978-0-415-78044-5 (hbk)
ISBN: 978-0-415-78045-2 (pbk)
ISBN: 978-0-203-58194-0 (ebk)

Typeset in Times New Roman
by Taylor & Francis Books

Contents

List of illustrations		viii
Foreword		x
Acknowledgments		xiii
List of abbreviations		xiv
	Introduction	1
1	Religion: An institutional portrait	9
2	Global religious bodies	48
3	Religious movements in a globalized world	93
4	Interfaith encounters: Institutions, approaches, and questions	129
5	Faith-inspired organizations at work	154
6	Emerging issues and future directions	184
	Notes	195
	Select bibliography	203
	Index	207
	Routledge Global Institutions Series	224

Illustrations

Figures

1.1	Mapping the major world religions	36
1.2	Major religious traditions by world region	37
1.3	Africa: an example of the revolution of changing religious demography	38
1.4	Smaller religious traditions by world region	42
1.5	Statistical measures of religious adherence	43
1.6	Institutional confidence	44
2.1	Catholic Church World Youth Day. Millions of young people gathered to welcome Pope Benedict XVI to World Youth Day in Madrid, Spain in 2011	65
3.1	Sri Sri Ravi Shankar visiting areas in Bihar affected by floods	102
4.1	Sant'Egidio at Georgetown University. The Annual Prayer for Peace interreligious gathering took place at Georgetown University in September 2006	141
5.1	The Dhammayietra. The mural, by artist Channa, shows the peace march led by Buddhist monk Maha Ghosananda from 1992 onwards. It features the Dhamma wheel pushed by Buddhist monks, peace-loving men and women, including people in wheelchairs, farmers, Catholic priests, nuns, and soldiers.	182
6.1	Religious minefields	194

Tables

1.1	Constitutional regimes and religion: selected countries	21
1.2	Major religions by world region	40
1.3	Smaller world religions by region	41
2.1	Religion and state: contemporary arrangements	52
6.1	Issues that often feature in secular/faith dialogue	192

Boxes

I.1	Terminology headaches	3
1.1	The Jewish diaspora	13
1.2	The Peace of Westphalia, nation-states, and religion's loss of authority	15
1.3	The Lisbon earthquake: disaster propelling change	17
1.4	Religious demography and fast-growing communities	38
2.1	Religion and secularism in India	53
2.2	China: approaching religion in new ways	55
2.3	Brazil: a dynamic approach to religious freedom and tolerance	56
2.4	Religion and governance in Muslim majority countries	58
2.5	State and church in Finland	59
2.6	The Order of the Knights of Malta	60
2.7	Pontifical Councils	63
2.8	France: defining and regulating cults	72
2.9	Muslim philanthropy on the rise	81
2.10	The World Islamic Call Society	82
2.11	Zionism and globalization	85
2.12	Zoroastrianism: the oldest of the revealed world religions	88
2.13	Bahá'í: a modern faith with a contemporary agenda	88
3.1	A movement's evolution: from the Oxford Group to Moral Re-Armament (MRA) to Initiatives of Change	95
3.2	Sri Sri Ravi Shankar's international organizations	101
3.3	A Japanese passion for peace	106
3.4	Modern religious figures: the case of Amr Khaled	116
4.1	A Common Word Between Us and You	144
4.2	Creation care and Christian-Muslim understanding	145
5.1	Caritas: a global confederation within the Catholic Church	158
5.2	The growth of World Vision, a faith-inspired Colossus	160
5.3	Islamic Relief: balancing faith traditions and international standards	162
5.4	The American Jewish World Service	164
5.5	A faith-inspired human development complex: the Aga Khan Development Network	165
5.6	From Christian Children's Fund to ChildFund International	166
5.7	Secrets to success? Compassion International	166
5.8	Charity and humanitarian work: religious roots in the Abrahamic faiths	168
5.9	Religious tensions and interfaith response in Sri Lanka	178

Foreword

The current volume is the seventy-fifth title in a dynamic series on global institutions. These books provide readers with definitive guides to the most visible aspects of what many of us know as "global governance." Remarkable as it may seem, there exist relatively few books that offer in-depth treatments of prominent global bodies, processes, and associated issues, much less an entire series of concise and complementary volumes. Those that do exist are either out of date, inaccessible to the non-specialist reader, or seek to develop a specialized understanding of particular aspects of an institution or process rather than offer an overall account of its functioning and situate it within the increasingly dense global institutional network. Similarly, existing books often have been written in highly technical language or have been crafted "in-house" and are notoriously self-serving and narrow.

The advent of electronic media has undoubtedly helped research and teaching by making data and primary documents of international organizations more widely available, but it has complicated matters as well. The growing reliance on the Internet and other electronic methods of finding information about key international organizations and processes has served, ironically, to limit the educational and analytical materials to which most readers have ready access—namely, books. Public relations documents, raw data, and loosely refereed websites do not make for intelligent analysis. Official publications compete with a vast amount of electronically available information, much of which is suspect because of its ideological or self-promoting slant. Paradoxically, a growing range of purportedly independent websites offering analyses of the activities of particular organizations has emerged, but one inadvertent consequence has been to frustrate access to basic, authoritative, readable, critical, and well-researched texts. The market for such has actually been reduced by the ready availability of varying quality electronic materials.

For those of us who teach, research, and operate in the area, such restricted access to information and analyses has been frustrating. We were delighted when Routledge saw the value of a series that bucks this trend and provides key reference points to the most significant global institutions and issues. They are betting that serious students and professionals will want serious analyses. We have assembled a first-rate team of authors to address that market. Our intention is to provide one-stop shopping for all readers—students (both undergraduate and postgraduate), negotiators, diplomats, practitioners from non-governmental and intergovernmental organizations, and interested parties alike—seeking insights into the most prominent institutional aspects of global governance.

Global Institutions of Religion

World religions and religious institutions were an understudied and underappreciated subject of public discourse and academic analysis, at least in the West, until the terrorist attacks of 9/11 served as a wake-up call to governments as well as policy analysts and scholars about the significance of religion in international affairs. As Katherine Marshall discusses in more detail in the Introduction to her book, one plausible explanation for this neglect is the relative dominance of a secular political discourse in the West, especially Europe, and a secular society that has been essentially disinterested in the academic study of religion. As a consequence, for example, Western scholars have underestimated the role of religion in the post-colonial resistance to dictatorships in the developing world, especially in the Middle East, and Central and South Asia. Since 9/11, of course, the appreciation for its influence has been evolving rapidly. Governments, think tanks, universities, and foundations have focused increasingly on feeding the vastly greater public and scholarly appetite to understand the global political role of religion and how religious institutions shape world events and processes.

We knew that we wanted a book on this vast topic and were delighted when Katherine accepted what might, for anyone else, have been an impossible assignment. She only recently stepped down after a 35-year career at the World Bank, a topic that she addressed in a well-received earlier volume in the series, *The World Bank: From Reconstruction to Development to Equity* (2008). In her last six years at the World Bank she served as senior advisor on topics not typically associated with international financial institutions—namely, faith, ethics, and values. Currently Katherine teaches about these topics at Georgetown University, where she is a senior fellow at the Berkley Center for Religion,

Peace and World Affairs. She is also the executive director of the World Faiths Development Dialogue, a non-governmental organization (NGO) based at the Berkley Center, and she serves on the boards of several other faith- and development-related NGOs. There are few people who have her extraordinary wealth of experience with religious institutions and their influence on world politics, and fewer still who can claim to be a participant observer in their machinations.

We are pleased to publish this book on such a crucial subject in the series. It fills a significant gap in the literature by providing a concise introduction to religious institutions and an insightful analysis of their role in world affairs. We wholeheartedly recommend it and, as always, welcome comments from our readers.

Thomas G. Weiss, The CUNY Graduate Center, New York, USA
Rorden Wilkinson, University of Manchester, UK
August 2012

Acknowledgments

This book is the product of a journey of learning and exploration of what was for me, in 1999, largely unknown territory: the worlds of religion. Asked by James D. Wolfensohn, then World Bank president and my boss, to help with a project to build bridges towards often hostile religious actors, I embarked on the task with some trepidation, discovering along the path vast reservoirs of knowledge, a complexity I had barely imagined, and constant challenges to the way I understood politics, society, history, values, and even geography. The book owes much to colleagues and critics who have challenged and enlightened me along the way. Among them are many within international institutions and especially at the World Bank (where I spent many years), at Georgetown University (especially my inquisitive and skeptical students), and at the World Faiths Development Dialogue (the NGO born of the creative visions of James D. Wolfensohn and Lord Carey of Clifton). Patrice Brodeur, Robert Calderisi, Michael Bodakowski, and Thomas Banchoff gave practical and thoughtful suggestions on manuscript drafts. Wonderful research support came from Berkley Center assistants and WFDD staff Anny Gaul, Louis Ritzinger, Audrey Wilson, Mary Grace Reich, Sam Scott, Alana Tornello, Vieshnavi Rattehali, Nafees Ahmed, Wendy Guardado, and Jessica Holland. I am grateful particularly to Rorden Wilkinson and Thomas Weiss, the thoughtful and diligent series editors, who supported my involvement in the project and for their incisive observations.

I dedicate this book to my daughter Laura, her husband Dan, my son Patrick, and my grandson Desmond Patrick Ryan, who give meaning to values and what lies behind them. My two now-adult children have journeyed with me the road to learning about the worlds of religion, with never-ending insights and questions.

Abbreviations

ADRA	Adventist Development and Relief Agency
AIPP	Asia Indigenous People's Pact
AJC	American Jewish Committee—Global Jewish Advocacy
AJWS	American Jewish World Service
AKDN	Aga Khan Development Network
BAPS	Bochasanwasi Shri Akshar Purushotam Swaminarayan Sanstha
BJP	Bharatiya Janata Party (India)
CAFOD	Catholic Overseas Development Agency for England and Wales
CRS	Catholic Relief Services
DESA	Department of Economic and Social Affairs (of the UN)
DfID	Department for International Development (UK government)
EAA	Ecumenical Advocacy Alliance
ECOSOC	United Nations Economic and Social Council
FBO	faith-based organization
FIO	faith-inspired organization
G8/G20	Group of 8, Group of 20, largest world economies
GMO	genetically modified organism
IAHV	International Association for Human Values
IARF	International Association for Religious Freedom
IDB	Islamic Development Bank
IFAPA	Interfaith Action for Peace in Africa
IHEU	International Humanist and Ethical Union
IMF	International Monetary Fund
IofC	Initiatives of Change
IR	Islamic Relief
ISESCO	Islamic Educational, Scientific, and Cultural Organization

MDGs	Millennium Development Goals
MRA	Moral Re-Armament
NAE	National Association of Evangelicals
NGO	non-governmental organization
NU	Nahdlatul Ulama
OCHA	Office for the Coordination of Humanitarian Affairs (of the UN)
OIC	Organization of Islamic Cooperation
SARA	State Administration for Religious Affairs (People's Republic of China)
SBNR	spiritual but not religious
SEEDS	Sarvodaya Economic Enterprise Development Services
SGI	Sōka Gakkai International
SSRVM	Sri Sri Ravi Shankar Vidya Mandir
TIMA	Tzu Chi International Medical Association
UK	United Kingdom
UMCOR	United Methodist Committee on Relief
UN	United Nations
UNAIDS	the Joint UN Programme on HIV/AIDS
UNAOC	UN Alliance of Civilizations
UNDP	UN Development Programme
UNESCO	UN Educational, Scientific and Cultural Organization
UNFPA	UN Population Fund
UNICEF	UN Children's Fund
URI	United Religions Initiative
US(A)	United States (of America)
VVKI	Vyakti Vikas Kendra India
VVMVP	Ved Vignan Maha Vidya Peeth
WBSC	World Buddhist Sangha Council
WCC	World Council of Churches
WCMP	World Congress of Muslim Philanthropists
WCRP	World Conference of Religions for Peace (now Religions for Peace)
WEA	World Evangelical Alliance
WFB	World Fellowship of Buddhists
WFDD	World Faiths Development Dialogue
WHO	World Health Organization
WICS	World Islamic Call Society
WLF	World Lutheran Federation
WVI	World Vision International

Introduction

Religion is a major factor in world politics today, with a mixture of much-debated positive and negative dimensions. Wars are fought where religious identities ignite and fuel tensions. Terrorists from different world regions claim the mantle of religious ideology. Religious voices enjoin us to work for peace and a just world order, to renounce greed, to protect the environment, and to care for those who are downtrodden. Others fuel the human passions that foster intergroup competition and conflict and encourage humankind's assumption of dominance over the earth. Religious institutions run countless schools and hospitals. They are often the first on the scene when disaster strikes and the last to leave when order and security vanish. Religious actors enter political spheres, directly in some cases, indirectly in others, contesting for power and shaping attitudes. Religion, it is wise to observe at the outset, is a source of problems, even as it is a wellspring of solutions and inspiration and a force for good.

Yet in the core disciplines of international relations—in the fields of diplomacy, economics, and political science, in the academy and in practice, at the United Nations (UN), and in large swaths of civil society—religion has rarely been a major area of focus, especially in the decades that followed World War II. While several global shocks (notably the Iranian Revolution of 1979, the terrorist attacks of 11 September 2001, and an array of other violent incidents and instances of religiously fueled tensions) have shone a new spotlight on the impact of religious organizations on world affairs, the topic still sits uneasily in many global institutions. This neglect of religion in international affairs and its consequences have generated considerable reflection. Former US Secretary of State Madeleine Albright's book *The Mighty and the Almighty* is a prime example of the argument that systematic neglect of religious factors has been the general rule and that this has blinded policy makers to important forces at work in the international arena.[1]

The reasons for neglect are generally ascribed to a strong "secular" bias that has prevailed in leading academic institutions, especially in the United States and Europe—a bias grounded in the assumptions that, first, religion belonged in the private sphere, and second, that with modernization of societies religion as a major factor in global politics was declining in importance. One consequence of this sidelining of religion was a widespread failure to appreciate important changes taking place in religious communities, notably in Muslim societies. A new dynamic has become unmistakably apparent within Western, largely Christian communities where Muslims who were on the frontlines have had to respond to the rise of modernity and positivist scientific discourse. However, the deep currents of religious responses to globalization and social change extend well beyond Muslim communities: witness the surge of charismatic Christian practices, for example, and the emergence of modern forms of religious exclusivism, popularly known as fundamentalism. Yet religion was rarely the subject of systematic analysis as a factor in international affairs.[2] A broad religious "illiteracy" within policy communities is another consequence. This began with gaps in educational programs as discussion and study of religion moved to the margins of or out of the classroom, and was accentuated by a lack of professional frameworks to encourage thoughtful analysis and strategic reflections where religious actors and issues were involved.

Clearly there were exceptions. In some situations, for example in India during the post-Independence partition, religion was front and center. There have always been wise analysts who appreciated the complex forces at work, among them changes in the religious landscape. One such voice was Samuel Huntington, whose 1993 article in *Foreign Affairs* postulating that the world faced a "clash of civilizations" where religious divides played central roles sparked debates that continue to this day.[3] However, various reviews that have pored through reams of academic literature, policy papers, speeches, and other documents recording the history of ideas and practice in international relations attest to a remarkable neglect of what now seems an obviously critical topic.

Two recent books, *God is Back: How the Global Revival of Faith is Changing the World*, and *God's Century: Resurgent Religion and Global Politics*, epitomize the renewed focus on religion and also suggest the theme that we are witnessing a "resurgence" of religion as a central factor in international affairs.[4] A report by the Chicago Council on Global Affairs, released in February 2010 and directed to the still-new Obama Administration, argued forcefully that engaging with religious communities should be a central element in America's foreign policy.[5] Various parts of the UN system and different national governments have taken to heart the need, as the Norwegian Development Minister put it in 2010, to "take God seriously." These are all illustrative of a growing appreciation that religion must be taken well into account in international relations and that deliberate steps are needed to remedy the decades of neglect. Among the responses are the Henry R. Luce Foundation's grant program to support work on religion in international affairs and the UK Department for International Development (DfID) support for an extensive research program on Religions and Development led by the University of Birmingham.

A first challenge, however, is to clarify what is meant by religion and to navigate dangerous shoals of vocabulary and frameworks for analysis. The worlds of religion are both enormous and enormously complex, involving perhaps six of the world's seven billion people in some fashion. "Religion" broadly refers to ideas and beliefs, elaborate schools of theology, a vast array of institutions, and practices that shape daily lives from the moment they begin until their final hours. Religion is rarely greeted with indifference: it evokes strong emotions from adherents and skeptics alike. The very definitions of concepts such as "religion," "faith," and "spirituality," are fraught with debate. Box I.1 highlights some commonly used definitions, with significant caveats, and explains briefly the terms that this book employs. First and foremost, though, the diversity of religious beliefs and institutions, even within congregations, not to speak of tendencies multiplied to the global level, must be well appreciated as context for the discussion here. Indeed, to speak of "religion" as a singular concept borders on foolishness. Many misunderstandings and distorted debates result from oversimplifications of the complexities that are involved.

Box I.1 Terminology headaches

Religion and faith are terms that loosely describe large and complex worlds. The most basic terminology itself is fraught: the sense conveyed by the terms religion, faith, spirituality, secular is hotly contested. This is in English; similar complexities arise in different languages—to say nothing of the challenge of translating complex concepts among different cultures and communities.

Religion for some is a straightforward description of institutions and approaches. It can imply formal institutions, in keeping with one of the word religion's Latin roots, "to bind." Religion is sometimes used to signify simply a broad and intangible set of beliefs tied to the transcendent. It can also describe very specific theological premises and practices. The *Oxford Dictionary* definition is: "the belief in and worship of a superhuman controlling power, especially a personal god or gods." Plainly religion is not a "thing," and some resist using it as a noun, suggesting that the adjective "religious x" better conveys its nature as an approach rather than any sort of tangibility. Yet religious actors and religious institutions do plainly exist and so the term religion is used, here as in commom usage, with appropriate cautions.

Spirituality can suggest the essence of religious belief and practice. Alternatively it may refer to something distinct and apart from, and contrasted with, organized religion. The *Oxford Dictionary* gives two definitions: "related to religion or religious belief," and "relating to or affecting the human spirit or soul as opposed to material or physical things."

Faith may be used in ways similar to religion, as in "world faiths," conveying different traditions that view themselves as religious in nature. It may also suggest a broader set of specific beliefs or convictions that go beyond the implied hierarchy and formality that the term religion conveys for some listeners. However, faith also suggests a broader concept of belief in something transcendent. The term faith in English has still wider connotations, a quality of belief in what is commonly unseen. Some comment that "everyone has faith; the question is, faith in what?"[1] The *Oxford Dictionary* gives two definitions: "a strong belief in the doctrines of a religion, based on spiritual conviction rather than proof"; and second, "complete trust or confidence in someone or something."

The assumption that believers are organized in formal communities (a church or congregation) is the core of what religion is about in some settings but it sits uncomfortably for some traditions. There are believers (another term that is used)—some Buddhists, for example—who maintain that they do not have "faith" in the commonly understood sense of the word.

While "secular" suggests clarity and virtue for some, a common set of principles and values that go beyond religion, in other settings it can imply a godless and, by implication, valueless approach. One *Oxford Dictionary* definition is "not connected with religious or spiritual matters." The historical origin of the term was to express the contrast between those living within and outside monastic orders, and those bound or not by monastic rule. Today the common use is rather to contrast the non-religious (as in a secular political party) with one with a base or inspiration that is explicitly religious. In essence, the most common modern meaning of "secular" is to describe a society where religious institutions do not play much if any role in politics.

The term "faith-inspired" institutions or organizations suggests a wider net than is commonly suggested by the term "faith-based organization" (FBO), with less assumption that there are formal institutional affiliations. Many organizations, for example, may derive a sense of institutional purpose from a specific religious tradition and yet operate independently from any formal religious body (church, mosque, temple, etc.).

In short, definitions are difficult. This book uses religion because that term is in more common usage, though faith can in some contexts convey a broader and less formal connotation. No definition satisfies all concerns. The definition conundrum should never obscure the intrinsic complexity of the worlds and issues that lie behind the terms.

[1] Interview with Saad Eddin Ibrahim, December 2007, berkleyce nter.georgetown.edu/interviews/a-discussion-with-saad-eddin-ibra him-founder-ibn-khaldun-center-for-development-studies-in-cair o-and-the-arab-organization-for-human-rights

This book focuses on one dimension of the worlds of religions: the formal institutions that are specifically dedicated to governing religious communities and especially those institutions that operate across international boundaries, and thus that take transnational forms. Therefore it does not seek to delve far into the underlying beliefs and practices that are an obviously critical dimension of religion. In no way does the book purport to be comprehensive. Rather, it serves as an introduction to a large and complex grouping of very different institutions. The focus is on the intersections between religious and other global institutions, set against the fundamental question: why and how do these intersections matter? Among the central issues that arise are human rights and the role of religion—whether it is religious freedom, the rights of women, or boundaries between proselytizing and cultural integrity. In addition, religion plainly plays myriad roles in human security, whether it is as a cause of or factor in conflict, or as peacemaker, involved in reconciliation and rebuilding. Religious institutions are also major players in international development and in humanitarian relief, whether as direct providers of services like education and health, forming part of social safety nets in times of crisis and disaster, or as advocates for policy change and for international aid to the world's vulnerable communities. Increasingly, religious institutions are directly involved in both debates and action to address climate change. Finally, many religious institutions argue that they are the global "keepers" or guardians of core moral values, and while ethics and values are plainly contested space, there is little doubt that ancient and modern religious traditions and the analysis of core moral issues that they provide are a rich fount from which many draw ideas and guidance on their moral responsibilities and distinctions between what is right and wrong.

Layout of the book

Chapter 1 presents an overview of religion in the contemporary world, lightly sketching the historical trajectory (largely with a view to highlighting how far religious institutions were the original global institutions and how this picture has evolved over the centuries), then presenting the major categories of religious institutions and bodies that are involved in contemporary global affairs. Religious demography and the underlying statistics present particular difficulties, but the broad categories of adherents are summarized, together with trends, because contemporary religion should be seen as dynamic. Among the central themes of contemporary analysis are the shift of gravity within the world's largest faith tradition (Christianity) to regions other than Europe and North America, the tendency towards more significant fundamentalism and extremism within various traditions, and religious participation of many kinds in a set of new, modern, and often interreligious movements that seek justice and human welfare (with peace at the fore). Both exclusivist and pluralist religious tendencies are fruits of modernity. A central driver of change is the increased significance of societies that are plural (that is, with various different religious communities living together or at least side by side), and the growing influence of technology in shaping both the speed of change and the nature of institutional forms and perceptions that influence those institutions.

Chapter 2 outlines the institutional forms that different religious traditions take today, with a focus on those with transnational structures. The most formal and the largest are the central institutions of the Catholic Church, although both Orthodox and Protestant Christian denominations tend to be organized with hierarchical structures as well. However, the recent and extraordinarily dynamic trend of expansion of pentecostal, evangelical, and charismatic forms of Christianity is marked by far more decentralized structures. The picture for other large and influential faiths is more complex. For Islam, there is no central authority in any sense equivalent to the Catholic Pope, though various organizations aspire to such roles. The Organization of Islamic Cooperation includes the governments of most Muslim majority nations and operates with specifically religious principles. Judaism has a specific character with the State of Israel as a Jewish state with an explicit (if complex) global vision and mission. When it comes to other religious communities, large and small, the absence of clear institutional structures is even more striking.

Chapter 3 looks to a different, still more complex group of religious entities, loosely termed "movements." They differ from the formal institutions and hierarchies that are the most visible face of contemporary religion. They take very different forms, ranging from vast and expansive, with millions of devoted followers, to small and purpose driven. The chapter focuses on a variety of illustrative communities, including several from the Indian sub-continent, Hindu, Muslim, Buddhist, and spiritual; Catholic organizations like the community of Sant'Egidio and the Focolare movement; Engaged Buddhists; and a range of spiritually driven movements that object to being categorized as part of the traditional religious entities. Many have charismatic leaders and some, but by no means all, engage in a wide range of activities beyond purely pastoral roles, from meditation and politics to peace building and reconciliation. Organizations like Al Qaeda and Hamas, to a degree, fall within this general category.

Chapter 4 focuses on inter- and intra-faith movements and organizations. While there are ancient traditions of outreach among different religious institutions, most look to the 1893 World Parliament of Religions in Chicago as the start of a modern, complex tradition of dialogue and exchange. The two impetuses for these movements are, first, to counter the tendencies toward conflict among religious traditions, where peace tends to be the central theme. Second, they aim to make common cause among the world's religious traditions, whether for international development and humanitarian ends or to work towards successful pluralistic communities. The various global interfaith organizations work at different levels and are characterized by often very different styles. An important recent trend is a sharpening focus on youth both because they are, as all agree, a large percentage of the present population, as well as the future of humanity, and because of concerns about the path that youth culture seems to pursue. While youth cultures vary widely, as do the responses of interfaith communities, there is agreement on one point: that they have great potential for dynamism. Intra-faith tensions may be more acute than among different traditions, and institutions like the World Council of Churches address both common causes and differences.

Chapter 5 focuses on what are, within international circles, often the most visible institutions associated with religion: the vast array of operational and advocacy institutions that have specific substantive purposes. Often collectively termed faith-based organizations (FBOs), they are central players in the broader non-governmental world. Because they take such widely different forms in different world regions, however, they are more aptly called "faith-*inspired* organizations." There is a vast difference between global giants like Caritas Internationalis, World Vision, and Islamic Relief and the rather fluid and generally under-resourced emerging networks of, for example, Muslim women's organizations or groups engaged in grassroots work for peace. The religious links that these institutions maintain vary widely, ranging from direct ties to a specific religious body, to others the inspiration of which is plainly religious but where formal ties are limited. The issue of religion as a source of conflict and as a force for peace and reconciliation is a central topic for many organizations but still more for those that observe and seek to interact with them.

Chapter 6 focuses on emerging trends and issues that relate to religious dimensions of contemporary global governance and challenges. It explores how the UN and other institutions (the European Union, the World Economic Forum, and the World Bank, for example) have grappled with their relationships with both institutions and issues involving religion. Likewise it reviews how some religious bodies view their relationships with international institutions and their systems of governance. Differing approaches to gender and to human rights alike highlight practical and complex issues that turn around the meaning of religious freedom as a fundamental human right. Taking the Millennium Development Goals and the Universal Declaration of Human Rights as two beacons of international agreement that underpin global institutional ideals and structures, the concluding section reflects on how religious partnerships and actors fit within these frameworks.

1 Religion

An institutional portrait

- Ancient movers: how religious beliefs and actors shaped history and how religion's roles have changed
- Religion and state in contemporary societies
- The "Islamic world" and "the West"
- Clash of civilizations?
- Contemporary religious dynamics
- Blessed are the peacemakers
- Religious demography and attitudes
- Religion's organizational forms
- Conclusion

The world's many religious traditions have given rise to an extraordinary range of institutions. This chapter situates these institutions within an historical context and in the framework of contemporary global institutions. To do so, a reflection on historic visions and manifestations of religion is an essential first step. Religious leaders and organizations often paved the way for transnational movements of people and institutions: in that sense, they were the original globalizers. For much of world history, religion was so central to belief systems, governance, and notions of authority as to make the distinctions among them—distinctions that we still labor to draw today—largely inconceivable. The first part of the chapter thus focuses on four critical topics: the mid-seventeenth-century European move towards the ideal of a nation-state that distinguished religious and secular authority and the subsequent rise of "secular" norms; the United Nations (UN) Universal Declaration of Human Rights and its assertion of the right to religious freedom, suggesting both freedom to practice a religion and freedom from rule by religion; contemporary debates around the roles of religious beliefs, laws, and authority that in some instances pit a "Western" versus a "non-Western" world (and its particular links to the idea of a clash of civilizations); and an exploration of the "secularization" of international relations in the post-World War II era, then followed by the current revival of interest in religious institutions and roles. The chapter also introduces a discussion of religion as a factor in violence and war as well as peace and social cohesion (this is treated in greater detail in Chapter 5). While religion remains a significant source of conflict today—often indirectly, sometimes directly—religious peacemaking is also an important force. These contrasting dimensions of religion are central elements of the institutional landscape.

Religious demography is also an essential part of understanding contemporary religious institutions. Three clear trends are notable: the growing weight of non-European and non-North American religious communities within major religious traditions; the transnational patterns that religious fundamentalism and extremism are taking; and the growing complexity of plural societies, juxtaposed with greater concentrations of adherence to the major global religions. The religious transformations of the twentieth century represent perhaps one of that era's most significant social developments and the worlds of religion are still today undergoing profound transformations that are linked *inter alia* to modernization, migration, and the impact of technology and new modes of communication.

Against the backdrop of this dynamic portrait of changing religious demography, patterns of religious adherence, and organizations, this chapter sets out a framework to help guide the navigation among very different types of religious institutions.

Ancient movers: how religious beliefs and actors shaped history and how religion's roles have changed

From the earliest recorded history religion and government were intertwined, and political authority was commonly associated with some mystical or spiritual force. This is still frequently the case in indigenous societies; in Africa, for example, many chiefs are seen as carrying a spiritual as well as a temporal role and authority. From the first millennium BCE, and especially after the middle of the first millennium AD, many religions, in an institutionalized form, took on vastly expanded roles as moral and political authorities and acquired significant worldly power and wealth. Government and religion were often *de facto* one and the same, with the authority that came from religion often trumping even power strongly based on military might. This was particularly the case for the Catholic Church and, after the seventh century, Islamic Caliphates, but there are parallels in other world religions and regions, notably China and Japan, Persia (under the Zoroastrians), and South Asia. Pope Innocent III (1198–1216), who represented an apex of Christian power, described the power relationships as a linking of day and night, sun and moon (with religious authority representing day and sun):

> In the same way for the firmament of the universal Church, which is spoken of as heaven, he appointed two great dignitaries; the greater to bear rule over souls (these being, as it were, days), the lesser to bear rule over bodies (those being, as it were, nights). These dignitaries are the pontifical authority and the royal power. Furthermore, the moon derives her light from the sun, and is in truth inferior to the sun in both size and quality, in position as well as effect. In the same way the royal power derives its dignity from the pontifical authority: and the more closely it cleaves to the sphere of that authority the less is the light with which it is adorned; the further it is removed, the more it increases in splendour.[1]

Part of this concept of the integration of religion and government was that a single faith was seen as essential to civil order, and a vital element of the social fabric. Having the right faith was essential to pleasing God, who upheld the natural order and averted disaster. Religious heresy was treason, and religious toleration was seen as admitting evil and dangerous elements into society.

For over a millennium, the stories of civilizations were thus to a large degree narratives of the ebb and flow of religious and temporal power. Conquests, conversions, and defeat involved many different authorities, and their ties to religion were elemental. During Europe's Middle Ages, the ideal was that a universal Christian empire and a universal church would hold sway, harking back to ideals of the height of the Roman and Carolingian Empires. The reality, however, was often quite different: fractured feudal rule with deep political divisions among many principalities, free cities, duchies, and feudal kingdoms. However, for centuries there was a religious unity in the Christian world and little question that the Church was a primary political force and actor. These assumptions and ideals were shattered by the Protestant Reformation which in turn gave rise to centuries of warfare, fought often in the name of religion—an experience which to this day shapes the views of many who look with unease to the explosive potential of religious conflicts and perceived dangers of religious involvement in governance. Likewise, as Islamic soldiers and merchants swept across vast regions of the world beginning in the seventh century, there were again ideals of the *Umma*, the united community that combined spiritual and religious authority, but here also sharp schisms emerged, notably between Sunni and various forms of Shi'a Islam. For centuries the Ottoman Empire combined political and spiritual rule, with the noteworthy characteristic that multiple religious communities were an accepted part of the regime. However, it was succeeded by a fractured set of communities that dreamed of unity but rarely came close to achieving it.

Alongside the epic power struggles that dominated geopolitics, the religion in which people believed and which dictated the rhythm of lives and days was in large measure either an inherited identity, not open to question, or an identity and rule imposed as the religion practiced by the rulers. Religion was important, shaping worldviews, influencing land tenure, defining ideals of family and community, and affecting financial matters at all levels, but choosing one's religion was hardly the norm and dissenters and religious minorities were often subject to discrimination or persecution. The Latin phrase *cuius regio, eius religio* means that the religion of the King was the religion of those he governed. A term coined by jurists in the Holy Roman Empire, which occupied much of Central Europe, it implied that each prince in the empire could decide which tradition his subjects would follow. In England in the 17th century, the monarchy shifted from Catholic to Protestant, back to Catholic and finally – under Elizabeth the First – to Protestant. The result was violent persecution of those who did not follow suit. The discriminatory laws and persecution of Jews in Europe, especially during the Spanish Inquisition, were emblematic of an era in which religion and authority were largely one and the same, and where tolerance of diverse beliefs was far from the norm. One of history's most extraordinary stories is that of the global movement of the Jewish people as they fled persecution and exercised their remarkable talent for creative solutions to their environment (see Box 1.1). The motivation for the emigration of colonists to North America was driven in large measure by persecution of groups termed "non-conformists." The early years of settlement and history have both a dark side and one with visionary ideals and courageous application. The exclusivism that characterized much colonial enterprise, including in North America, resulted in the destruction of indigenous communities as the colonies that became the United States of America expanded. The contrasting courage of people who stood behind their beliefs and opened themselves to different traditions is equally part of the legacy. American concepts of religious freedom as they were hammered out in the United States Constitution were marked by this experience.

Box 1.1 The Jewish diaspora

Realities and myths of the Jewish diaspora evoke the many links between globalization and religion. Diaspora, or "dispersion," from the Greek word "to scatter" and the Hebrew "to be exiled,"[1] refers to the movements of Jews through history. More specific usage ties diaspora to voluntary and forced migrations out of the ancient homeland: *Eretz Israel*, or the Land of Israel. The timing and circumstances of the earliest diaspora are disputed, but the first significant migration out of the Kingdom of Judah is said to have occurred in 586BC, when Jews were deported into slavery by the Babylonians. Many Jews returned to the Kingdom of Judah, but four-fifths remained voluntarily in exile, establishing autonomous sociopolitical systems throughout the Middle East, Asia Minor, and the Balkans. The diaspora proper involved the mass migrations that followed the destruction of Jerusalem in 70AD by the Roman Empire. Widespread Jewish conversion during the first and second centuries in these far-reaching communities increased the size and global distribution of Judaism: "the fervor of proselytism was indeed one of the most distinctive traits of Judaism during the Greco-Roman epoch"[2]; (today Judaism is not a proselytizing religion).

During the Middle Ages, Jewish populations divided into geographic groupings. The Ashkenazi held sway in Jewish centers in Northern and Eastern Europe and Sephardic Jews settled in Iberia, North Africa, and the Middle East. Communities adopted distinctive languages, rituals, and cultures, though Jewish autonomy was maintained through voluntary and forced exclusion from mainstream cultures.[3] The post-1492 movement of Jews from Andalusia created new communities especially in North Africa and the Balkans.

As nation-states took form in Western Europe in the eighteenth and nineteenth centuries, fears of Jewish communal separatist states within the state emerged. This plus increases in Jewish populations fueled anti-Semitism. The result was a significant shift in the Jewish diaspora to the Western hemisphere (notably to the United States), southern Africa, Australia, and East Asia. With rising nationalism and the horror of the Holocaust, the desire for a homeland grew among the scattered diasporic communities and the Jewish national movement developed. The Zionist movement to restore Jewish statehood in Eretz Israel was officially launched with the First Zionist Congress in 1897 and led to the eventual establishment of the State of Israel in 1948. The return of Jews worldwide to the Israeli state changed the notion of the diaspora, though most Jews still live in global diasporic communities.

Scattered Jewish communities have relied on various mechanisms to preserve their Jewish identity and traditions. Though Jewish institutional structures have lacked the clear hierarchy of other religious traditions like the Catholic Church, throughout antiquity, Jews made pilgrimages, paid an annual Temple tax, and accepted the authority of Jerusalem's Sanhedrin.[4] Within the Arab caliphate, Jewish educational systems (*yeshivot*) in Babylonia had authority over 97 percent of the world's Jews. Even with divisions in Jewish communities in the Middle Ages, local decision-making bodies communicated with authorities from all parts of the Jewish world to maintain the *halakhic*—a formal constitutional structure created out of the collective body of religious law.

This structure weakened with the rise of Western nationalism and the dispersal of Jews globally. A "voluntarism" arose as communities took the form of Orthodox, Conservative, and Reform movements. Institutions changed dramatically over the twentieth century, shaken by World War II, communist regimes, and emigration to Israel. Jewish institutional frameworks in North Africa and the Middle East were weakened as much of the Jewish population left. New frameworks arose in North and South American Jewry as diaspora communities remained and formed new, complex relations with Israel. Jewish communities have formed government-like institutions, local civil societies, fraternal organizations, and special interest groups that offer services and representation for Jews in their prospective countries and with Israel-based frameworks.

[1] Used in Deuteronomy (28:25; 30: 4–5), meaning dispersion as a temporary condition of dislocation. Tessa Rajak, "The Jewish Diaspora," in *Origins to Constantine*, ed. M. Mitchell, F. Young, and K. Bowie (Cambridge University Press, 2006).

[2] Sibyllines, iii. 271; compare I Macc. 15 (Hachette & Co., 1906, "Diaspora").

[3] D.J. Elazar, "The Jewish People as the Classic Diaspora: A Political Analysis," The Jerusalem Center for Public Affairs:

Daniel Elazar Papers Index Online, 1986, jcpa.org/dje/articles2/
classicdias.htm.
[4] Hachette & Co., "Diaspora," from "Judæi," in *Dictionnaire des
Antiquités*, 1906.

In reflections on the relationships between religious and political
authority in the modern era, the signing of the Treaty of Westphalia in
1648 is held up as a watershed. Its main goal and result was a peace
agreement that recognized what has come to be known as the nation-
state. It also broke the perceived and actual power hold of the church.
Box 1.2 elaborates on some of the Westphalian principles and agreements. Westphalia, in effect, represented the end of the dream of a
unified Christian Empire, yet in France the continuing influence of the
ideal of *une foi, une loi, un roi* (one faith, one law, one king) was an
indication that lingering assumptions and practical experience still
reflected an ideal where state, society, and religion were bound together. Religion still formed the basis for the social consensus and the
church sanctified the state's right to rule in exchange for military and
civil protection.

Box 1.2 The Peace of Westphalia, nation-states, and religion's loss of authority

The 1648 Treaty of Westphalia, which ended the Thirty Years War
(1618–48), heralded a reorganization of Europe into a network of
nation-states in which religious and temporal authorities were
formally distinct and the principle of sovereign rule was formally
recognized. It is often cited as a critical stage in defining the
respective roles of religious and non-religious political institutions
as well the concepts of national sovereignty that mark the world
order to this day.

The Peace of Westphalia was in fact a series of peace treaties
signed between May and October 1648 (in Osnabrück and
Münster) that settled a complex set of military conflicts involving
the Holy Roman Empire, Spain, and the Dutch Republic.
Wars had split what is now Germany and much of Europe into
hostile religious camps, and the Peace marked a major change in
the relationship between church and state—as well as in notions
of the rights and duties of separate nation-states vis-à-vis one

another—by recognizing the right of sovereign rule and bringing the Reformation era to a close.[1]

The wars had made it clear that a new system was needed that responded to the needs of emerging states and their quite different relationships with the church as rulers of distinct domains. In a sense, however, the treaty displeased all the parties involved. The Protestants lost Bohemia, and were left with an inferior place in the electoral college and the Diet. The Catholics, on the other hand, were forced to permit the exercise of heretical worship, and church lands were left in the grasp of sacrilegious spoilers. The princes could not throw off the burden of the Emperor's imperial supremacy, while the Emperor could turn that supremacy to no practical account. Most disparaging was Pope Innocent X, who scathingly pronounced the provisions of the treaty, "*ipso iure nulla, irrita, invalida, iniqua, iniusta, damnata, reprobata, inania, viribusque et effectu vacua, omnino fuisse, esse, et perpetuo fore*"—in short, useless and evil in every way.

Yet, for all its shortcomings, to this day Westphalia is looked to as the foundation for the international system of sovereign nation-states.

[1] avalon.law.yale.edu/17th_century/westphal.asp.

Two other major watersheds still color approaches to religion and power today: the French Revolution and the emergence of Marxist-Leninist thought. The French Revolution represented a fierce, outright rejection of the authority of the "Two Estates": the royals and noblemen, and the church. The two were linked as the enemies of the people, and in the heyday of the Revolution all signs of religious authority and practice, starting with landed estates and extending to the very names of days and months, were eliminated. Many clerics died or fled and church properties were confiscated. What was promoted instead was a civic religion—a deeply secular state stripped of the symbols as well as the practical power embodied in religious institutions. The ideas behind the French Revolution emerged from the prior centuries of Enlightenment thinking and notably, where religion was concerned, of Spinoza and Voltaire. The crux of Enlightenment thinking was to question the authority of religion and other uncritically accepted beliefs. One impetus for this thinking was the catastrophe of the 1755 Lisbon earthquake, which shook beliefs and encouraged a deep rethinking of accepted authority (see Box 1.3). Free examination of the concepts and practices that religious authorities had called for without question was the goal. Voltaire was an especially vocal and influential critic of organized religion, arguing forcefully for a complete separation of state and religion that went well beyond Westphalian principles. Writing about Christianity, he once observed: "[Our religion] is without a doubt the most ridiculous, the most absurd, and the most bloody to ever infect the world," although he was also a vocal supporter of religious freedom and tolerance of different traditions.[2]

Box 1.3 The Lisbon earthquake: disaster propelling change

In 1755, on All Saints' Day, an enormous earthquake followed by fires and a tsunami devastated Lisbon, virtually destroying the city and the region around it. The earthquake may have had a magnitude of 8.5–9.0, although it is impossible to know for certain, while the death toll is estimated to have been as high as 100,000 people—about one-third of Lisbon's population, ranking it as one of history's deadliest earthquakes. As with many disasters (the 2010 Haiti earthquake, the 2011 Japanese earthquake and tsunami, and Central American hurricanes among them), the events prompted a profound ideological upheaval. The Lisbon earthquake was a precursor to the French Revolution, accelerating the intellectual and political changes that shook confidence in both religious and political authority.

The earthquake took place on a religious holiday and destroyed the city's major churches. Priests blamed the destruction on Lisbon's sins and inquisitors roamed the streets seeking heretics to hang, but in reality the grip of the medieval church was weakening. Bourgeois forces (merchants, tradesmen, and the like) were growing stronger. The French Revolution, beginning a mere 34 years later, was evidence of just how far the traditional constraints and rules of the game of traditional society had changed. The earthquake led to political turmoil in Portugal and inspired major developments in theodicy and in the philosophy of the sublime.

Voltaire was deeply affected by the earthquake. His poem on the earthquake and the novella *Candide* questioned blind faith in God and the fatalism that the dominant philosophy promoted. Voltaire's poem observed ironically: "All is well, the heirs of the dead will increase their fortunes, masons will make money rebuilding the buildings, beasts feed off the bodies buried in the debris: this is the necessary effect of the necessary causes; your particular misfortune is nothing, you will contribute to the general welfare: such talk would have been as cruel as the earthquake was dreadful." In *Candide* Voltaire comments that "After the earthquake, which had destroyed three-fourths of the city of Lisbon, the sages of that country could think of no means more effectual to preserve the kingdom from utter ruin than to entertain the people with an auto-da-fé, it having been decided by the University of Coimbra, that the burning of a few people alive by a slow fire, and with great ceremony, is an infallible preventive of earthquakes." Candide laments: "If this is the best of all possible worlds, what are the others like?"[1]

[1] Voltaire, *Candide*, first published 1759, chapter 6.

The French Revolution was followed by the Napoleonic era and a turbulent succession of counter-revolutions, restorations, and new revolutions, during which relations between church and state were in flux. Developments culminated in the December 1905 law that established for France a distinct separation of church and state. One of the clearest legal articulations anywhere of what a lay state involves, it stated that "The Republic neither recognizes, nor salaries, nor subsidizes any religion," establishing the backbone of the proud French principle of *laïcité*. As France today confronts the roles in French society of Muslim and other immigrant communities, the principles of *laïcité* and of the 1905 law are often invoked as bedrock concepts governing the role of religion in society. Both the French and American revolutions, as well as the long-fought efforts to define the role of religion in the United Kingdom, have exerted significant influence on comparable efforts, in Turkey and Egypt, for example, to define the respective roles of religion and governmental authority.

A second major shaper of attitudes and approaches to religion and the state was the thinking of Marx, Lenin and the communist "century." Arguably, these exerted as lasting an influence on the relationships between religion and state in the modern world as the Enlightenment and Revolutionary eras (and of course they are linked both intellectually and in practice). Marx famously denounced religion as a major factor in the oppression of working people:

The struggle against religion is, therefore, indirectly the struggle against that world whose spiritual aroma is religion. Religious suffering is, at one and the same time, the expression of real suffering and a protest against real suffering. Religion is the sigh of the oppressed creature, the heart of a heartless world, and the soul of soulless conditions. It is the opium of the people. The abolition of religion as the illusory happiness of the people is the demand for their real happiness. To call on them to give up their illusions about their condition is to call on them to give up a condition that requires illusions. The criticism of religion is, therefore, in embryo, the criticism of that vale of tears of which religion is the halo.[3]

The years of harsh opposition by communist regimes to religions and their institutions shook religious establishments the world over and for decades meant that in large parts of the world religion was essentially invisible, and deliberately so. The impact of Marxist thinking extended well beyond formally communist states, influencing approaches to religion in Mozambique, Cambodia, Vietnam, and many other societies. The framing of many UN covenants that relate to religion bears the marks of communist thinking and influence and their prevailing suspicion of religion. The resurgence of religion across the nations that constituted the former Soviet Union and its allies in Eastern Europe and Asia in the post-1989 era is one of the most remarkable stories of the late twentieth century. There, in most places religion is back in forms that often have a political cast, though they rarely extend to formal links with the official government.

Religion and state in contemporary societies

The relationships between religious authorities and governments in practice take many different forms today. This is a dynamic field of evolving and sometimes sharp shifts in law and practice. In some countries, for instance, there is an established religion. The United Kingdom, where the Anglican Church occupies a key position in the very concept of the state, is an example. Several other European nations still have official churches, while others offer special protections or guarantee freedom of religion through equitable financial support to different faith communities (Germany and the Netherlands, for example). In Latin America, with the exception of Mexico (influenced especially by French traditions), for many decades the Catholic Church had constitutionally defined roles in many countries, though this has declined as one country after another has modified both the formal and *de facto* roles that the Catholic Church plays in relation to the state. A number of countries define themselves as Islamic, among them Saudi Arabia, Pakistan, the Sudan, Mauritania, Morocco, and Iran. Cambodia's constitution is based on "King, Nation, and Religion," giving the Buddhist faith the role of a national religion. It is important to underline the extent to which arrangements that each nation has with its religious communities and institutions are distinctive—the product of history and often of hard-fought battles. Most nations today provide for freedom of worship and belief in their constitutions. The practical issues of what influence religious institutions exercise in politics and in society often are subject to a host of legal and financial regulations, but in many cases turn less on formal recognition of space for religion than on the implementation of legal provisions. Indeed, the reality "on the ground" where religion and the state are concerned can often look quite different from what is spelled out by law. Table 1.1 summarizes the broad patterns of constitutional approaches to religion in the different regions of the world.

Freedom of belief is one of the foundational principles behind the Universal Declaration of Human Rights, agreed upon in 1948:

> Everyone has the right to freedom of thought, conscience and religion; this right includes freedom to change his religion or belief, and freedom, either alone or in community with others and in public or private, to manifest his religion or belief in teaching, practice, worship and observance.[4]

This basic principle is elaborated in a succession of subsequent instruments and in many respects can be considered as the spirit and law governing international approaches to religion. Legal scholars Witte and Christian observe that "Human rights have emerged today as one of the richest products of the interaction of religion and international law—the common law and common power of the emerging cosmopolitan world order."[5] The human right to freedom of religion, however, is not always easy to apply in practice. Progress toward genuine agreement on what this freedom involves and how it should be applied in different societies has been far from smooth. In particular, tensions exist around three issues: proselytizing and evangelizing, apostasy (or freedom to change one's religion), and blasphemy. Each of these topics has provoked intense conflicts that drive home underlying differences in approach to the roles of religion in society and in law. Underlying many of the disputes is unease by many religious authorities about the implications of true equality between men and women.

Table 1.1 Constitutional regimes and religion: selected countries[1]

Country	Constitutional Guarantee of Religious Freedom	Registration Requirement for Religious Groups?	Religious Freedom in Practice
Afghanistan	Restricted in law and practice	No	Publicizing and promoting religions other than Islam is prohibited.
Algeria	Guaranteed; restricted in other laws and policies	Yes	Proselytizing banned; minority religious groups denied registration
Bolivia	Guaranteed	Yes; Roman Catholic Church exempted; unregistered groups practice unimpeded	Religious freedoms generally respected; government has formalized Catholic social service organizations.
Brazil	Guaranteed	No	Religious freedoms generally respected; racism or religious intolerance punishable by imprisonment.
Cameroon	Guaranteed	Yes; indigenous groups exempted	Religious freedoms generally respected; government television regularly broadcasts Christian and Muslim services.
Cape Verde	Guaranteed	Yes, but failure to register does not result in restrictions	Religious groups may not be armed or promote violence, racism, or xenophobia.
Central African Republic	Guaranteed	Yes; indigenous groups exempted	"Witchcraft" is a criminal offense; government media services broadcast a multitude of religious ceremonies.
Chad	Guaranteed; some restrictions in practice	Yes; indigenous groups exempted	Certain Muslim groups banned; require permission to proselytize; reports of preferential treatment of Muslims
Cote d'Ivoire	Guaranteed	Yes	Religious freedoms generally respected; some reports of discrimination in national media outlets.

Table 1.1 (continued)

Country	Constitutional Guarantee of Religious Freedom	Registration Requirement for Religious Groups?	Religious Freedom in Practice
Democratic Republic of the Congo	Guaranteed; some restrictions in practice	Yes; but unregistered groups generally operate freely	Religious freedoms generally respected; isolated reports of abuse.
Egypt	Guaranteed; restricted in practice	Yes	Freedom of religion does not apply to Bahá'ís; restrictions on conversion; proselytizing restricted.
Eritrea	Guaranteed, but Constitution not implemented	Yes	Government has not approved registration of some churches; must receive permission to distribute literature; political activity by religious groups banned.
Ethiopia	Guaranteed	Yes; Ethiopian Orthodox Church and Ethiopian Islamic Affairs Supreme Council exempted	Religious freedoms generally respected; illegal to incite one religious group against another.
France	Guaranteed	No, but must register for tax-exempt status and official recognition	General respect for religious freedom in practice; however religious symbols are banned in schools.
Ghana	Guaranteed	Yes	Religious freedoms generally respected.
Kenya	Guaranteed	Yes; indigenous groups may choose not to register	Religious freedoms generally respected; some accusations of discriminatory practices against Muslims.
Liberia	Guaranteed	Yes; same process as all NGOs	Religious freedoms generally respected.
Madagascar	Guaranteed	Yes; can register as "simple associations" if do not meet criteria	Religious freedoms generally respected; religious. organizations granted free access to state media for "public service" purposes.

Table 1.1 (continued)

Country	Constitutional Guarantee of Religious Freedom	Registration Requirement for Religious Groups?	Religious Freedom in Practice
Malawi	Guaranteed	Yes	Religious freedoms generally respected; isolated accusations of discrimination by minority groups.
Mali	Guaranteed	Yes; required of all public associations; indigenous religions exempted	Religious identity not designated on official documents; may not wear religious headdress in official photos if face is obscured.
Mauritania	Islam	Restricted in law and practice	Government requires all groups receive official authorization before meeting, even in private homes.
Morocco (Including Western Sahara)	Guaranteed; restricted in practice	Yes	Restrictions on conversions from Islam, proselytizing, and religious literature; government monitors religious groups.
Mozambique	None	Guaranteed	Yes, but unregistered groups generally operate freely.
Nepal	Guaranteed	No	Religious freedom generally respected; prohibits proselytism.
Nigeria	Guaranteed	Yes	Publishing of non-Islamic religious literature and proselytizing Muslims banned in practice; practicing of minority religions restricted.
Pakistan	Restricted in law and practice	Yes	Restrictions on Ahmadis; strict laws against blasphemy; restrictions on minority religions.

Table 1.1 (continued)

Country	Constitutional Guarantee of Religious Freedom	Registration Requirement for Religious Groups?	Religious Freedom in Practice
Palestinian Occupied Territories (Including Regions Governed by the Palestinian Authority	Guaranteed	Yes, but not strictly enforced	Religious freedoms generally respected; government unable to prevent discrimination in some regions; security policies can restrict access to religious sites.
Republic of Congo	Guaranteed	Yes; same process as all NGOs	Religious freedoms generally respected; discrimination based on religious denomination prohibited.
Russia	Guaranteed	Not required, but must register open a bank account, own property, publish literature, enjoy tax benefits, or conduct services in prisons, hospitals, or the armed forces.	Some laws restrict religious expression in public. Certain laws restrict religious freedom by discriminating denying groups legal status.
Rwanda	Guaranteed	Yes; if not registered, public gatherings must be pre-approved	Religious freedoms generally respected; missionary groups permitted on case-by-case basis.
Saudi Arabia	Restricted in law and practice	Yes	Public practice of any religion other than Islam prohibited; religious freedoms severely restricted, particularly for minorities.
Senegal	Guaranteed	Yes	Religious freedoms generally respected as long as order is maintained; government provides financial and material assistance to religious groups.

Table 1.1 (continued)

Country	Constitutional Guarantee of Religious Freedom	Registration Requirement for Religious Groups?	Religious Freedom in Practice
Sierra Leone	Guaranteed	Not required, but most do in practice	Religious freedoms generally respected; intermarriage between Muslims and Christians common.
Singapore	Guaranteed; some restrictions in practice	Yes; actions deemed damaging to public order can result in deregistration;	Proselytizing discouraged; some religious texts banned; government approves weekly Islamic sermons.
Somalia	Guaranteed; government unable to enforce Constitution in practice	Varies by region; government has little authority to enforce rule of law	Proselytizing any religion other than Islam prohibited; transitional government ratified legislation to implement Sharia law nationwide in 2009.
South Africa	Guaranteed	No	Religious freedoms generally respected; discrimination based on religious denomination prohibited.
Sri Lanka	Guaranteed; some restrictions in practice	No	Accusations of government discrimination in service provision; religious tensions.
Sudan	Guaranteed; restricted in practice	Yes; but not widely enforced	Non-Muslims face discrimination in the North; religious freedoms generally respected in the South; no legal remedies for discrimination.
Syria	Guaranteed; restricted in practice	Yes	Conversion from Islam not recognized; restrictions on groups deemed "extreme"; all groups monitored; proselytizing restricted.

Table 1.1 (continued)

Country	Constitutional Guarantee of Religious Freedom	Registration Requirement for Religious Groups?	Religious Freedom in Practice
Taiwan	Guaranteed	No; may do so voluntarily for tax benefits	Religious freedoms generally respected.
Tajikistan	Guaranteed, restricted in other laws and policies	Yes	Number of Mosques and distribution of religious literature restricted.
Thailand	Guaranteed; some restrictions in practice	Yes; no new groups recognized since 1984; unregistered groups operate unimpeded	Some ethnic/religious tensions in southern regions; insulting Buddhism prohibited.
Tunisia	Guaranteed; some restrictions in practice	Yes; same process as all other NGOs	Illegal to proselytize Muslims; "sectarian dress" banned; restrictions on freedom of assembly.
Union of Comoros	Guaranteed; some restrictions in practice	No	Illegal to proselytize Muslims or convert from Islam, but prosecutions are rare.
United States	Guaranteed	Must register to receive tax-exempt status.	Religious freedom is generally respected and upheld by the law.
Venezuela	Guaranteed, provided it does not violate public order	Yes	Religious freedoms generally respected; all registered religious groups may receive government funding, but majority goes to Roman Catholic Church.
Vietnam	Guaranteed; restricted in practice	Yes; some reports of delays in registration process	Reports of government harassment of some religious groups; government oversees all religious activity.

Notes:
[1] This summary draws on various sources including the US Department of State country reports on religious freedom. Note that several countries are in transition on governance of religions.

At one level the disputes around the meaning of the universal human right to freedom of belief brings to the surface a debate about how universal the 1948 Declaration truly is. One line of argument holds that the framers of the Declaration drew primarily if not exclusively on Christian and Western principles and that Asian and Islamic values in particular are not well reflected. Witte and Green, drawing on the compelling account by law scholar and diplomat Mary Anne Glendon about the framing of the Universal Declaration, argue that the human rights norms that underlie much of international common law are neither Western and Christian nor static:

> They are fluid, elastic, and open to challenge and change. The human rights regime is not a fundamental belief system. It is a relative system of ideas and ideals that presupposes the existence of fundamental beliefs and values that will constantly shape and reshape it … The human rights regime is neither the child of Christianity and the Enlightenment, nor a ward under exclusive guardianship of either.[6]

It is, of course, foolish to deny the historical fact that Western Christendom and Enlightenment liberalism contributed disproportionately to the evolution of the modern human rights region. However, that does not mean that they are the sole basis nor that human rights as hammered out over the past 65 years do not reflect a broader understanding of values drawn from a wider history and cultural backdrop. Even so, the Organization of Islamic Cooperation (OIC) has framed its own statement of human rights grounded in Islamic principles.

Issues of freedom to worship and to propound one's faith and, above all, the rights of religious minorities subject to persecution and discrimination are often on international agendas. In the United States, the 1998 International Religious Freedom Act gave a special place to religious freedom as a foreign policy objective, and the State Department is required to report each year on the status of religious freedom in all countries and to rate how far this complies with international norms.[7] Countries of special concern are singled out for particular focus.

In many respects, religious institutions have benefited from the human rights revolution, which has contributed to what many term the "great awakening" of religion around the globe. Human rights protections for and by religions have increased in tandem with the democratization of the world. Witte and Green estimate that more than 200 major new statutes and constitutional provisions on religious rights have been promulgated since 1975—many of them including generous protections for liberty of conscience and freedom of religious exercise; guarantees of religious pluralism, equality, and nondiscrimination; and other special protections and entitlements for religious individuals and groups.

However, the global human rights revolution has also coincided with intensifying religious and ethnic conflict, oppression, and belligerence. Infringements on people's right to choose and practice their religion are commonplace in many regions of the world. These infringements are particularly acute where extremist religious groups seek to impose norms of behavior and conformity with their vision of proper social order. In some regions, a "new 'war for souls' has broken out—a battle to reclaim the traditional, cultural, and moral fabric of these changing societies and a struggle to retain adherence and adherents to indigenous faiths."[8] This was especially evident during the 1994 Cairo Conference on Population and Development as well as the Beijing Conference on Women the succeeding year, where what many term an "unholy alliance" of Muslim nations and the Catholic Church, supported by some Christian evangelical bodies, fought hard against articulations of human rights that focused on women's equality and reproductive health.[9] Recently there has been heightened tension at the UN regarding the significance of human rights, notably the rights of women and the definition of "gender rights" (specifically regarding homosexuals). Again, those who pose the greatest challenges come, for the most part, from religious communities. Indeed, some religious activists argue that a paradigm of "human flourishing," falling more in line with socially conservative religious doctrines, should replace that of "human rights." Semantics aside, in many respects what is occurring is that local religious groups are joining forces with political leaders to adopt statutes and regulations that restrict the constitutional rights of their foreign religious rivals and, in their view, arrest the processes of social change in their communities that they see as undermining their culture and traditional authority.

The "Islamic world" and "the West"

The rise of political Islam is a critical part of the history of global religion, and especially the tensions surrounding it. Muslim communities and the Islamic faith are discussed in different chapters, but both the rapid rise of Islam in the centuries after the Prophet Mohammed's death and contemporary tensions between "the Muslim world" and "the West" are part of the broad history of religious institutions in international politics, as are deep divisions among different parts of the global Muslim community. The long and sorry history of the Crusades, which from the eleventh through the thirteenth centuries pitted European Catholicism squarely against Muslim communities across the Middle East, with devastating effects also on Jewish and Eastern Christian communities, left deep wounds and legacies evident in the acute sensitivity that is often the swift reaction whenever the word "crusade" is applied to a cause or event. These were clearly wars of religion, blessed by the Pope, even as a host of other motivations, economics among them, played important roles.

As a geopolitical phenomenon intricately linked to religious beliefs and authority, the narrative of the Muslim "golden era" is nothing short of remarkable. Within three centuries of Mohammed's death Muslim armies had conquered lands extending from the Atlantic Ocean to Central Asia, and a succession of extraordinary empires and rulers shaped the emergence of civilization, learning, science, and notions of governance and power. They included, for example, the Umayyads, Abbasids, Fatimids, Ghaznavids, Seljuqs, Safavids, Mughals, and Ottomans—clearly among the most influential and distinguished powers in the world. The narrative, however, is also forced to confront a decline, both in the political power and in the wealth, of many Muslim societies from the nineteenth century onward. Intricately tied to this global decline is a sense of humiliation and anger at what is perceived as a lack of respect for Muslims and their faith from the world's currently dominant societies— particularly Europe and the United States. The emergence of oil wealth, the successful and rapid development of certain nations, and a number of impressive leaders temper that general sense of alienation, but recent decades have witnessed angry rhetoric, an increasing sense of Muslim identity (as opposed to national or others), and of course violent terrorist attacks of which 11 September 2001 was the worst, but far from the only, example. The stalemated conflict between Israel and its neighbors exacerbates the problem and is a constant point of reference, framing many discussions of human rights in international bodies, where "Zionism" has become the political wedge issue. Efforts to address and resolve the tensions in the Middle East as well as those between a larger group of Muslim majority nations and leading world powers are two of the international community's leading issues. Following the Arab uprisings of 2011, one of the central questions in the Arab Middle East is how changing societies will balance the often competing claims of religious adherents and leaders and broader, often more secular, proponents of democracy. Violence and the threat of violence from extremist groups, many claiming the legitimacy of Islamic ideals for a global Muslim community, are shaping daily life in many corners of the world as nations and communities worldwide have to respond to the threat of terrorism.

Clash of civilizations?

Samuel Huntington, in his 1993 article, "The Clash of Civilizations," set out the argument that the future geopolitical tensions of the world would be concentrated in clashes between what he termed "civilizations": "The fault lines between civilizations will be the battle lines of the future."[10] He framed the issue also as a struggle between the "Western" world that had for centuries dominated geopolitics and the "non-Western" world that would take its place in international affairs, not as the subjects they had been in the past but as prime actors. He argued that differences among civilizations turn on critical elements of life, including beliefs in God, and attitudes towards such crucial matters as liberty and authority as well as rights and responsibilities (not to speak of relationships between men and women). These are, he argued, far more important and potent sources of deep-rooted conflicts than distinctions that are linked to political ideologies and regimes. Islamic civilization was at the center of his concern but he also pointed to tensions between the West and powerful Asian societies, notably the Chinese. Huntington maintained that as globalization distances many from their tight identification with their nation-state, religion moves in to fill the gaps. He set this against the backdrop of a revival of religion, and especially religion in its more fundamentalist forms, citing scholar Giles Keppel, who describes this religious resurgence as the "revenge of God." Defining identities in cultural, civilizational terms encourages a "we versus them" polarity. Huntington argued that tensions along the Muslim-Christian fault line have existed for 1,300 years and that he did not believe they would decline. The divide between "the West and the rest" is even seen as a "human rights imperialism," as the varying conceptions of rights and duties discussed earlier in this chapter become tied to inter-civilizational power struggles. Perhaps his central and most pertinent message is that "the West" will need to develop a profound understanding of the basic religious and philosophical assumptions underlying other civilizations and the ways in which people in different situations see their interests.[11]

Huntington's thesis has sparked lively controversy, with many contesting both his definitions of what identities and civilizations entail and his observation that they clash and are likely to continue to do so. Yet his article and subsequent book are full of important insights, practical ideas, and counsel. The efforts to promote dialogue and an alliance of civilizations, as well as the heightened interest in interfaith relations and dialogue which have become important features of contemporary international affairs, can be viewed in no small measure as a response to Huntington's arguments and the significant forces that inspired his concern at a clash of civilizations.

Contemporary religious dynamics

The assertion that we are witnessing a "revival" or a resurgence of religion has elements of truth, but what is also involved is what writer Karen Armstrong has termed a "revelation,"[12] by which she means the removal of a veil from phenomena that were present all along. This presents three important questions: first, if religion was an important force throughout recent history, why were analysts so blind to it? Second, is there indeed a resurgence of religion, and if so, why? Third, with religion clearly a central factor in modern international relations, what is distinctive about modern forms of religion, and how is it changing and in which directions?

Answers to the first question lie in the much-critiqued secularization assumptions that dominated social science disciplines and professions in the decades following World War II and, it is argued, in the highly secular cultures of the places where leading international affairs public intellectuals were based. Perhaps the most telling account of the significance of the secular bias is by sociologist Peter Berger. A well-known scholar (now at Boston University), Berger argued throughout his early career that religion was in decline and indeed increasingly would be relegated to the private sphere. He then changed his mind and became a strong proponent of the need to take religion far more seriously as a force in economic and social transformation, national, and international affairs.[13] Other "converts" include columnist David Brooks, who described himself once as a "recovering secularist." Former US Secretary of State Madeleine Albright, former US President William J. Clinton, and former British Prime Minister Tony Blair have all argued publicly and forcefully that they often gave far too little importance to religion in their policy analyses while in office. In the light of unfolding world politics and hotspots of tensions, including religious conflicts in Iraq and Afghanistan, multiple religiously linked terrorist attacks across the globe, religious and political turbulence in Iran, and the religious dimensions of Somalia's failed state, to name but a few, it would indeed be hard to argue that religion is not an important force. The secular bias, however, is still significant and core academic courses on religious factors are still rare within international relations, diplomacy, and international development programs, as well as in executive education in the diplomatic services of most countries. Religious illiteracy, even among educated elites, is an unfortunate product of the secularization trends of modern Europe and the United States.[14]

One of several systematic reflections on the importance of religion for US foreign policy is represented by a task force organized by the Chicago Council on Global Affairs, which produced a report largely directed at the Obama Administration but also to the foreign policy "establishment" more generally.[15] Titled *Engaging Religious Communities Abroad: A New Imperative for U.S. Foreign Policy*, the 2010 report argued that religious communities are central players in the counterinsurgency war in Afghanistan, development assistance, the promotion of human rights, stewardship of the environment, and the pursuit of peace in troubled parts of the world. Its central conclusion is that "[t]he success of American diplomacy in the next decade will not simply be measured by government-to-government contacts, but also by its ability to connect with the hundreds of millions of people throughout the world whose identity is defined by religion."[16] The report highlighted President Obama's Cairo speech on 4 June 2009, when he promised that the United States would engage with Muslim communities. The core message: savvy religious observers and leaders need to be far more actively engaged in the foreign policy arena if important foreign policy progress is to be achieved in today's world.[17]

The second question (is there indeed a resurgence of religion?) is more difficult to answer because of fierce data and definitional issues. It seems likely that the preponderance of global citizens have not fundamentally or sharply changed their religious beliefs or practices in recent decades, but that several factors have changed the way their religious identities are manifested. The increased visibility of broader religious communities, the reach of evangelists from different faiths (in person and through various media), and the sense of "the other" that comes with mass and instant communications all appear to be altering the face of religion as it is perceived by millions of people, in rich and poor communities alike. The polarization of global politics, the hegemony of the United States, rapid social changes punctuated by successive and severe economic crises, and especially the shifting global politics of the post-1989 era appear to offer fertile ground for extremist tendencies within most, if not all, faith traditions. These extremist tendencies are frequently associated with fundamentalist beliefs, often fueled by reactions to change. They are accentuated, as Karen Armstrong[18] and other observers argue, by fear of the unknown and a profound sense of injustice in the face of blatant inequalities among nations and within communities, as well as uncertainties about the directions the future will take. So while there may not be a resurgence of religion *per se*, there are significant changes at work within every faith tradition, and there is clearly an increase in both mainstream and extremist groups playing active roles on the political scene.

The third question asks how modern religion is changing. It is important to distinguish here between the nature of religious practice, organization, and beliefs in the more prosperous democratic nations of the world and in those of economically poorer regions. In wealthier societies, religion has changed profoundly from the pattern of obligatory common religions that prevailed before the French Revolution. To a very significant extent, religious affiliation today is a matter of choice and many elect to change their religion or to practice it in their own way, if at all. The most rapidly growing religious demographic in the United States is termed SBNR—spiritual but not religious—a category of people who consider themselves as motivated by spiritual factors but do not associate with any formal religious body. Non-denominational "megachurches" respond to a desire for spiritual roles without the tight communities of the past. How individuals apply their beliefs varies widely by community and individual. Interesting studies suggest that religiously engaged people give more generously to charitable causes and that they are generally happier, but the diversity of experience is enormous. A large number of American adults have changed their religion over their lifespan. Avowed atheists are a relatively small but growing group, active in politics. Plural societies are increasingly the norm, evident in the explosion of diverse religious buildings and communities that scholar Diana Eck has made the focus of her Religious Pluralism Project at Harvard University.[19]

In most poor communities around the world, however, few have a practical choice of what religious tradition they will follow, and religious identities tend still to be conferred at birth, forming a central part of lifelong associations that are both spiritual and cultural (and sometimes legal). Religious traditions and beliefs affect attitudes on marriage and childbirth, child rearing, family relationships, illness, and death. Religion is also involved in land tenure, attitudes towards gender relations, and in political engagement. Religion, in short, is a central part of daily lives (and thus of politics) at every level, from the family to international institutions.

Blessed are the peacemakers

Nowhere are the debates around the roles and directions of religion in the modern world as significant as in relation to violent conflict. Wars of religion are hardly a modern matter, but the forms that religiously inspired violence takes today differ markedly from their historical ancestors. Stalin questioned how many army divisions the Pope possessed (a disparaging observation as to whether or not religion was a significant political force), but there were times when religious leaders raised armies and inspired their forces with reference to the will of God. Today, few religious conflicts are so straightforward, even in those instances where state and religion are joined (as in Iran or, arguably, Israel). The deep-seated conflicts that perturb Nigeria, often framed in terms of conflict between a largely Christian south and a majority Muslim north, clearly have far deeper and more complex causes. Among them are the lack of education and job opportunities for many youth, tensions among largely pastoral and agrarian communities, and the incendiary roles of political leaders who focus on religious identities, sometimes deliberately, in ways that fuel conflicts rooted in different causes. A similarly complex frame of analysis would apply in virtually every conflict termed religious, including, for example, the Sudan, South Sudan, Kashmir, the Balkans, and Sri Lanka.

The peacemaking roles of religious leaders and communities are another important and often neglected topic. While Mahatma Gandhi, Martin Luther King, Jr, and Desmond Tutu are renowned as religious leaders who have worked passionately for peace, far less attention is given to ongoing work by countless religious communities both to settle conflicts and to work for reconciliation and rebuilding. Former diplomat Douglas Johnston and Cynthia Sampson term religion "the Missing Dimension of Statecraft" in the very title of their book that points to examples of constructive peacebuilding across the globe.[20] More significant is the untapped potential of religious ideas, communities, and leaders to help in alerting political and social leaders to brewing conflicts, to mediate and broker peace settlements, and to help rebuild wounded communities.

The prominent Swiss theologian Hans Küng consistently repeats his central belief that there can be no peace among nations without peace among religions and no peace among religions without dialogue among religions. At one level, the call for peace is a strong common theme that links virtually all religious traditions: "blessed be the peacemakers," "peace be upon you," "*shalom.*" The realities, however, are more complex. Raw tensions among religious communities are a stark reality that is linked to the strength of conviction that one's tradition is right and that God calls for the conversion of those who do not share one's beliefs—also an element found in many religious traditions. The politics of competition for adherents, with its links to power and finance, also plays a role. The work of several organizations in the interfaith movement (Chapter 4) aims to build on the common calls for peace and to address those sources of tension that are amenable to better understanding and reconciliation. Of particular interest is the quite recent emergence of peacebuilding approaches, techniques, and institutions (Chapter 5).

Also of note are the traditions of different communities that have particular relevance for international relations. Among these are the "peace churches"—Quakers, Mennonites, and others—which have worked for centuries to bring an end to war even as they fight for justice. The Catholic Church is engaged in active efforts to rekindle ancient traditions of peacebuilding that draw, above all, on community engagement, reconciliation, and forgiveness. Muslim peacebuilding practices are the topic of increasing focus; examples include the Common Word Initiative, which promotes dialogue between Muslims and Christians, and efforts to delve deeper into Sufi traditions and cultural heritage through ideas, music, and poetry as an inspiration to peaceful and sustainable societies. The Fes, Morocco Festival of Global Sacred Music and its Forum for dialogue represent a creative and bold effort to build on Muslim, Sufi traditions to transcend barriers of culture and faith.[21] Notwithstanding bellicose traditions in some regions (notably Sri Lanka), Buddhist doctrine actively speaks to inner peace as well as harmony within society as central precepts for living. Conflict resolution programs and think tanks (the United States Institute for Peace among them) are working to identify these ideas, document practical experiences, and bring them closer to the mainstream, so that religion is no longer a "missing dimension" of global affairs.

Religious demography and attitudes

Data on religious adherents, even at the most basic level, are difficult to obtain and, above all, difficult to evaluate. There is first the problem of how to define a believer. Most data are based on reporting by religious communities or institutions themselves or by self-reporting, for example where census questions seek information on religious affiliation. Many countries, however, do not seek such information and there is plenty of reason to believe that, where it is reported, much of the data reported are distorted or simply false. Depth and nature of religious belief is another question: the Catholic Church, for example, counts all who are baptized as Catholics without regard to how they lead their lives from that point on, and several Muslim majority countries (Saudi Arabia among them) report that 100 percent of their citizens are Muslim. For some areas, religious affiliation is known with great precision and there a plethora of studies can plausibly assess how belief influences, for example, health and attitudes towards education and marriage. Elsewhere such efforts have little concrete evidence on which to build. The well-respected World Values Surveys, for example, have examined multiple aspects of religion in its various assessments, contributing

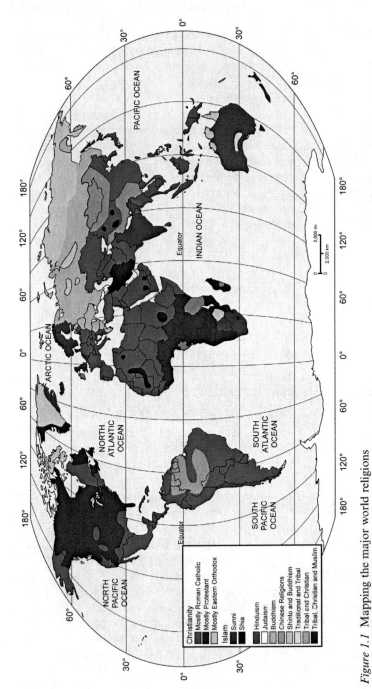

Figure 1.1 Mapping the major world religions
Source: From Matthews. *World Religions*, 7E. © 2013 Wadsworth, a part of Cengage Learning, Inc. Reproduced by permission. www.cengage.com/permissions

important insights. At a broader, global level, however, the data on religious adherence should be taken with some reserve.

In looking to global religious demography a first objective is to establish the broad size of the largest world religious communities (by size, Christianity, Islam, Buddhism, and Hinduism), the patterns of growth (are they increasing or declining?), and the geography of this picture, in both static and dynamic terms. Broadly, both Christianity and Islam as religious communities are growing, and the center of gravity (meaning the geographical focus and concentration of believers and of power) has shifted, and it is projected to shift far more from "north" to "south."[22] The tables and figures present this picture, with due caveats on their precision. In particular, Figure 1.3 offers an example of the dynamic nature of Christianity and Islam. It focuses on Africa, termed

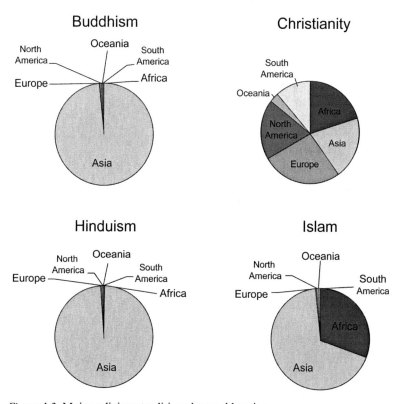

Figure 1.2 Major religious traditions by world region
Source: Todd M. Johnson and Brian J. Grim, eds., *World Religion Database*, www.worldreligiondatabase.org, Leiden: Brill Online (6 July 2012)

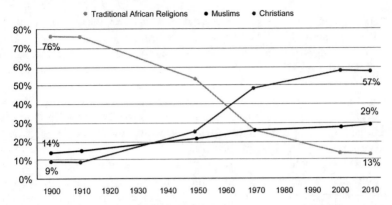

Figure 1.3 Africa: An example of the revolution of changing religious demography
Source: *World Religion Database.* Historical data draw on government records,
historical atlases, and reports of religious organizations at the time. Later figures draw on UN population estimates, surveys, and censuses. Chart produced
with permission of the Pew Research Center's Forum on Religion & Public Life,
from "Tolerance and Tension: Islam and Christianity in Sub-Saharan Africa,"
© 2010, Pew Research Center, www.pewforum.org.

by some the world's most religious continent, and highlights the dramatic
changes in religious demography over the past century. The expectation
is that change will continue to characterize Africa.

A second objective is to ensure that in looking to the major trends
and actors, less sizeable and visible actors are not ignored. Table 1.3
and Figure 1.4 show the size and location of such traditions. Box 1.4
summarizes some recent research on relative birth rates among religious communities, suggesting significant shifts in their balance. An
important dimension, neglected until recent years is the role of traditional, indigenous religious and spiritual communities. On the African
continent, for instance, indigenous religious traditions amount to an
estimated 90 million people.[23]

Box 1.4 Religious demography and fast-growing communities

Rates of population growth worldwide have slowed in recent
decades but one understudied topic is sharp differences in rates of
growth among some religious communities. University of
London Professor Eric Kaufmann's 2010 book *Shall the Religious Inherit the Earth? The Demographic Contradictions of*

Liberal Capitalism[1] argues that the population of the developed world will become increasingly religious and conservative in the long term, reversing decades—even centuries—of liberal secularization. There will be no mass conversions or sudden shifts in the cultural mood, however. Instead, religiosity will spread largely through demographic advantage in a world where secular religions and sources of enchantment have exhausted themselves. The promise of science and rational inquiry, once a source of intrigue and optimism, has been replaced with "relativism and managerialism," poor substitutes for the rich emotional connections, sense of higher purpose, and identity needs fulfilled by religious (and particularly fundamentalist) traditions. The calls to "be fruitful and multiply" found across many faith traditions continue to be answered among the most devout, and advances in medical technology further multiply the demographic advantage of the highly religious. Among the examples he highlights are the impact of rapid population growth among Orthodox Jewish communities in Israel and the relatively rapid population growth of some Catholic and Muslim communities. While some have argued that Kaufmann's models neglect the potential impact of cultural assimilation, he concludes that the projected rise in religiosity across the developed world may well exert a strong influence on future global politics.

[1] Eric Kaufmann, *Shall the Religious Inherit the Earth? The Demographic Contradictions of Liberal Capitalism* (London: Profile Books, 2011).

A special challenge is to understand the global and regional trends affecting extremism and fundamentalism. A wide variety of causal factors and trends have been proposed by scholars. Economic stagnation and political repression are often pointed to as leading causes of religious extremism and violence, although uneven concentrations of religious fundamentalism across impoverished regions of the world clearly point to other elements as well. Local cultural and political factors often play a role, and trailblazing research in the fields of psychology and sociology continue to explore the impact of Huntington's notions regarding a globalization backlash and the hardening of religious identities in the face of perceived cultural intrusions by the West, worsened by persistent economic inequities. Different but with related elements is the extraordinary vibrancy of

Table 1.2 Major religions by world region (millions)

	Buddhists	Catholics	Hindus	Muslims	Orthodox Christians	Other Christians	Protestants	Total
Africa	0.30	177.00	3.00	425.80	43.50	108.30	188.30	946.20
Asia	487.00	137.00	941.80	1,078.00	18.50	132.40	87.40	2,882.10
Europe	1.80	276.90	1.20	41.50	203.80	14.50	94.20	633.90
North America	4.50	246.30	2.20	5.20	7.60	82.40	78.60	426.80
Oceania	0.60	8.90	0.50	0.50	1.00	1.90	12.60	26.00
South America	0.70	321.70	0.40	1.30	0.90	37.30	42.60	404.80
Total	494.90	1,167.90	949.00	1,552.30	275.20	376.90	503.70	5,319.90

Note: The sum of the Christian communities (Catholics, Orthodox, other Christians, and Protestants) exceeds the total Christian count displayed in Figure 1.1. This inconsistency in the data available is indicative of the challenges that face quantifying religious populations.

Source: Todd M. Johnson and Brian J. Grim, eds., *World Religion Database*, www.worldreligiondatabase.org, Leiden: Brill Online, 23 July 2012.

Table 1.3 Smaller world religions by region (millions)

	Bahá'ís	Confucianists	Daoists	Jains	Jews	New religionists	Shintoists	Sikhs	Spiritists	Zoroastrians	Total
Africa	2.10	0.00	0.00	0.10	0.10	0.10	0.00	0.10	0.00	0.00	2.60
Asia	3.40	8.00	8.40	5.10	6.00	59.00	2.70	22.80	0.00	0.20	115.60
Europe	0.20	0.00	0.00	0.00	1.90	0.40	0.00	0.60	0.10	0.00	3.20
North America	0.80	0.00	0.00	0.10	5.80	1.80	0.10	0.60	3.20	0.00	12.40
Oceania	0.10	0.00	0.00	0.00	0.80	0.10	0.00	0.00	0.00	0.00	1.10
South America	0.60	0.00	0.00	0.00	0.10	1.70	0.00	0.00	10.30	0.00	12.80
Total	7.30	8.10	8.40	5.30	14.80	63.00	2.80	24.10	13.70	0.20	147.70

Source: (Todd M. Johnson and Brian J. Grim, eds., *World Religion Database*, www.worldreligiondatabase.org, Leiden: Brill Online, 23 July 2012.)

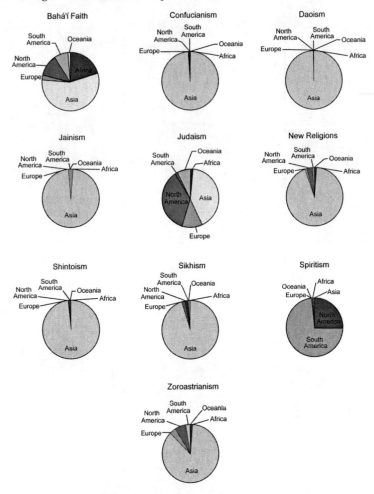

Figure 1.4 Smaller religious traditions by world region
Source: (Todd M. Johnson and Brian J. Grim, eds., *World Religion Database*, www.worldreligiondatabase.org, Leiden: Brill Online, 6 July 2012.)

charismatic churches, arguably the fastest-growing religious phenomenon in the world today. The rapid expansion of many new or relatively new Protestant denominations (termed variously charismatic or Pentecostal) and, largely in the wake of their spread, the transformation of more traditional religious communities (Protestant and Catholic) throughout much of the developing world has caused considerable consternation among the religious communities that often were long established there. This includes traditional religions (Maya in

Guatemala, for example), Muslim communities, and the Catholic Church. They have often greeted these new actors and their tendencies toward proselytization with dismay, fearing a loss of cultural heritage with continued conversions. The topic of evangelization or proselytizing has emerged as one of the most sensitive issues around religion, especially in (both) Christian and Muslim communities. Other Christian groups, which continue to make up a sizeable majority of faith-inspired development organizations, often view the expansion of charismatic churches with suspicion as well. Overt proselytization is frowned upon in most development circles, and many Christian communities in the developing world see tensions between indigenous religious groups and evangelicals as damaging to their mission. The extent to which competition for adherents plays a role must, of course, also be considered.

Finally, Figure 1.5 and Figure 1.6 focus on the evidence suggested by some statistical measures of strength of religious adherence and, related to that, levels of relative trust in various entities, religious leaders and communities among them.

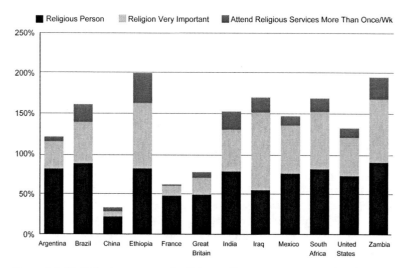

Figure 1.5 Statistical measures of religious adherence
Source: The World Values Survey, *2005–2008 Wave WVS Online Data Analysis*, www.wvsevsdb.com/wvs/WVSAnalizeStudy.jsp (accessed 6 July 2012)
Note: Questions: Independently of whether you go to church or not, would you say you are: A Religious Person?; For each of the following aspects, indicate how important it is in your life: Religion; Apart from weddings, funerals and christenings, about how often do you attend religious services these days?

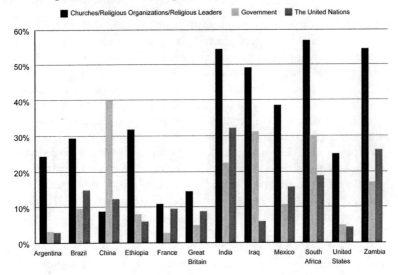

Figure 1.6 Institutional confidence
Source: (The World Values Survey, *2005–2008 Wave WVS Online Data Analysis,*
www.wvsevsdb.com/wvs/WVSAnalizeStudy.jsp (accessed 6 July 2012))
Note: Question: I am going to name a number of organisations. For each one,
could you tell me how much confidence you have in them: is it a great deal of
confidence, quite a lot of confidence, not very much confidence or none at all?
Answer: Quite a lot of confidence.

Religion's organizational forms

Religious institutions are extraordinarily diverse, varying by tradition
and by region, extending from the tiniest community level to vast global
institutions. Many are formal and are governed by an array of legal
regulations, some specific to religion (for example, those that exempt
religious institutions from taxation), others applying more broadly to
civil society as a whole. Many leaders of and workers in religious institutions are professionals, trained through formal programs in seminaries or comparable institutions. Religious organizations, however, also
mobilize vast numbers of volunteers who work without salaries, both
to support the religious community as well as to practice good works
that are part of the religious enterprise.

Six categories of religious institutions are the principle focus of this
book. They are briefly introduced here, then treated in greater detail in
subsequent chapters.

• Formal structures of religious traditions and communities: a prime
  example is the formal hierarchy of the Catholic Church. Others

would include a Buddhist Sangha, the Anglican Communion, and the Imamate of the Ismaili community. For many, but not all faith traditions, these structures extend from global to local communities. Many are actively and deliberately involved in both transnational and national politics.

• Various religiously inspired movements: these range from vast to small, and very formal to very informal, and would include the Community of Sant'Egidio, a Rome-based lay Catholic organization working in some 80 countries; Opus Dei, also a lay Catholic movement; Engaged Buddhist movements; the Art of Living, a Hindu-inspired spiritual movement; and both Sufi Muslim and Salafi Muslim movements. Religiously inspired movements could also be said to include violent organizations with a strong religious character, like Boko Haram in Nigeria, the various parties to conflict in Sri Lanka, the Branch Davidians in the United States, and Al Qaeda. Many such movements play political roles both in mobilizing communities and shaping ideas and in specific practical programs (running schools, hospitals, and youth programs, for example).

• Global interreligious or ecumenical bodies: these include global bodies like Religions for Peace, the Parliament of the World's Religions, and the World Council of Churches that work for specific causes (peace, interfaith dialogue, advocacy), and to mobilize common faith voices and initiatives. There are also regional and more specifically focused entities. Among the latter would be the Ecumenical Advocacy Alliance (EAA), which works primarily on issues of HIV/AIDS and fair trade.

• Community or congregation level groups: here there is a wide array of women's, youth, and other groups of countless descriptions, many of them informal in institutional terms. They represent the essence of the social capital which many ascribe to religion as its primary asset. They have the power to mobilize action, communicate, and serve their members, but in general tend to be rather informally defined and often poorly coordinated.

• Faith-inspired organizations: this vast array of institutions, taking many different forms, works directly on humanitarian relief and on community development. This category consists of a largely uncounted, highly diverse set of entities, ranging from enormous and structured (World Vision, Catholic Relief Services), to informal and tiny. Many work directly at the community level, while others are global advocates for specific causes or for a broad view of social justice or peace (the World Peace Prayer Society is an example).

• Religiously linked academic institutions: these include seminaries and religious training institutions, universities, schools, literacy programs, peace education efforts, and many others. This body of institutions deserves special focus due to its role in shaping ideas and theologies and because the institutions train both future religious leaders and many young people. Jesuit Universities, Al-Azhar University, and Union Theological Seminary are examples of pivotal institutions. Also of note are foundations and organizations that in whole or in part relate to religious organizations. Examples might include the Templeton Foundation, the Tony Blair Faith Foundation, and the Chautauqua Institute.

A perennial and thorny question is how religion relates to the concept of and the various structures that represent civil society. At a broad level and essentially by definition, most religious institutions are non-governmental bodies and share many characteristics with a range of civil society organizations. This is especially true for those organizations categorized as faith-based or faith-inspired, as they share many characteristics with the even broader category of non-governmental organizations. In different country settings and for varied purposes, religious organizations are considered part of civil society more generally to a greater or lesser degree. Some governments and institutions make a point of not distinguishing religiously linked organizations from others with similar functions or organizations at all. However, in alternate settings they may be treated differently in important respects, ranging from inclusion in (or exclusion from) policy discussions, financial relationships, access to information, etc. In the United States the issues of discrimination in hiring, obligations to report information, and financial treatment set religiously linked organizations apart from other segments of civil society. Faith leaders often resist being lumped together with other parts of civil society. They argue, justly, that religious institutions and their memberships dwarf other parts of civil society. Many also contend that religious institutions have deeper and longer roots in communities; depending on the nature of other civil society institutions, this may or may not be the case. Whatever the formal definitions and the significant legal privileges or obligations that go with the designation and categorization of religious entities under the wide umbrella of civil society, these organizations together weave the richest "social capital" fabric known today, with by far the most intensive presence in communities. They also have extraordinarily wide national, regional, and global presence and networks.

Conclusion

In reflecting on the dynamic picture of religion's roles in international affairs, a central question is what, in fact, is happening to religious institutions and beliefs: are they in decline, as the long-standing secular assumptions maintained, or is there a global resurgence and a rethinking of religious roles as part of globalization? A related issue is how the nature and dynamics of religious institutions and their changing character are understood by those engaged in international affairs. Because he began his career with one appreciation of religion's role and came explicitly to change fundamentally the way he understood the forces at work, sociologist Peter Berger is an influential analyst of both the factors at work and how they have been and are perceived, including the tendency towards what he terms a "cognitive contamination" that has led to wide acceptance of certain beliefs, warranted or otherwise. The secular theory that dominated international relations thinking until recently held that modernity, "both because of the spread of scientific knowledge and because modern institutions undermined the social bases of religious faith, necessarily led to secularization (understood as the progressive decline of religion in society and in the minds of individuals)."[24] It is clear, however, that "it cannot be plausibly maintained that modernity necessarily leads to a decline of religion."[25] In short, a fresh look at religion suggests a different view of important dimensions of international relations. There are indeed fundamental changes afoot. They include, apart from shifting demographics in religious institutions and their global reach, a sharp increase in the religious plurality of many modern societies. This has major effects on diversity, civic peace, and social interaction the world over. Plurality increases the individual's ability to make choices between and among worldviews. Religion is almost always an important element. Increasingly plural societies are also resulting in changes in the character of religious institutions and their relationships with one another. In many societies, churches and their equivalents in other faith communities have become voluntary associations, often in competition with one another. This change in the plural character of societies affects not only religion, but also morality, as it contributes to a greater diversity of values—which are the foundation of morality. In many respects, this ethical diversity is more difficult to cope with than religious pluralism where identities are fairly rigid, and it is a fundamental challenge of modern, diverse societies where, notwithstanding the broad agreements on human rights and other norms, values (for example, in understanding and acting on inequalities of wealth and opportunity and relations among men and women) are in contest, in both subtle and fundamental ways.

2   Global religious bodies

- Religious institutions at the national level
- Catholic Church institutions
- Protestant churches
- The Orthodox world
- Cults and reformers?
- Ecumenical movements and organizations
- The Muslim world and contemporary geopolitics
- Global institutions for Islam
- Global organizations of Buddhism
- Hindu organizations
- Prominent smaller faiths
- Conclusion

An institutional map of global religions would show an extraordinarily large and diverse field of institutions, taking many forms and ranging widely in size, composition, and organizational culture. The challenge of categorizing them bears some resemblance to that presented by non-governmental organizations (NGOs) as a whole.[1] Not only are the core missions of the organizations perceived differently by actors and observers, but their official status varies: ranging from bodies mandated in national constitutions or formally accredited by the United Nations (UN), to informal, clandestine, and sometimes illegal groups. Religious institutions are also dynamic. An observer in Uganda, for instance, compared evangelical churches there to "mushrooms," suggesting that they emerge rapidly, seemingly from nowhere, and can vanish just as quickly. Not all institutions evolve so rapidly, but religious organizations everywhere are affected by the modernization and transformation of communications, international migration, and other facets of globalization. The roles of diaspora communities that often rely on and value religious ties are a prominent example of how networks spurred by globalizing forces today serve to link communities that in earlier times were essentially autonomous. These forces have both accentuated and accelerated tendencies towards greater unity, as well as sharpened distinctions between communities. A literal map of institutions, needless to say, does not exist, even at a very local level. Even so, a priority task in appreciating the complex worlds of global religious bodies and assessing the political roles they play in international relations is to get a sense of what institutions exist, by place and function, and how they work in practice.

With these caveats in mind, this chapter's objective is to introduce and illustrate the institutions that govern the largest religious communities, with special attention to those that have a transnational presence or character. The focus is on institutions that govern religious communities themselves (thus the Catholic Church, as opposed to Catholic faith-inspired organizations like Catholic Relief Services (CRS) or Georgetown University). A first challenge is that the governance of spiritual and material dimensions of religious institutions overlap, and disentangling the two is rarely straightforward. For this discussion, however, the focus is explicitly material and centered on the ways in which institutions organize themselves and subsequently present this practical dimension to the external world. They employ staff, manage revenues and finance, buy and develop land, and oversee a wide range of subordinate bodies with various functions, religious and non-religious. In these respects they share many of the demands on, as well as qualities of, secular institutions. In the same vein, global religious institutions relate continuously to others in different categorical spheres. Partnership is as common a notion among these institutions as it is, for example, among private companies. Complexity is a second challenge. Many of the institutions involved have centuries if not millennia of history involving institutional schisms and rivalries as well as ancient yet vibrant traditions that color the structures themselves, the way in which they are presented in relation to adherents and rivals, and the language and terminology they use. Straightforward institutional biographies would be most helpful, but they are often unavailable and are rarely unambiguous and uncontested.

The chapter begins with a brief review of the formal statuses of religious institutions nationally (constitutional approaches to religion are discussed in Chapter 1 and relationships at the international level in Chapter 4). At issue is the relationship between "church and state." In practice arrangements vary widely, shaped by each nation's history and social and political ideals. The arrangements range from clear separation, wherein religious institutions are defined as private, to tight integration of religious institutions and leaders in structures and practices of national governance. In most situations relationships are complex—even where a national church is "established"—and appreciating this complexity is foundational to an understanding of contemporary religious institutions.

The institutions of the Catholic Church and the Holy See represent the largest and most formally structured religious bodies in the world, and they are thus treated in some detail. Other Christian organizations—especially the wide array of Protestant denominations as well as the Orthodox Church—also have distinctive if widely varying institutional forms that are significant on the global stage. Several organizations, described as ecumenical, are working to overcome some of these barriers of dispersion and division as they seek to link together different segments of a single family of religious traditions.

Institutional governance within both global and more local Islamic communities is, by contrast, rather more difficult to describe succinctly as there is no structure comparable to the Catholic Church hierarchy. There are, however, important institutions that govern and represent Muslim nations as well as different Muslim communities. These take several different forms.

Where other religious traditions are concerned, the task of identifying formal institutions and responsibilities is still more challenging. Buddhist, Hindu, Jewish, and other communities all have an array of institutions with formal leaders who carry both spiritual and temporal responsibilities (for example, managing facilities), but rarely are these transnational bodies widely recognized as "speaking for" even segments of the religious community, much less the faith at large. Transnational arrangements in these traditions tend to involve a combination of formal and informal structures, and there are many instances of institutional rivalries and clashes. With many thousand religious entities not all can be analyzed, but some distinctive communities with global reach and structures are described to serve not only as examples of the diversity in the field, but also of historical depth (Zoroastrians, for example) or the governance dynamics of newer religions (the Bahá'ís and new branches of Hinduism).

Diversity and complexity also characterize governance arrangements for indigenous religious communities. Sadly, indigenous traditions have long been the subjects of neglect and even outright persecution as proselytizing traditions, imbued with deeply ingrained notions of cultural superiority, swept across the globe. At one global interreligious meeting, for instance, a spokesman for indigenous people who were gathered on a stage commented to the formal religious leaders who constituted the audience, "We are what is left when you got through with us."[2]

Often located in remote and far-removed places, these traditional communities are governed in many different ways. Only recently have institutions emerged that aim to represent the broad and diverse community of indigenous traditions globally, but these are assuming increasing importance as the UN and other international entities focus on the special attributes and rights of indigenous communities. For very different reasons, similar comments apply to actively non-religious traditions (humanists, for example) and Pagan or Wiccan followers. There are many relevant institutions but how far they represent all who might adhere to their beliefs is not easy to discern.

Religious institutions at the national level

The statuses and roles of religious institutions are defined country by country, often following intense reflection, controversy, and even violence. Broadly speaking, relationships between religious bodies and the state in many parts of the world have tended, as outlined in Chapter 1, to move from established roles for religious bodies in national governance (theocratic states being the prototypical form) towards the "Westphalian" model, where many if not most religious actors are excluded from formal political and legal authority. Even in Europe and North America, however, where separation of church and state is the official ideal, this by no means suggests that religious institutions are irrelevant to national governance. A wide range of laws and practices determine, country by country, how religious institutions function within the society and whether and how they enter the political sphere. The complexities of church-state relationships are the stuff of daily politics: witness the continuing debates in the United States about what the Constitution means for the nation's religious character and where religious institutions can and cannot intervene in practical matters (abortion, school prayer, and even regulation of insurance).

What is less well appreciated is how far specific national arrangements vary across states. Many European countries have established churches, yet even there the understanding of religious freedom in several nations means, in effect, that different denominations must receive equal treatment by the state. This can translate, for example, into state support for clergy salaries or schools across a wide range of denominations. In many parts of the world, especially Muslim majority nations, religion is an explicit part of the political system. In many others, religious groups play a less formally articulated, but nevertheless prevalent, role in national politics—for example, through political parties that have an explicit religious link and ethos. The specific roles that religious authorities

Table 2.1 Religion and state: contemporary arrangements

Jurisdictions recognizing Catholicism as their state or official religion

---

Vatican City (a theocracy), Costa Rica, Liechtenstein, Malta and Monaco. Andorra, Argentina, Dominican Republic, El Salvador, Italy, Haiti, Honduras, Paraguay, Peru, Poland, Portugal, and Spain give special recognition to Catholicism in their constitution although it is not the state religion.

All cantons in Switzerland give official recognition to a church except Geneva and Neuchâtel. Roman Catholicism is recognized as official in several cantons, including Appenzell Innerrhoden, Nidwalden, Schwyz and Uri. Switzerland itself has no official religion.

Jurisdictions recognizing one of the Eastern Orthodox churches as their state religion

---

Greece: Church of Greece; Finland: Finnish Orthodox Church has a special relationship with the Finnish state (Orthodox Church Act); Georgia: Georgian Orthodox Church

---

Jurisdictions recognizing a Lutheran church as their state religion

---

Denmark (Church of Denmark); Iceland (Church of Iceland); Finland: Evangelical Lutheran Church; Sweden relegated their state church, the Church of Sweden, to a national church in 2000.

Jurisdictions recognizing a Reformed church as their state religion

---

Scotland (Church of Scotland); Tuvalu (Church of Tuvalu); several cantons in Switzerland give official recognition to the Swiss Reformed Church as the cantonal religion, including Appenzell Ausserrhoden, Bern, Schaffhausen, Vaud, and Zurich. Switzerland itself has no official religion.

Jurisdictions recognizing an Anglican church as their state religion

---

England (Church of England)

Countries recognizing Islam as their state religion

Afghanistan; Algeria; Bangladesh; Brunei; Comoros; Egypt; Aceh Province of Indonesia; Iraq; Jordan; Libya; Maldives; Malaysia; Mauritania; Morocco; Pakistan; Qatar; Saudi Arabia; Somalia; Tunisia; United Arab Emirates; Iran (theocracy); Ibadi; Oman; Kuwait; Yemen; Bahrain; Somalia

---

Governments recognizing Buddhism as their official religion

Cambodia; Sri Lanka (constitution accords Buddhism the "foremost place," but Buddhism is not recognized as the state religion); Thailand (Thai constitution (2007) recognized Buddhism as "the religion of Thai tradition with the most adherents"; Laos; Bhutan; Kalmykia, a republic within the Russian Federation

---

Others

Israel is defined in several of its laws as a "Jewish and democratic state" (*medina yehuditve-demokratit*).

Nepal was the world's only Hindu state, but is no longer following a declaration by the parliament in 2006.

---

play in law, legislative bodies, judicial matters, and executive bodies may be the subject of sharp tensions, or they may be broadly recognized as integral parts of a national system.

A detailed review of national arrangements is far beyond this book's scope. To convey a sense of the complexity and relevance of "church-state relations," Table 2.1 lists countries where there are now state or established religions.[3] Four "mini case studies" illustrate the wide diversity of arrangements in various countries. A fifth frames issues for a distinctive group of countries with majority Muslim populations. Box 2.1 outlines India's approach to religion in relation to government. Box 2.2 summarizes the complex issues of religion in China. Box 2.3 takes Brazil as an example of the dynamics of national approaches to religion in Latin America. Box 2.4 outlines differing approaches to religion and state in several Muslim majority nations. Box 2.5 illustrates the complexity of state-church relationships with the example of Finland.

Box 2.1 Religion and secularism in India

India today has no official religion, considers itself a secular state, prides itself on its commitment to religious freedom and tolerance, and, despite significant religiously marked conflicts over its history, has a generally remarkable history of adhering to its principles of tolerance and pluralism. India's religious landscape, however, is complex and there are tensions within and among traditions, as well as a legal system that, in some areas, relies on religious authorities for purposes of family law. The most significant challenges involve the status of India's large Muslim minority, which lags behind other groups in education, employment, and welfare. The role of religion in India's dynamic democracy, however, continues to evolve.

Four of the world's major religions were born in India: Hinduism, Buddhism, Jainism, and Sikhism. As such, religion has always been part of India's identity and ethos, and in few countries is religion as visible and palpable as it is in contemporary India. Religious diversity and tolerance are well established in India by law and custom, and the vast majority of Indians associate themselves with a religious identity and set of beliefs.

Approximately 80 percent of Indians are Hindus (in a sense they are Hindu by default since it is considered a cultural as well as a religious identity). India's Muslim population (the world's second largest) is about 13–14 percent of the population. Christians and

Sikhs represent about 2 percent of the population each, and Buddhists and Jains under 1 percent. This remarkable religious diversity is the product of conquest, assimilation, and integration of religion by traders, travelers, and rulers over the years. Another unique dimension of Indian religion is its global influence, as the Indian diaspora in the West has popularized many aspects of Hindu philosophy (yoga and vegetarianism, for example). Indian spiritual organizations like the Hare Krishna movement and the Brahma Kumaris have also had a considerable influence on the spreading of Hinduism outside India. One distinctive feature of India is that all the major religions are the majority faith in at least one state.

India's constitution declares the nation to be a secular republic that upholds the rights of citizens to worship freely and spread their faith, subject to "reasonable restrictions" for the sake of morality, law, and order. Freedom of religion is a fundamental right guaranteed by the constitution. When religious tensions or conflicts do occur, the general view is that they are political rather than religious in nature. The word "secular" was added to India's constitution by an Amendment Act of 1976, which mandates equal treatment and tolerance of all religions. There is no religious instruction in government-supported schools, and the Supreme Court of India has upheld freedom of religion as a fundamental right.

An important policy measure with religious dimensions is the system of reservations, essentially a constitutionally guaranteed quota system. It was initially introduced for Christians. Applied at the state level, it currently affects primarily Christians and Muslims, and has particularly significant ramifications at higher education levels and in the civil service. It has been highly contentious since it was introduced in colonial times.

None of India's religious communities have a supreme religious authority, nor is there any body that purports to represent or speak for the plethora of religious communities, though interfaith activity is on the increase. A distinctive feature of Indian law and society is the established authority of independently administered religious legal systems over significant sections of the law (family law, for example). Muslims, Christians, Zoroastrians, and Jews, for instance, have personal laws exclusive to their communities. Meanwhile, Hindus, Jains, Buddhists, and Sikhs are governed by a single legal system known as Hindu personal law.

Box 2.2 China: approaching religion in new ways

The People's Republic of China was notoriously hostile to religion in its early decades, subscribing to the communist suspicions of religion as an "opium" that distorted the energies of citizens and of clerics whom it saw as deeply inclined to undermine revolutionary change. Opposition to the Dalai Lama, crackdowns of Buddhists in Tibet and Muslim Uighurs, and tensions with the Vatican over who is authorized to anoint bishops are part of this history of tensions around religious beliefs and above all religious organizations. Yet China's citizens, the government asserts, enjoy freedom of religious belief, and the state, public organizations, and individuals are not to compel citizens to believe—or not believe—in any religion. The constitution and laws protect "normal religious activities" that are overseen by five state-sanctioned "patriotic religious associations" (Buddhist, Taoist, Muslim, Catholic, and Protestant). By law, only these associations can register religious groups and places of worship. Others, the Falun Gong among them, are prohibited and infractions bring down a heavy state hand. Members of the Chinese Communist Party are discouraged from participating in religious activities, an indication of continuing official qualms. Proselytizing in registered places of worship and in private settings is allowed, but with restrictions. Punishments for infractions range from fines to imprisonment.

This long-standing story of unease and regulation is changing, albeit gradually. One sign is a shift in the official position towards Confucianism, once denigrated as a relic of the past, now more honored as a cherished heritage. Similar thawing towards Taoism is occurring and Buddhist groups now operate more freely than they did a few decades ago. The backdrop for these changes are both the general opening up of social and economic space in China and the evident growth in interest in and commitment to religious practice by what are thought to be hundreds of millions of Chinese. As an example, there are (official statistics) over 36,000 Islamic places of worship and over 45,000 imams.[1] One 2007 survey found that over 31 percent of adult Chinese considered themselves religious believers. The Pew Research Center estimated the number of Christians practicing in illegal (house) churches at 50 million to 70 million and some estimates go much higher.[2]

The government's State Administration for Religious Affairs (SARA) oversees relationships with a wide range of religious communities and has reached out especially to academic institutions in recent years. After the 2010 Qinghai earthquake, religiously linked NGOs moved swiftly to organize help, and the government took note. Some foreign religious groups are finding a new openness to cooperation—for example, the Amity Foundation, Taiwan-based Tzu Chi, and Christian Action. Local governments have allowed some religious groups and practices besides the five nationally recognized religions, including Orthodox Christianity, in some provinces and also have been more accepting of indigenous religious practices. The changing roles of religion in China offer one of the world's most dynamic developments, and it turns in part around the state's institutional roles vis-à-vis both citizen beliefs and the active roles that religious institutions play in shaping values and behaviours and in concrete social support and services.

[1] Cited in US State Department *July–December, 2010 International Religious Freedom Report: China*, www.state.gov/j/drl/rls/irf/2010_5/168351.htm. The figures are SARA data.

[2] The Pew Forum on Religious Life, *Global Christianity*, December 2011, www.pewforum.org/Christian/Global-Christianity-china.aspx.

Box 2.3 Brazil: a dynamic approach to religious freedom and tolerance

Brazil has a vibrant contemporary religious dynamic that is characterized by strong *de facto* religious tolerance, rapid growth of a wide range of charismatic protestant denominations, and considerable syncretism among religions, overlaid on a long history of active Catholic Church involvement in Brazilian policies and politics. Brazil's long history of encouraging immigration—for example, from the former Ottoman lands in the nineteenth century—and promoting internal migration to populate the interior has contributed to its rich religious diversity. These policies brought in large numbers of Christians, Jews, and Muslims, including large numbers of Protestant northern Europeans. All constantly redefine the Brazilian religious landscape. Thus Brazil enjoys remarkable diversity in its ethnic and religious make-up across an enormous territory, with a notable absence of ethnic and religious tension.

The Catholic Church was involved from the very start in defining Brazil as a distinct entity, and today Brazil has the largest number of Catholics living in a single country in the world. In 1493 (just after Columbus's first voyage of discovery to the Americas), Spanish-born Pope Alexander VI issued a Papal Bull parceling out newly discovered lands between Spain and Portugal; although the exact lines were later modified, this agreement opened Brazil to Portuguese colonization and Christian (originally Jesuit) evangelization. Colonization proceeded there as elsewhere with cross and sword united, and during the Empire (1822–89), the Church operated as part of the state bureaucracy.[1] However, a series of clerical squabbles and scandals coupled with severe government repression led to clashes among bishops and imperial officials and the Church's institutional breakdown. The positivist-inspired military officers who toppled the monarchy ended subsidies for Catholic activities, secularized education, and wrote religious freedom into the Constitution of 1891. Liberty from state control was seen as an asset, but the Church never fully recovered its earlier power and status. During much of the twentieth century, however, strong ties with the government were reestablished, particularly at local and regional levels. The Church once again came to be seen as a bulwark of social stability, regaining quasi-official recognition.

Today, Brazil's constitution guarantees freedom of religion and prohibits the establishment of any religion, banning government support or hindrance at all levels. Nonetheless, the Church, whether through movements like liberation theology (essentially born in Brazil), or exemplary programs like the remarkable national early childhood development program Pastoral da Criança[2] is still a force that shapes both society and politics.

Brazil's other religious traditions also play active roles in politics and, increasingly, in international affairs. Brazil's Afro-Brazilian Candomblé tradition is extending its influence across Latin America and Africa. Dynamic evangelical Protestant denominations like The Universal Church of the Reign of God and the Assemblies of God are powerful actors with "megachurches," radio stations, and a global presence. Virtually every world religion, large or small, has a presence in Brazil.

[1] A more detailed account of this history is *inter alia* in Kenneth Serbin, "Church-State Reciprocity in Contemporary Brazil: The Convening of the International Eucharistic Congress of

1955 in Rio de Janeiro," Working Paper #229, August 1996, kellogg.nd.edu/publications/workingpapers/WPS/229.pdf.

[2] For an account of the foundation of this program and its links to the Catholic Church see author's interview with Dr Zilda Arns Neumann, berkleycenter.georgetown.edu/interviews/a-discussion-with-dr-zilda-arns-neumann-founder-pastoral-crianca-brazil.

Box 2.4   Religion and governance in Muslim majority countries

Religion, and specifically Islam, plays widely differing roles in Muslim majority countries. The varying roles are products of history and of political forces that balance temporal and religious authority. A common topic of debate today is the role of Sharia in legal systems which, again, takes many forms. At a simplistic level, reference to Sharia suggests a strict application of Muslim law in matters ranging from family relations to charging interest on loans. In practice, however, it suggests a broad approach to honoring Islamic principles in society, both in specific framing of law and in attitudes towards social relations.

Saudi Arabia, known as the most strictly Muslim community in today's world, is governed in practice by a complex and often tacit agreement among the Crown, religious authority, and state bureaucracy. Morocco's king, known as the Commander of the Faithful, traces his authority to an early imam and his personal religious authority blends with a rather French-style bureaucracy and a constitutional monarchy in Morocco's governance. Pakistan, the product of the partition of British India largely on religious lines, from its creation has wrestled with the issue of how Islam as a religion relates to the state in all government branches, most notably the judiciary. Indonesia, with the world's largest Muslim community, also has developed a complex balance that defines a state respectful of but not defined by religious identity. The guiding state principle, *pancasila*, comes from two Javanese words: *pañca*, meaning five, and *sīla*, meaning principles. The five principles, held to be inseparable and interrelated, are belief in the one and only God, just and civilized humanity, Indonesia's unity, democracy guided by inner wisdom in the unanimity arising out of deliberations amongst representatives, and social justice for all. Iran, the largest Shi'a Muslim nation, is currently the nation most closely approaching a theocracy. The December 1979 Constitution, as amended in 1989, defines the political, economic, and social order of an Islamic Republic, and Shi'a Islam of the Twelver school of thought as Iran's official religion. Iran's elected president and parliament (*majlis*) govern with a Guardian Council. The most powerful political figure is the Supreme Leader, a position held in recent times by the highest religious authority, the Ayatollah. The role of religion and of religious authorities in Muslim minority African and Middle Eastern nations is in most instances less formalized and tends to vary over time. In countries affected by the 2011 Arab uprisings, notably Egypt, the role that religious authorities and religion will play is in flux.

Box 2.5 State and church in Finland

The Evangelical Lutheran Church of Finland has a special relationship with the Finnish state. Its internal structure is described in a special law, the Church Act, which can be amended only by a decision of the Synod of the Evangelical Lutheran Church and subsequent ratification by the parliament. Thus, it can be changed only by changing the constitution. The church has a power to tax its members and all corporations, unless a majority of shareholders are members of the Finnish Orthodox Church. The state collects these taxes for the Church for a fee. The Church is required to give a burial place for everyone in its graveyards (79 percent of the population were members at the end of 2009). The Finnish president also decides the themes for the intercession days. The Church does not consider itself a state church, as the Finnish state does not have the power to influence its internal workings or its theology, although it has a veto for changes of the internal structure that require changing the Church Act. The Finnish state does not accord any precedence to Lutherans or the Lutheran faith in its own operations.

Catholic Church institutions

The Catholic Church is one of the world's oldest and most elaborate institutions, with a vast global reach, countless distinct and separate branches and affiliated organizations and networks, and a complex history, the telling of which fills many libraries. Few purport to understand the full panoply of institutions within the Catholic Church, much less their inner workings, although many analyses have set out explicitly to "demystify" it.[4] The Church also has the unique characteristic of being simultaneously a religious body (the Catholic Church) and a sovereign state (the Holy See). The Church functions as a global network of territorial jurisdictions (dioceses) which serve the spiritual and material needs of the world's estimated 1.2 billion Catholics. Besides the formal episcopal hierarchy of cardinals, bishops, and priests, the Church also includes a remarkable array of religious orders and other organizations that are part of the Church but function as more or less distinct entities (the Knights of Malta, described in Box 2.6, are an example). The Vatican refers to the tiny state (108 acres) inside the city of Rome, Italy, the sovereignty of which was established by international treaties. The Vatican State itself was officially born in 1929, with the signing of the Lateran Treaty by Italy and the Holy See. Vatican City administers a unit of Swiss Guards, has a post office and bank, and issues coins, stamps, and passports. However, it is the Holy See itself that accredits ambassadors from most nations, and administers its own diplomatic service, consisting of Papal Nuncios (the equivalent of ambassadors) who serve in virtually all countries and many international institutions. Needless to say, administrative matters in the Vatican are quite complex and need not be further elaborated on here. For our purposes it is useful to note the unique status of the Catholic Church as both a highly significant international religious body, as well as a sovereign state.

Box 2.6 The Order of the Knights of Malta[1]

A unique global institution, the Order of the Knights of Malta (officially the Sovereign Military Hospitaller Order of Saint John of Jerusalem of Rhodes and of Malta) is a sovereign authority recognized by many nations but without any formal territory. It functions today largely as a charitable organization that manages medical relief in disasters and as a support and advocate for the disabled. It has operated in over 120 countries. Its name notwithstanding, the order has had no military function since the late eighteenth century.

Based in Rome, the Order is a Roman Catholic organization that counts about 13,000 members worldwide. It traces its foundation to 1048 when Amalfian merchants in Jerusalem formed a monastic order to run a hospital that tended to Christian pilgrims in the Holy Land. At the height of its power the order took on substantial military functions for Rome, defending Christians from the local Muslim population. The Knights of St John were one of many Christian military orders founded during this period—including the fabled but now defunct Knights Templar. The Knights of St John went into exile when the Sultan of Egypt retook Jerusalem in 1291, and settled in Rhodes 20 years later until the Sultan's forces once again sent them into new exile in 1523. Settling in Malta, they ruled the island until Napoleon's army ousted them in 1798. They then moved to Rome, where they have kept their base ever since.

When the Order was originally founded, knights were expected to take a vow of poverty, chastity, and obedience; nowadays, obedience is sufficient. Membership is still by invitation, but members no longer have to be nobles; indeed, the Knights have become increasingly American in membership. The Order's leader, referred to as the prince and grand master, is elected for life in a secret conclave and must be approved by the Pope.

The Order of the Knights of Malta is considered a sovereign entity under international law and prints its own postage stamps and coins (though these have mostly novelty value today). It enjoys observer status at the UN, which classifies it as a non-state entity, like the Red Cross, and maintains diplomatic relations with 104 countries. The Order does not have official relations with the United States, though it has offices in New York for the UN delegation, and in Washington for its representation at the Inter-American Development Bank.

[1] www.foreignpolicy.com/articles/2011/01/19/who_are_the_knights_of_malta_and_what_do_they_want, 11 January 2011.

The Catholic Church's reputation as a highly centralized and strictly hierarchical institution is apt, at least formally. The Pope and the papacy (the offices that directly serve the Pope) administer a tiered structure that extends to some 2,800 dioceses, territorial divisions each led by a bishop, and then to some 409,000 priests serving in almost 220,000 parishes across the world. The hierarchy is truly and formally patriarchal in a literal sense, in that women cannot hold office, though they play many important roles, ranging from administering hospitals and schools to serving the formal clerics.[5] The authority of the Pope is, according to Canon law, absolute: "He is the head of the College of Bishops, the Vicar of Christ, and the Pastor of the universal Church here on earth. Consequently, by virtue of his office, he has supreme, full, immediate and universal ordinary power in the Church, and he can always freely exercise this power."[6] In short, the Pope has full executive, legislative, and judicial power over the Catholic Church. Indeed, many rulers might aspire to the idea of infallibility that is part of both the aura and reality of the Pope's authority. In practice, his directives constitute part of a vast body of thought and teaching presented in the form of Encyclicals and other pronouncements. Of special interest for international affairs are the social teachings of the Church, which touch on topics ranging from theory of just war to gender relations, and from labor practices to environmental protection.

The Pope is among the world's most admired and revered world leaders, as well as the one perhaps most subject to vilification as a personification of what are viewed as the flaws of religious authority. When he travels, he is greeted by crowds numbering in the millions and he meets regularly with heads of state and other religious leaders; when he speaks, millions listen. While the temporal authority of the Papacy today is far different from the days when a Pope was an absolute monarch, he is still a leading global authority. Stalin famously queried disparagingly how many divisions the Pope commanded (the answer, of course, was none), but his influence is nonetheless a force to be reckoned with.

Veteran Vatican commentator John Allen deciphers the complex and often mysterious structures around the Pope as a series of concentric circles. These emanate from the Pope's various functions. He is first Bishop of Rome, then leader of the church itself (setting policy, deciding matters of personnel and finance, and serving as the final appeal within the vast church system). The Pope is, beyond the Church itself, generally acknowledged as the most authoritative and respected among global religious leaders and thus has a unique convening power. The Pope, for good and sometimes for less good (the sex abuse scandals come to mind) is a unique source of moral authority in the world and in his domain. The church has vast, if not fully tabulated, material wealth in land, works of art, buildings, and investments.

New popes are not selected often, but when they are, all eyes are on Rome. The world tunes in to follow the distinctive selection process of a man who will inevitably be the subject of great reverence and fascination. All eligible cardinals (under the age of 80)—some 120 today—meet in Conclave in the Sistine Chapel, where they pray, reflect, and cast ballots until a Pope is elected. The world follows the process informed by different colors of smoke emerging from the chimney of the chapel that convey how the process is progressing. When white smoke emerges, the world knows: *Habemus Papam*—we have a Pope.

The heart of the church is seen by its leaders as the episcopal structure: that is, the bishops and cardinals who serve as the connections between the Vatican and Catholics worldwide. The Pope appoints both and has supreme authority over them. The nature of this authority and the system itself were materially affected by the watershed event of the Vatican II Council, which met from 1962 to 1965. The bishops who convened in Rome, led by the Pope, thrashed out many of the issues confronting the modern church as a global institution, and the process in many respects fundamentally transformed what had been a rather stultified organization. Key institutions of the Church today—notably the Synods, in which bishops meet periodically, and the Conferences of Bishops, which represent regional groupings of bishops that engage with national and regional authorities on wide-ranging issues—trace their current form to Vatican II. Likewise, a new (and continuously evolving) approach to modern communications and media stemmed from Vatican II.[7]

The formal administrative structures in the Vatican are known as the Roman Curia, or dicasteries, and they involve a complex web of institutions. All formally report to the Pope, but in practice report to the secretary of state (an office dating from 1644), who is in charge of administering both internal church affairs and foreign relations. The offices of the Curia are known as congregations and their functions and focus center on the religious administration of the Church. The nine congregations include: the Congregation for the Doctrine of the Faith, the authority on theological matters; the Congregation for the Cause of Saints, handling beatifications; the Congregation for Bishops, administering all personnel functions; and the Congregation for Catholic Education, overseeing the vast Catholic education system. Each functions as an administrative entity, with cardinals, bishops, and lay employees as staff. The Curia also has a judicial branch, which follows the Code of Canon Law. Finally, there is a so-called "New Curia" that has functioned since Vatican II. It includes 11 councils; each, like the Congregations, is organized as an autonomous office with staff and demanding work programs (see Box 2.7).

Box 2.7 Pontifical Councils

- Pontifical Council for Laity
- Pontifical Council for Promoting Christian Unity
- Pontifical Council for the Family

- Pontifical Council for Justice and Peace
- Pontifical Council Cor Unum (fostering charitable works)
- Pontifical Council for the Pastoral Care of Migrants and Itinerant Peoples (for example, the Roma and sailors)
- Pontifical Council for the Pastoral Care of Health workers
- Pontifical Council for the Interpretation of Legislative Texts
- Pontifical Council for Interreligious Dialogue
- Pontifical Council for Culture
- Pontifical Council for Social Communications

The picture of the Catholic Church is far from complete without introducing the hundreds of religious orders the sizes, structures, and administrations of which each have a distinct individual character, often shaped by more than 1,000 years of history. The orders are generally administered with considerable autonomy and have wide-ranging functions. Many run schools and hospitals and have other social roles. Many have a truly international reach, found in far-flung corners of the globe, while others are small and locally focused. Worldwide, there are far more religious women in these orders than men: the respective numbers were estimated at 770,000 religious women and 194,000 religious men in 2000.[8] Two of the best-known women's orders are the Benedictines and the Sisters of Charity. Since the Middle Ages, the Benedictines have been known for their commitment to hospitality and peace and represent a sizeable organization. In 2000, there were 7,179 Benedictine nuns and 10,000 Active Benedictine sisters organized in independent communities, each led by an abbess. The Sisters of Charity, another well-known order, focus their work on the very poor. Among the best-known men's orders are the Jesuits, the Dominicans, and the Franciscans. The Jesuit Order (the Society of Jesus) was founded in 1534, and today some 19,000 Jesuits serve in 115 countries.[9] The order has its own hierarchy and is well known for its independence of thought and action, even vis-à-vis the Pope. A passionate commitment to education is another Jesuit hallmark. The Jesuits' leader is known as the superior general, and is selected by election among Jesuits. Provincials hold office at the regional level.

The Roman Catholic Church also includes a set of churches known as the Eastern Catholic Churches. These are autonomous and self-governing, but "in communion" with Rome (meaning that they share a common view of liturgy and authority). They have centuries-old theological traditions that are similar to different Orthodox Churches but differ in important respects, including recognition of the Pope's authority. Maronite

Figure 2.1 Catholic Church World Youth Day. Millions of young people gathered to welcome Pope Benedict XVI to World Youth Day in Madrid, Spain in 2011
Source: © Godong/Robert Harding World Imagery/Corbis

Christians, centered in Lebanon, are one such example. Historically, Eastern Catholic Churches were located in Eastern Europe, the Asian Middle East, North Africa, and India, but are now quite widely dispersed across all world regions.

Chapter 5 focuses on the vast array of institutions like hospitals, universities, lay institutions, and other institutions that are part of the Church (these number in the hundreds of thousands) and Chapter 3 describes the many lay movements, including the Focolare, the Community of Sant'Egidio, and Opus Dei, that are also part of the Catholic world.

Protestant churches

The Roman Catholic Church is highly complex, but from an institutional perspective it can be understood as a single set of organizations. This is far from the case for the Protestant churches that emerged beginning with the Reformation in the sixteenth and seventeenth centuries, when a series of schisms split the Catholic Church and gave rise to many churches that have come to function quite independently. Indeed, the number of different Protestant denominations today is estimated at about 38,000, involving some 800 million people. There are an estimated 1,500 in the United States alone. As is the case for the Catholic Church, reams of history trace the personalities, theological beliefs, and social movements that have given rise to the complex kaleidoscope of contemporary Protestantism. Summarizing this history falls well beyond the scope of this discussion, which instead focuses on organizational forms and, where they are readily traced, highlights common forms and patterns. For the most part, the Protestant world presents a story of distinctive forms of organization, a high degree of decentralization, federation-type structures allowing sharing of experience, successive efforts to repair rifts and schisms, and a long history of transnational relationships and, often governance.

Navigating the Protestant world is complex—hardly surprising given the plethora of different churches and the complex theologies that distinguish them. Roughly speaking, Protestant churches today can be described as falling into five, often overlapping, groups:

1   the historic Protestant churches, prominent among them the Anglican and Episcopal churches, Lutherans, Presbyterians, Methodists, and Baptists;
2   the peace churches: Quakers, Mennonites, and Seventh-day Adventists;
3   churches specific to different regions, like the Church of Latter-Day Saints and the African independent churches;
4   the new charismatic churches, overlapping with evangelical and pentecostal churches; and
5   non-Trinitarian churches, like the Unitarians. Each has its distinct organizational structures and theology; many, if not most, have a global dimension.

Christian churches, but especially many within the Protestant denominations, are often known for their missionary work and for the roles that churches played as part of the colonial enterprise of the seventeenth through twentieth centuries. Like the Catholic Church, most Protestant churches have an explicit missionary purpose, seeking to evangelize— literally to "share the good news." However, different denominations and individuals approach and undertake this dimension in very different ways, which range from active proselytizing and seeking converts to far more nuanced approaches that see the example of selfless service as the proper response to the call to mission. That said, the missionary history of churches was a central focus of globalization and remains so to this day.[10] It has shaped many institutional relationships across boundaries, often forging close links that have lasted for centuries (the Anglican Communion is an example, as are Lutheran denominations in the United States that maintain some ties with the "old world"). In some instances, where a nation or region has sought to move away from colonial histories, new and different relationships have emerged, sometimes in the form of newer churches (African independent churches, for example) or greater receptivity to more contemporary religious entities like pentecostal churches or Mormon missionaries.

The Church of England and the Anglican Communion are examples of both the particularity of a specific denomination and of its global reach. The global significance of the denomination and its leaders are a blend of their history, of colonial legacies, of the contemporary reality of the Commonwealth bonds among nations, and of personal leadership and influence. Apart from its exemplary function, the Anglican Communion and its leader, the Archbishop of Canterbury, have, like the Catholic Pope, a special position of acknowledged and respected religious leadership, conferring on them a distinctive form of convening power.

The contemporary form of the Anglican Communion grew directly from the English history of the Reformation and is inextricably linked to British colonization and decolonization. After King Henry VIII separated his church from the Catholic Church in Rome following disputes about his determination to divorce and remarry, the Church of England (with bitter interludes under Catholic sovereigns) became the established, legal religion in England. It remains so to this day, and in that sense is a prime example of an "established church." The Archbishop of Canterbury is a critical public figure—considered third in order of precedence in the United Kingdom (after the queen and prime minister), bishops sit in the House of Lords and thus legislate, prospective ambassadors are briefed by the office of the Archbishop of Canterbury on religious affairs in their post, and parishes in England are defined by territory, not by believers or church attendance. Notwithstanding the many debates about the rights and wrongs of this system, the Church of England is very much part of the British government structure.

To a degree, the established Church of England was spread to Britain's colonies, but in very different forms. Many British colonies were formed initially by dissenters from the established church. Nonetheless, in most British colonies the Church of England in its different forms (the Episcopal Church in the United States, for example) took on the role of a church of elites. In some places the Anglican Church has retained its established role in some form, while in others (the United States is a prime example) the colonial religious experience shaped different church-state relationships. The historic legacies are illustrated in one case: Trinity Wall Street, a small church in the shadow of the New York City twin towers, benefits still from a gift of farmland from Queen Anne in the sixteenth century which translates into fabulous wealth in the contemporary urban setting of downtown Manhattan. The Trinity Wall Street Foundation has supported Anglican churches all over the world.

Today, Anglican and Episcopal churches form a loose federation, known as the Anglican Communion, consisting of member churches, known as provinces, in 165 countries with 85 million members. The

Communion is a unique geographic and moral entity that ties together quite independent churches in Southern Africa, Nigeria, East Africa, and Australia. Today that community is challenged and deeply split over issues of "culture wars," especially gay priests and bishops, gay marriage, and even women priests, but it is committed to a common set of beliefs and commitment to service—for example, on HIV and AIDS. The Communion is led by the Archbishop of Canterbury (as a "first among equals," without direct executive authority). It operates through the Lambeth Conferences held every 10 years, periodic primates meetings (primates are bishops), and the Anglican Consultative Council that meets every two-to-three years. A small office in London provides administrative support, and the Communion is active at the UN and also through a variety of networks that work on topics like the environment, HIV and AIDS, and indigenous peoples. It is in many senses through these common practical collaborations that the Communion derives its strength and influence. The Communion lacks anything smacking of the absolute authority attributed to the Catholic Pope; its global ties are largely moral and cultural, and sometimes financial and pragmatic.

It is difficult to trace common patterns among the many other traditional Protestant churches, since each one has evolved with a distinctive history and ethos. What is most interesting here is the complex web of international affiliations—more often than not in the form of elaborate institutional links—that are vibrant and significant despite often wide gulfs and distance. The Lutheran World Federation is a prominent example. A "global communion of Christian churches in the Lutheran tradition," the Federation was founded in 1947 in Lund, Sweden, and today has 145 member churches in 79 countries representing over 70 million Christians. It is governed by a Global Assembly that meets every six-to-seven years and an elected chief executive officer, the secretary general, who has pastoral, diplomatic, and executive functions. What does the Federation do? In contemporary terms the answer would likely be common advocacy, fellowship, and developing a sense of common purpose, as well as leading and coordinating charitable work. The Federation has a headquarters in Geneva, Switzerland, which is active as an advocate and connector. It does not bridge divides even within the Lutheran churches but presents an important face of commitment to a global purpose to the world.

The common global links of the Baptist Church are quite different and emerge from another historical journey. Diverse from their beginnings, those identifying as Baptists today differ widely from one another in what they believe, how they worship, their attitudes toward other Christians, and their understanding of what is important in Christian discipleship. The earliest Baptist church was founded in 1609 in Amsterdam, with an English separatist (John Smyth) as its pastor. Baptist practice spread to England, with General Baptists considering Christ's atonement to extend to all people, while Particular Baptists believed that it extended only to the elect. In 1638, Roger Williams established the first Baptist congregation in the North American colonies. In two historic "awakenings" that colored American history, Baptist membership grew rapidly in both New England and the South. Baptist missionaries have spread their church to every continent. In 2002, there were over 100 million Baptists worldwide and over 33 million in North America. Baptists worldwide are not united. Today, the Baptist World Alliance reports more than 41 million members in more than 150,000 congregations.

Likewise, Methodists represent a Protestant grouping with a wide variety of denominations and organizations, claiming 70 million adherents. They trace their roots to John Wesley's evangelistic revival movement within Anglicanism. Known for its missionary work, and its establishment of hospitals, universities, orphanages, soup kitchens, and schools, Methodists are found in countries around the world. Methodism spread throughout the British Empire and colonial America. Early Methodists were drawn from all levels of society, including the aristocracy, but the Methodist preachers took the message to laborers and criminals who tended to be left outside of organized religion at that time.

Each denomination, and often subdivisions within a denomination, has its own distinctive form of organization. Presbyterians focus on the role of Elders, while other denominations may look to the leadership of a charismatic individual (or the memory of such a leader). The Society of Friends (Quakers) is noteworthy for its lack of formal leadership and its highly participatory approach to governance. This in turn shapes very different transnational organizations. For the Seventh-day Adventists, a General Conference (with headquarters in Silver Spring, Maryland) governs the world church, with smaller regions administered by divisions, union conferences, and local conferences. It considers itself the 12th-largest religious body in the world and the sixth-largest highly international religious body, with a missionary presence in over 200 countries and territories. The Church of Latter-Day Saints also has a global organization, run from the Salt Lake City, Utah headquarters. These networks stand in sharp contrast to tiny denominations that maintain links with congregations in different countries, perhaps forged by an historic contact or personal encounter. Transnational links, large and small, take countless forms and can be found everywhere in the world. German churches, for example, have been particularly active in supporting congregations in South America.

Of special importance are organizations that link evangelical churches worldwide, and especially the World Evangelical Alliance (WEA), which works with local churches around the world. WEA's network extends to churches in 128 countries, each of which has formed an evangelical alliance. Over 100 international organizations give a world-wide identity, voice, and platform to more than 600 million evangelical Christians. The WEA traces its origins to a meeting of Christians from 10 countries in London in 1846 to launch "a new thing in church history, a definite organization for the expression of unity amongst Christian individuals belonging to different churches."[11] In 1951 believers from 21 countries officially formed the World Evangelical Fellowship. The Fellowship works to strengthen local churches, supporting national alliances and grassroots leadership. It works through a series of commissions on specific topics that include religious freedom and advocacy. The Micah Challenge, which advocates for the UN Millennium Development Goals, emerged from the WEA.

Perhaps the most startling religious development in recent years is the rapid spread of a variety of "charismatic" churches, most of them falling into a grouping termed pentecostal.[12] Others describe themselves as "non-denominational," while there are some that are outgrowths of Catholic or traditional protestant groups. The respected Pew Forum suggests that a quarter of the world's 2 billion Christians fall into this category of "lively, highly personal faiths." Distinguishing features include speaking in tongues, faith healing, and prophesying. A sub-set fall into a grouping described as the "prosperity gospel," which contend that virtue and adherence to church teachings will bring the reward of wealth. That such churches are spreading like wildfire is clear; the significance of and reasons for the explosion of such churches are not. Looking here for global institutions, however, is difficult if not impossible. There are some large churches and some strong international links: the role of the Saddleback Church and Pastor Rick Warren is a case in point, as he distributes sermons online to a reputed 100,000 pastors and dispatches congregants to work in what he terms "purpose-driven countries" like Rwanda.[13] Several Brazilian churches are active and influential in Africa, and a "reverse missionary" trend is apparent in Europe, where charismatic preachers from Africa and other regions are attracting huge congregations. Generally, however, the new movement and its churches are characterized by their decentralization and fragmentation. Some are welcomed by established churches but many are not, viewed with suspicion and labeled as "sects." However, the new churches are increasingly players in global affairs, shaping ideas, attitudes, and practices (for example, encouraging savings and investment), but this rarely, if ever, takes place in the context of formal, identifiable transnational organizations.

The Orthodox world

A rich and complex set of Orthodox Christian churches are important actors in much of Eastern Europe and in other world regions. They trace their origins to the fifth century, when a split within Christianity separated Oriental Orthodoxy from Chalcedonian Christianity and thus from the Catholic Church in Rome. Notwithstanding efforts over many years to bring the churches together and a series of continuing dialogues to achieve greater harmony, the Catholic, Protestant, and Orthodox worlds remain quite separate.

The Orthodox Church calls itself a communion that is made up of 15 separate hierarchical churches; the name used is autocephalous, meaning that each has its own head—a Patriarch or a Metropolitan. They recognize no single head comparable to the Pope of Rome. The highest-ranking bishop among these Orthodox churches is the Patriarch of Constantinople, who is also primate of one of the separate churches. Based in Istanbul, the current Patriarch is one of the world's most respected religious leaders, sometimes called the "Green Pope" because of his active support for protection of the environment. While each local or national Orthodox church is a portion of the Orthodox Church as a whole, there is in effect no common structure that links these very separate churches. Bishops and patriarchs meet but they do not form a distinct organization. Other important Patriarchs include the Patriarchs of Moscow (a leading figure in Russia and also within global religious circles), and of Albania.

The Oriental Orthodox churches, which today include the Coptic Orthodox Church of Alexandria, the Armenian Apostolic Church, the Syriac Orthodox Church, the Malankara Orthodox Church of India, the Ethiopian Orthodox Church, and the Eritrean Orthodox Tewahedo Church, are generally referred to as "Non-Chalcedonian," and sometimes by outsiders as "monophysite" (meaning "One Single Nature," in reference to Christ). However, these churches themselves describe their Christology as miaphysite (meaning "One United Nature," in reference to Christ).

A special place is occupied by the Ethiopian Orthodox Tewahedo Church. One of the few pre-colonial Christian churches of sub-Saharan Africa, the Ethiopian Church has a membership of 40–45 million and it is the predominant Oriental Orthodox Christian church in Ethiopia. Administratively part of the Coptic Orthodox Church until 1959, it was granted its own Patriarch by Coptic Orthodox Pope of Alexandria and Patriarch of All Africa Cyril VI. The Church is an integral part of the culture and life of Ethiopia. It has a huge presence throughout the country, and is highly influential in politics and in daily life. To convey an idea of its scale, the Church counts some 450,000 deacons.

As an illustration of complex interreligious relationships, it was the Coptic Orthodox Church that served as a "godfather" to the formation of an association of African instituted churches. An important but often neglected group of churches that grew up largely in reaction to institutions perceived as elitist and colonial in character, these churches are important institutions in many very poor regions. The association has for the first time given voice to these churches and makes possible transnational exchanges, training, and targeted programs, for example, on HIV and AIDS.[14]

Cults and reformers?

Global attention focuses, understandably, on several distinctive organizations, often termed sects. These include some that are violent: the Jim Jones group and the Branch Davidians who precipitated violent conflict in Waco, Texas, are prime examples. The mass suicide of Jones' followers in Guyana in 1978 by drinking poisoned Kool-Aid shocked the world and still permeates some understandings of the perils of unquestioning belief (as well as providing a continuing metaphor for the brainless following of a leader). Others are perhaps more an illustration of human diversity: Quiverfull might fall in that category, a group committed to bearing the maximum number of children possible. Box 2.8 highlights the distinctive and unique history of France's process of defining and regulating cults.

Box 2.8 France: defining and regulating cults

France has elaborated a system for setting limits on what are seen as dangerous religious groups, or "cults." Oversight and monitoring of cults has a long history, but a tightening of regulations in 1994–95 was prompted by mass suicides in a group called the Order of the Solar Temple and violent incidents in other countries (e.g. the Japanese Aum Shinrikyo group). A parliamentary commission on cults was established in 1994 by the French National Assembly to determine what constituted a cult. Its 1995 Gest-Guyard report (unanimously adopted) set out categories that focused on their supposed threat to group members or to society and the state and listed 173 cults that met at least one criterion that it defined as dangerous. The group recognized the difficulty in objective classification, while it did not question the ethical or political need to do so. In 1995 Prime Minister Raffarin issued a circular that broadened the scope of oversight from a list to criteria set by an Interministerial Commission whose mission is to "monitor and combat cultic deviance."[1] Later parliamentary commissions on cults reported in 1999 and in 2006 and the About-Picard Law of 2001 strengthened legislation against cults. The 1999 commission focused on financial and tax dimensions of cults and their relationships with business, and the 2006 commission focused on the effects of cults on minors.

Defining a cult has always been the crux of the matter. The main categories of threat that emerged in 1995 are, first, threats to people (mental destabilization, excessive financial demands, separation from home environment, danger to physical integrity, indoctrination of children), and second, threats to the community (anti-social speech, public disorder, negative financial activities). Efforts to infiltrate public bodies were defined as a key threat. Novelty, small size, and eccentricity were not to be criteria. One of the few official efforts anywhere to define threats from cults, the criteria came under criticism as vague. Bishop Jean Vernette, the national secretary of the French episcopate to the study of cults and new religious movements, observed that the criteria might be applied to almost all religions. Sociologists like Bruno Étienne emphasized that mental manipulation should not be defined by the police. Questions were raised about the absence of Opus Dei and the Freemasons and the presence of Scientology and Jehovah's Witnesses. Some movements engaged in legal proceedings to obtain the secret documents that were the basis of their inclusion. The US State Department's 2004 religious freedom report also criticized the report, accusing it of not having heard the groups accused. Its concern was that "official government initiatives and activities that target 'sects' or 'cults' have fueled an atmosphere of intolerance toward members of minority religions in France."[2] It viewed the initiatives as troubling because they were "serving as models for countries in Eastern Europe where the rule of law and other human rights are much weaker than in France."

[1] www.legifrance.gouv.fr/affichTexte.do?cidTexte=JORFTEXT00
 0000809117&dateTexte=&categorieLien=id.
[2] www.state.gov/j/drl/rls/irf/2004/35454.htm.

Ecumenical movements and organizations

From the mid- to late nineteenth century, the fracturing within Protestant churches especially inspired an ecumenical movement. The 1910 Edinburgh Missionary Conference is seen as a landmark event in a new determination to bridge divides and to establish a set of common institutions that would link different denominations and help them to work towards common ends (missionary work was a central element). In 1937 a group of church leaders agreed to establish a world council of churches that would merge two organizations, the Faith and Order Movement, and the Life and Work Movement. World War II deferred the plans, but in August 1948 delegates from 147 churches met in Amsterdam, then in Lund in 1950, and the World Council of Churches (WCC) was formed. With its headquarters today in Geneva, Switzerland, the WCC is formed of some 525 member churches, which claim a total membership of about 525 million people. The WCC includes most "historic protestant" churches, as well as most of the Orthodox churches. It does not include the Catholic Church, though there is a working cooperation agreement. Many, if not most, pentecostal and evangelical churches are not members.

The WCC has an elaborate structure, with delegates sent from the member churches for a global assembly that is held every seven or eight years. The Assembly elects a Central Committee that governs between Assemblies. A variety of other committees and commissions answer to the Central Committee and its staff. Assemblies have been held since 1948. The last Assembly was in Porto Alegre, Brazil, in February 2006, with the next planned for South Korea in 2013.

The WCC thus has a 65-year history that includes activities on many fronts. Peacemaking is among them, and the WCC, for example, played significant roles in the negotiations processes that led to agreement on independence for South Sudan. It has also played important roles in health, first in encouraging the World Health Organization towards greater focus on primary health care, and, more recently, on HIV and AIDS. The WCC historically has viewed itself as a prophetic voice representing the poor and marginalized, and in this context has issued strong statements against international organizations including the International Monetary Fund (IMF) and the World Bank.[15]

A continuing issue for many churches (and a source of friction in many parts of the world) is proselytizing, or evangelizing. This is subject to various international legal instruments, especially in relation to humanitarian aid, but there remain grey areas, notably as religious freedom comes into tension with national laws, cultural landmines, and the ethics of engagement among different cultures. An important step was an historic agreement in June 2011 on a code of conduct on proselytizing, reflecting long years of negotiation. Three organizations, representing about 90 percent of world Christianity, launched on 28 June a global code of conduct for proselytizing in a bid to reduce tensions between different religious convictions. Described as "an historic moment in our shared Christian witness," the document was issued by the WCC, the WEA, and the Pontifical Council for Interreligious Dialogue of the Holy See.[16] The agreement, "Christian Witness in a Multi-Religious World: Recommendations for Conduct," addresses four areas of primary concern: Christian unity, human rights, a positive outlook on mission and evangelism, and religious freedom.

The Muslim world and contemporary geopolitics

Widely diverse, what is commonly termed the Muslim world counts some 1.5 billion people living in every country in the world. The concept of a "Muslim world," though widely used, is highly problematic. The Muslim faith originated in Arabia in the seventh century, spreading rapidly behind conquering armies. However, Muslims, living as far apart as Senegal and Indonesia, Russia and Dubai, over many years shared little beyond the core beliefs of Islam. Today's sharpened focus on Islam as a global religion and force is the result of various factors. These include the common sense of a religious identity that modern communications and the forces of globalization have encouraged, shared religious beliefs and practices (for example, the *Hajj* and fasting during the month of Ramadan), and threads of a common culture. However, the differences are at least as great as what is held in common. Today's focus on Islam is also the product of fears of a current or impending "clash of civilizations" (see Chapter 1) and of terrorism perpetrated in the name of Islam and by terrorist organizations (like Al Qaeda) that claim to be following Islamic ends and beliefs. This discussion addresses briefly some of the cultural and geopolitical challenges that center on contemporary understandings of a Muslim world, but its primary focus is an effort to "map" the various institutions that link Muslims across national boundaries.

The Iranian Revolution of 1979 and the series of devastating terrorist attacks—most notably on 11 September 2001—are watershed events in contemporary history and they have led to sharply increased attention to Islam as a religious tradition. Huntington's "clash of civilizations" theory focused especially on the cultural and religious dimensions of Islam which, in his argument, were likely to produce conflict and "bloody

borders" between Muslim and non-Muslim communities. To respond
to both the perceptions and realities of cultural and religious clashes, a
wide range of efforts have proliferated with the central theme of promoting peace and harmony through dialogue and active collaboration.
Institutions have emerged with the purpose of understanding and communication, an end much to be desired in the light of surveys demon-
strating both dismally low levels of knowledge about the Muslim faith
in many countries and low levels of mutual trust.

At the UN level, the Alliance of Civilizations is the main outgrowth
of this concern. Following an initiative launched in 2004 by the prime
minister of Spain, a High-Level Group for the Alliance of Civilizations
was appointed by then-UN Secretary-General Kofi Annan in 2005 and
issued its report in December 2006. The report focused on tensions with
Muslim nations, proposing a series of initiatives ranging from redefining
narratives on the Israel–Palestine conflict to media outreach and job
training. Consideration of the report launched the Alliance of Civilizations, which began in 2007 to organize a series of annual high-level fora
(for example, in Doha in December 2011). While the remit of the Alliance
is certainly not explicitly focused on Muslim-West relations, in practice
improving these relationships has been a core objective. Other parallel
efforts include the World Economic Forum's Council of One Hundred, a
multidisciplinary group of leaders from "the West" and "the Muslim world"
that launched analysis and supported projects aimed at bridging divides.[17]
Educational programs at all levels and a host of other programs address
the phenomenon of Islamophobia and the welfare of immigrant communities from Muslim majority countries, especially in Europe. Public
diplomacy, cultural, and other programs in very different settings share
the aim of addressing the widespread distrust and anger directed towards
non-Muslim countries, which is a central contemporary threat.

Religious leaders and institutions are deeply involved in these efforts,
some spontaneously responding to goals of interfaith harmony, others
prompted by crises like the Danish Mohammed cartoon controversy in
2005, Pope Benedict XVI's September 2006 Regensberg speech deemed
insulting to Islam, and damaging incidents like the US torture of pris-
oners in Abu Ghraib and the provocative burning of copies of the Qur'an
in various settings. Among these efforts, the Common Word initiative
stands out.[18] Shortly after Pope Benedict XVI's Regensburg address, 38
Islamic authorities and scholars from around the world, representing
all Muslim denominations and schools of thought, sent an answer to
the Pope, in the form of an open letter. This represented an historic
first, as Muslim scholars from every branch of Islam spoke with one
voice about Islam's teachings. A year later, the message was expanded

and 138 Muslim scholars, clerics, and intellectuals agreed on a document called *A Common Word Between Us and You*, highlighting the common ground between Christianity and Islam. Both religious and political leaders support the initiative and the continuing effort at dialogue that it represents.

Global institutions for Islam

First and foremost, the Muslim faith and Muslims as a community have no institution comparable in its hierarchy and authority to the Catholic Church and the Roman Catholic Pope, or even as hierarchical as the rather loosely structured Anglican Communion and its leader, the Archbishop of Canterbury. While the sentiment of solidarity is an intrinsic part of the Islamic faith, and the image of an *Umma* (Muslim community) organized under a spiritual and temporal leader is deeply held, there was rarely an organized form along these lines (though some contend that at its height the Ottoman Empire was a close approximation in terms of its global reach). Since the early nineteenth century, however, there has been a succession of efforts to establish a unifying body. The efforts have given rise to a number of institutions but their forms are diverse, rather fragmented, and often contested. Apart from often fractious politics, from a religious perspective, there are quite deep divisions within the religion, most notably between Sunni and Shi'a denominations of Islam, which date back to the earliest years after the Prophet's death in 632. Figures are quite rough but the general understanding is that most Muslims are Sunnis (about 90 percent), and the remaining 10 percent Shi'as. Most Shi'as belong to the Twelver tradition and the remainder are divided among several other groups, including the Ismailis, led by the Aga Khan. In Southeast Asia, South Asia, China, Africa, and most of the Arab world Sunnis predominate, while Shi'as are the majority in Iran, Iraq, Azerbaijan, and Bahrain. Pakistan has the world's largest Shi'a Muslim population. Many fundamental beliefs are shared between Sunnis and Shi'as, but there are sharp differences in understandings of leadership and authority. Sunni–Shi'a relations have been marked by both cooperation and conflict, with deadly violence at times. A period of relative harmony for most of the twentieth century gave way to bitter conflicts, especially after the start of the Iraq War in 2003. Put simplistically, Sunni Muslims do not look to a formal religious hierarchy of authority, while Shi'a Muslims have Ayatollahs who represent a strong temporal and spiritual authority.

Another important, broad element of the Muslim faith is exemplified in Sufi traditions. Some view Sufism as something of a distinct sect, and the tendency to revere saints and follow specific teachers as leaders and the structure of groups known as brotherhoods support this understanding of how Sufi communities are organized. However, most view Sufi Islam as something that is much broader: a cultural Islam expressed in poetry and music, a mystical tradition. In areas like West Africa and Morocco, where most Muslims would consider themselves Sufis, the tradition is diverse and open to a wide range of teachings and understandings. Sufis look especially to the great Persian poet Rumi as a symbol and an inspiration for the Sufi focus on love and beauty.

Looking at the institutional dimensions of Muslim believers as a community worldwide, two entities have particular contemporary significance: Al-Azhar University and the Sheikh of Al-Azhar, and the Organization of Islamic Cooperation (OIC). Other leading institutions include the World Muslim Congress, the World Prayer Call Society, and newer institutions such as the Association of Muslim Philanthropists. Various distinct bodies have also emerged as authorities on Muslim finance, which is considered as core to following the Muslim faith. Several national leaders, notably the King of Morocco and the Aga Khan, imam of the Ismaili community, trace their lineage and thus their authority to the Prophet Mohammed and thereby carry both religious and political authority.

The Grand Sheikh of Al-Azhar is considered the highest religious authority for Sunni Islam, and the Al-Azhar University, located in Cairo, Egypt, is the world's most respected center of Islamic learning, as well as on related subjects like Arabic literature. Founded in around 970–972 as a *madrasa* (that is, school), it is Egypt's oldest degree-granting university. The University is associated with the Al-Azhar Mosque and the University combines education across a wide range of disciplines with its role as a religious training center and authority. Islamic scholars there issue *fatwas* (edicts) in response to disputes and questions submitted from all over the Sunni Islamic world. An example of a *fatwa* is the Sheikh's 2011 ruling that female genital cutting is not sanctioned or required by Islam. Al-Azhar trains Egyptian government-appointed preachers and it has an outstanding library. In sum, Al-Azhar's Grand Sheikh and its University have no formal authority beyond Egypt, but, because of their rich history and tradition, they are often looked to as leaders and, in some circumstances, authorities in matters related to the Islamic faith. The Grand Sheikh often represents Muslim voices in many interreligious settings and in some political fora. For example, he co-chaired the 2005 Alexandria Process, which aimed to bring religious leaders together to support peace efforts for the Middle East, with Lord Carey of Clifton, then Archbishop of Canterbury.

The OIC is a political, essentially intergovernmental organization with significant religious character and goals. Headquartered in Jeddah, Saudi Arabia, it is the largest international organization outside the UN. Formerly known as the Organization of the Islamic Conference, it was established in 1969; the impetus was in large part the 1967 defeat of Arab armies by Israel. This brought leaders together in 1969 for a summit in Rabat, Morocco. They agreed on a new, inclusive Islamic institution. Its members are 57 countries, predominantly in the Middle East and North Africa. They include the world's Muslim majority nations, as well as a few countries with Muslim minorities (Gabon, for example). A few countries with significant Muslim populations, notably Russia and Thailand, sit as observer states while others, such as India and Ethiopia, are not members. Members meet in triennial summit conferences and a host of other events and initiatives. The OIC's stated goal is "to galvanize the Ummah [the global community of Muslims] into a unified body," as the OIC represents the values and causes close to the "hearts" of Muslims. In this capacity, OIC consults and works with the UN, seeking to represent and protect the "interests of the Muslims" as it works to settle conflicts and disputes involving its member states. In 2005 the OIC established a Ten-Year Program of Action that "envisages joint action of Member States, promotion of tolerance and moderation, modernization, and extensive reforms in all spheres of activities."[19]

The OIC's supreme authority is the Islamic Summit, composed of kings and heads of state and government of member states. It convenes once every three years to deliberate, take policy decisions, and provide guidance on all relevant issues. The Council of Foreign Ministers meets once a year and focuses on policy implementation. The OIC's executive organ is its General Secretariat. OIC also has a long series of affiliated organizations: notably, the Islamic Development Bank, the Islamic Educational, Scientific, and Cultural Organization (ISESCO), the Islamic Broadcasting Union, the International Islamic News Agency, and the Islamic Committee of the International Crescent (an organization that aims to intervene in disaster situations).

One product of the OIC is the Cairo Declaration of Human Rights in Islam, agreed to in 1990.[20] Presented as a document intended to be complementary (rather than competitive) to the Universal Declaration of Human Rights (UDHR), the Cairo Declaration is quite explicit in its religious, Islamic foundations. Article 24 states that "All the rights and freedoms stipulated in this Declaration are subject to the Islamic Shari'ah." Likewise, Article 25 states that "the Islamic Shari'ah is the only source of reference for the explanation or clarification of any of the articles of this Declaration." OIC efforts to have the UN Human Rights Council adopt the Declaration have not succeeded, because of tensions or contradictions seen with the UDHR. Human Rights Watch contends that OIC has "fought doggedly" and successfully within the UN Human Rights Council to shield its member states and many others from criticism, unless those criticisms involve Israel.[21]

An important part of the OIC complex is the Islamic Development Bank (IDB). Its primary mission is to "foster the economic development and social progress of member countries ... in accordance to Islamic law."[22] A further objective is to develop and promote Islamic finance instruments. The IDB was established in 1973 by the Conference of Finance Ministers of Muslim Countries and began operations two years later with its headquarters in Jeddah, Saudi Arabia. It has regional offices in Rabat, Kuala Lumpur, Almaty, Kazakhstan, and Dakar, Senegal, and fields representatives in member countries including Afghanistan, Azerbaijan, Bangladesh, Guinea Conakry, Indonesia, Iran, Nigeria, Pakistan, Sierra Leone, Sudan, Uzbekistan, and Yemen. IDB members must be members of the OIC. The IDB is governed by a Board of Governors that votes on key issues; voting power is based on shares in the Bank and thus essentially economic strength. The Board of Executive Directors has delegated authority to oversee general operations and policies. The Board of Governors increased the Bank's capital stock to 30 billion Islamic dinars in 2005 as part of a strategy to widen the IDB's scope and impact. The IDB is in many respects similar to other regional development banks, with the distinctive feature that it has developed considerable expertise in Islamic finance. In keeping with its Islamic character, no interest is charged on its loans (as interest is considered to be against Islamic principles). A core IDB activity is an ambitious anti-poverty program focused on its poorer member states that is also seen as part of its Islamic mission to attend to the welfare of those in need.

There are a number of other transnational Muslim organizations, the history and relationships of which are complex and intertwined. They include the Muslim World League, or *Rabita*, from the Arabic. This organization focuses on religious matters. Founded in 1962 and supported in substantial measure by the government of Saudi Arabia, it includes religious representatives from 22 states. It is generally considered to reflect a conservative interpretation of Islam. Among the topics covered by its mandate are the peaceful propagation of Islam, Islamic education, and coordination among Muslim preachers. It does involve itself in global political affairs in various ways. Contrasting statements include its support for interfaith dialogue and condemnation of terrorism, and a letter to the UN secretary-general in 2009 describing the Israeli operation in Gaza as "the worst form of state-sponsored terrorism ever known to mankind."

The World Muslim Congress was founded formally in 1949, but its roots go back to a congress of eminent Muslim leaders in Mecca in 1926, making it one of the oldest operating global Muslim organizations. It is based today in Karachi, Pakistan, and its stated goals are to work for world peace and Muslim unity. It has been the recipient of several prominent international awards, including the Templeton Prize and the Niwano Peace Prize. However, as an illustration of how religious and political issues overlap, the 1988 Templeton Prize award was delayed because of accusations that the Congress was anti-Semitic and had supported extremist causes and contributed to the sense of victimization of Muslims that had contributed to the emergence of Islamist movements.

Many other organizations have a Muslim religious character and specialized functions. An example is the Malaysia-based Sisters in Islam, which promotes women's rights within an Islamic framework. Of special note is the Aga Khan Development Network (AKDN), led by His Highness the Aga Khan (Chapter 5). The outstanding work of its various entities is widely recognized and admired in fields ranging from education to ethical investment. Another striking modern development is the rise of Muslim philanthropy (see Box 2.9). The World Islamic Call Society (Box 2.10) is an example of a primarily religiously oriented organization, this one with its base in Libya, which developed a reputation for serious engagement on interfaith issues, garnering interest and support from organizations including the Vatican and leading Jewish organizations, but the shadow side of which emerged after the Libyan revolution opened new windows into the activities of the Gaddafi regime.

Box 2.9 Muslim philanthropy on the rise

A noteworthy and relatively new organization is the World Congress of Muslim Philanthropists (WCMP), established in 2007. As the Muslim world is characterized by both large wealth and some of the world's poorest nations and communities, a sharpened focus is going to Muslim charity, as one of the fundamental pillars of Islam. WCMP comprises a global network of affluent individuals, grant-making foundations, and socially responsible corporations. The aim is to bring together philanthropists to increase philanthropic knowledge, exchange ideas, coordinate, and further understand challenges. An annual forum provides a platform for hundreds of international leaders, partners, and institutions to meet.

Box 2.10 The World Islamic Call Society

Established in 1972 in Libya as a nonprofit entity, the World Islamic Call Society (WICS) comprises over 250 Islamic organizations from around the world. Activities include programs in religious, cultural, social, and economic development, and the society has been particularly active (often with lavish financing) in many African countries. Governance is led by an International Council for Islamic Call. Many WICS activities were noteworthy for their openness to different ideas and serious analysis behind positions. The organization participates actively in various international interfaith efforts, representing the Islamic world. It has been an important advocate for Muslim women and has cooperated closely with the UN Children's Fund (UNICEF) and the UN Educational, Scientific and Cultural Organization (UNESCO).

After the fall of the Gaddafi government in 2011, revisionist thinking about WICS emerged. A Reuters report in March 2012 described it as one of the world's leading Islamic missionary networks, "the smiling face of his [Gaddafi's] Libyan regime, and the world smiled back."[1] Highlighting the often sterling work of the organization, the report noted its dark side—essentially, serving as an organization to promote Gaddafi's search for power and influence and even direct support for terrorist activities and insurgent groups. This has, in short, been an organization deeply engaged in a double game and life. Its future? To be determined.

[1] Tom Heneghan, "Special Report: Gaddafi's Secret Missionaries," Reuters, 29 March 2012, www.reuters.com/article/2012/03/29/us-libya-missionary-idUSBRE82S07T20120329.

Global organizations of Buddhism

Buddhism is both a religion and a philosophy, and it encompasses a variety of traditions, practices, and beliefs. These are based on the teachings of Siddhartha Gautama, or the Buddha (awakened one), who lived in what is today eastern India between the sixth and the fourth centuries BCE. Two major branches of Buddhism have developed over the years—Theravada and Mahayana—and are generally specific to various regions. Theravada, for example, is the main school in Sri Lanka and Southeast Asia, while East Asia's Buddhism mainly follows the Mahayana school. There are wide ranges in estimates of the total number of Buddhists worldwide: 350–500 million is considered a conservative (if rather wide) estimate.

There is no global authority for Buddhism, and practice and teaching tend to be highly decentralized. Monks in a given area form a Sangha, but the practical (and even theoretical) authority it exercises varies widely by country. A recent tendency is the development of organizations reflecting an explicitly Engaged Buddhism. The formation of the tradition is attributed to the leadership of the Vietnamese monk Thich Nhat Hahn, who coined the phrase. A Network of Engaged Buddhists with global reach is based in Thailand, with related traditions and organizations in other regions.[23] Figures like the Dalai Lama exercise wide influence in the world (and also spark considerable conflict, given the tensions around China's role in Tibet). His organization is a complex hybrid of religious and political nature, at one level advocating pure philosophy and faith, but also a *de facto* government in exile in India. Finally, lay Buddhist movements mobilize millions of followers. Examples include two Japanese movements, Risho Kossei-Kai and Soka Gokkai, and the organization launched by Ven. Sheng Yen from Taiwan (Chapter 3). All have large transnational organizations.

There are several global Buddhist movements that seek to organize and, to a degree, represent the voice of Buddhist believers. There is some rivalry among them and their relationships, and respective mandates are not easy to discern. An example is the World Fellowship of Buddhists (WFB), founded in 1950 in Colombo, Sri Lanka, by representatives of Buddhists from 27 nations. Theravada Buddhists are most influential in the organization (their headquarters are in Thailand and all of the presidents have been from Sri Lanka or Southeast Asia), but members of all Buddhist schools are active in the WFB. It now has regional centers in 35 countries, including India, the United States, Australia, and several European and African nations in addition to traditionally Buddhist countries. The WFB aims to promote Buddhist teachings and unity and solidarity among Buddhists. Another is the World Buddhist Sangha Council (WBSC), an international NGO founded in Sri Lanka in 1996. Its aim is to develop exchanges among the Buddhist religious and monastic communities of different traditions worldwide and to help carry out activities for the transmission of Buddhism.

Hindu organizations

The world's Hindus are almost all from India, and in many respects the label Hindu, derived from the Indus River, describes a geographic as much as a spiritual category. Thus it is hardly surprising that Hindu beliefs and traditions vary widely. With millennia of history, the texts, stories, and traditions are rich and diverse. Among the beliefs commonly associated with Hinduism are the notion of caste and reincarnation: humans are born into social categories, in part owing to experience in previous lives. Hindu spiritual beliefs include the understanding that the universe undergoes endless cycles of creation, preservation, and dissolution. Hindus believe in karma, the law of cause and effect by which each individual creates his own destiny by his thoughts, words and deeds.

There is no central Hindu organization, though there are dozens if not hundreds of organizations that are inspired by Hindu beliefs. To a degree, spiritual authority is vested in regionally based Acharyas, but their authority is minimal. A number of political parties profess to advance and follow Hindu nationalism, or state that they represent Hinduism or Hindus. Of these the most powerful and best known is the Bharatiya Janata Party (BJP, or Indian People's Party). The Party, generally considered conservative and right of center, has questioned India's secular constitution and has at the least contributed to interreligious tensions in various instances. With global migration, the Indian diaspora is taking on increasing importance in different regions, and often works through organizations cast in spiritual terms.

Prominent smaller faiths

Many other faith traditions with long histories are actively shaped by forces of globalization and play roles as global institutions. Perhaps the most prominent on the international stage is Judaism, but several others deserve special note. These include the Bahá'í faith, which is particularly active within the UN and stands as a progressive force advocating, for example, for women's rights; the Sikh tradition, with its strong ethos of service and wide international presence; the Zoroastrians, perhaps the world's oldest faith; and newer traditions which fall outside the scope of traditional religions. A prominent example is the set of organizations led and inspired by Indian spiritual guru Sri Sri Ravi Shankar (Chapter 3).

Judaism

Judaism occupies a special and complex place among global religions and among global religious institutions. This distinctive role is the product of the sheer depth of Jewish history (see Box 1.1). With well over 3,000 years of continuous Jewish identity, the texts, traditions, and values of Judaism have directly and indirectly shaped many of the world's religious and spiritual institutions and beliefs, as well as secular ethics and civil law. Migration and global links are deeply embedded in Jewish history and in the contemporary religious and social realities of Jews. Jews have for millennia lived in many societies, distinct and often relegated to special places to live with specific legal regimes, but their cohesiveness as a community and drive made them pivotal members of far-flung communities over many centuries.

The long history of persecution of Jews is a dark chapter in humanity's history and it culminated in the unspeakable horror of the Holocaust during World War II, when over 6 million Jews were murdered; as the first government-sanctioned effort to eradicate the existence of an entire people, nothing comparable has happened before or since. The Zionist movement, rooted in 3,000 years of Israel as the historic homeland of the Jewish people and spurred by a response to persecution and to the Holocaust, was not strictly religious but had religious elements in its strong sense of common identity that was linked to the Jewish faith (see Box 2.11). The creation of the State of Israel as a Jewish state in 1948, and the continuing international tensions around Israel's role and its very right to exist color international relations in countless ways.

Box 2.11 Zionism and globalization

Zionism refers to the movement to restore the Jewish people to the region now known as the state of Israel. The term, however, has broader religious, secular, and nationalist connotations that include the national liberation movement of the Jewish people, the return of the Jewish people from diaspora, and the spiritual rebirth of the Jewish people. Zionism and its territorial claims have weathered much controversy, labeled as everything from "socialist to fascist, secular to religious, territorially minimalist to expansionist."[1]

Zionist thought draws on memories preserved through generations of a return from exile—a "noble and divinely sanctioned adventure ... prefigured in the chronicles of the return from Babylonian exile led by Ezra and Nehemiah."[2] The modern political idea is commonly identified with the movement's late nineteenth-century founder, Theodore Herzl. Herzl linked anti-Jewish violence to the rising nationalism in Europe and to Jews' minority status. Jewish intellectuals like Herzl questioned whether emerging norms of human rights would include Jews. Zionist political organizing began formally in 1897, with the First Zionist Congress. Jewish communities around the world were organized, governments were lobbied for support, and land settlement began in Palestine.

World War II and the Holocaust profoundly affected the Zionist movement: it was seen as convincing proof that Jews had no safe future in diaspora. It spurred mass immigration by refugees and survivors to what was, until the late 1940s, Palestine. After the state of Israel was created in 1948, waves of Jewish immigrants arrived also from the Middle East and Africa.

Zionist ambitions have come under increasing scrutiny with Israel's independent status. The core issue is the role of the Palestinian population. Originally assured that Jewish immigration would bring economic prosperity for them, early Zionists called the space a "land without a people"[3] and an estimated 700,000 Palestinians fled or were expelled from the region. The rest is history.

[1] Joshua B. Friedman, "Zionism," in *Encyclopedia of Activism and Social Justice* (Thousand Oaks, CA: SAGE, 2007), 1517–18, sage-ereference.com/view/activism/n955.xml.
[2] William A. Darity, Jr., ed., "Zionism," in *International Encyclopedia of the Social Sciences* 2 (9) (Detroit, MI: Macmillan Reference USA, 2008), 178–80.
[3] Ibid.

Judaism embodies an ethnic, national, and religious identity (like most of the civilizations at the time it arose), and those counted as Jews include both those who are born Jewish and converts to Judaism. The question of who is a Jew and thus how Jewish institutions can be defined is complex. The 2010 world Jewish population was estimated at 13.4 million, or roughly 0.2 percent of the total world population. About 42 percent of all Jews live in Israel and about 40 percent in the United

States and Canada, with most of the remainder living in Europe with smaller communities elsewhere.[24] The distinct sub-divisions within Judaism, the largest being Orthodox, Conservative, and Reform, play roles in global Jewish politics and ethos but are not reflected in distinct sets of accepted institutions. Differences center on approaches to Jewish law, which in turn affects social and cultural life. Historically, in Ancient Israel and in self-governing Jewish communities until the nineteenth century, special courts enforced Jewish law; today, these courts still exist but the practice of Judaism is mostly voluntary.

The role of Israel as the world's only Jewish state is a distinctive facet of Judaism today. There are many complexities in this national identity, even within Israel, involving the roles of religious and secular authorities. Ethnic and religious identity are intertwined and at times in tension in the complex political and social dynamics of Israel's plural democracy. Israeli Judaism has no global authority but holds substantial global influence, as Jews in different regions have complex but deeply engaged ties with Israel.

In sum, the world Jewish community and Judaism as a religious tradition has no central authority, nor is there a single organization that "speaks" for Judaism or for Jews. Authority on theological and legal matters is not vested in any one person or organization, but in the sacred texts and the many rabbis and scholars who interpret them. Jews are a quintessentially global people, and many Jewish organizations are transnational in character and involve a blend of ethnic and universal, and religious and secular. Each of the various streams has international arms and takes various forms. Among the most prominent institutions with an international presence and a wide array of partnerships is the American Jewish Committee (AJC), established in 1906. It works for the security and welfare of Jews worldwide, promoting pluralistic and democratic societies where all minorities are protected. "AJC is an international think tank and advocacy organization that attempts to identify trends and problems early—and take action."[25] A rather different organization is the World Jewish Congress, founded in Geneva in 1936. Its initial mandate was to unite the Jewish people and advocate for action against the Nazi onslaught. Today it describes itself as the representative body representing all Jews in 100 countries, with a mission to address the interests and needs of Jews and Jewish communities throughout the world, to foster the unity and creative survival of the Jewish people, and to maintain its spiritual, cultural, and social heritage. B'nai B'rith (which means children of the covenant) was founded in 1843 in New York, to confront what the founders called "the deplorable condition of Jews in this, our newly adopted country." From a basic mission of humanitarian aid and service, a system of fraternal lodges and chapters grew in the United States and, eventually, around the world. The Jewish institutional picture, however, goes far beyond these organizations: in the United States one website lists some 95 Jewish organizations.

Box 2.12 **Zoroastrianism: the oldest of the revealed world religions**

Zoroastrianism may have had a greater influence on mankind, directly and indirectly, than any other single faith. Founded in Persia (modern-day Iran) by Zarathushtra, Zoroastrianism is considered the world's first monotheistic faith. Once the religion of the Persian Empire, today it is small, with only 200,000 adherents. The largest group lives in India. Religious historians believe that the Jewish, Christian, and Muslim beliefs about God, Satan, the soul, heaven and hell, the resurrection, and the final judgment were all derived from Zoroastrians. With few adherents and a people scattered all over the world, Zoroastrians are said to have benefited from new communications technologies to keep their ancient faith and community alive in the modern era.

Box 2.13 **Bahá'í: a modern faith with a contemporary agenda**

The Bahá'í faith is a monotheistic religion founded by Bahá'u'lláh in nineteenth-century Persia. It emphasizes the spiritual unity of all humankind. There are an estimated 5 to 6 million Bahá'ís around the world in more than 200 countries and territories; the world headquarters is in Haifa, Israel. The Bahá'í faith stands out for its consciously global view, reflected in an active presence at the UN and in interfaith bodies. Their representatives advocate for human rights, including the rights of women. Religious freedom is a central issue, accentuated by the persecution of Bahá'ís in Iran.

As is the case with three other world religions (Judaism, Christianity, and Islam), it is ties of historical circumstance that bind the Bahá'í faith to the Holy Land. Before he died (in exile, in Israel), Bahá'u'lláh indicated that the world headquarters for the faith he had founded would be in the Acre/Haifa area in the north of what is now Israel, and today that is the spiritual and administrative heart of the Bahá'í Faith. The houses and other places associated with the exile there of Bahá'u'lláh and 'Abdu'l-Bahá have been restored meticulously by the Bahá'í community. The community has impressive houses of worship on every continent, the most dramatic, perhaps, the Lotus Temple in Delhi.

The Bahá'í faith's administration is a unique system created by Bahá'u'lláh and based on principles of consultation and cooperation. After Bahá'u'lláh's death, the faith was led first by his eldest son, 'Abdu'l-Bahá, and then by his great-grandson, Shoghi Effendi. It has been governed internationally by the Universal House of Justice since 1963.

The community's collective life is administered by nine-member consultative councils that are democratically elected without nomination or electioneering at the local, national, and international levels. These are Local Spiritual Assemblies, National Spiritual Assemblies, and the Universal House of Justice. In addition, appointed advisors assist and counsel local and national communities and institutions in their development. There is no clergy in the Bahá'í faith. Local Bahá'í communities meet every 19 days for a "feast," a gathering that includes consultation on community activities as well as devotional and social portions.

Indigenous religious communities

Within both academic and political global institutions that focus on religion there is an increasing focus on indigenous traditions. These are not strictly or at least consciously religious institutions, and yet the spiritual and religious nature of their beliefs has prompted a somewhat uneasy sense that in discussions of world religions these long-neglected groups should be included. The groups are by their nature rather difficult to define and generally widely scattered, with virtually no links among them until very recently. Estimates for the total population of the world's indigenous peoples are complicated by difficulties in identification and the variances and inadequacies of available census data. Recent estimates range from 300 million to 350 million at the start of the twenty-first century, or some 6 percent of the total world population, divided among at least 5,000 distinct peoples in over 72 countries.

Each community has its own governance arrangements, the variance so great that anthropologists have barely begun to describe—much less to understand—them all. At a global level, there has never been an institution that could be considered representative. The World Council of

Indigenous Peoples, based in Canada, was an attempt to address indigenous issues globally and push for indigenous priorities at the UN, but it went defunct in the mid-1990s. Currently the most legitimate entity is the UN Permanent Forum on Indigenous Affairs, but it is not truly representative. Among its 16 members, eight are nominated by governments and eight by indigenous councils. Some regional networks are fairly effective. They include the Asia Indigenous People's Pact (AIPP), which fields representatives from many of the indigenous associations across Asia. It has primarily a capacity-building function, training and educating members. There are similar networks in Latin America and emerging entities in Africa. All these entities are assuming increasing importance at the UN. Several focus on the special attributes and rights of indigenous peoples, as interreligious bodies seek to address the blind spot that has kept this rich trove of traditions and the issues they face away from mainstream dialogue.

Wiccan/Pagan organizations

Paganism (from Latin *paganus*, meaning "country dweller," "rustic") is a blanket term referring generally to religious traditions that are polytheistic or indigenous. Primarily used in an historical context, referring to Greco-Roman polytheism and the polytheistic traditions of Europe and North Africa before Christianization, it is also applied to contemporary religions, extending to most of the Eastern religions and the indigenous traditions of the Americas, Central Asia, Australia, and Africa, as well as non-Abrahamic folk religion in general. Characteristic of Pagan traditions is the absence of proselytism and the presence of a living mythology, which informs religious practice. Ethnologists tend to avoid the term "paganism," with its uncertain and varied meanings, preferring more precise categories such as polytheism, shamanism, pantheism, or animism. Some scholars apply the term to three groups of separate faiths: historical polytheism (such as Celtic polytheism, Norse Paganism, and Hellenic Polytheistic Reconstructionism, also called Hellenismos); folk, ethnic, and indigenous religions (such as Chinese folk religion and African traditional religion); and Neopaganism (such as Wicca and Germanic Neopaganism). Since the late twentieth century, "paganism," or "neopaganism," has come to be quite widely used to describe adherents of various New Religious Movements, including Wicca. In short, it includes a wide range of adherents.

Some pagan and neopagan individuals and communities have formed their own organizations; there are hundreds, most small and quite decentralized. Some have chosen to achieve formal legal status by becoming nonprofit corporations. In the United States, examples include the Aquarian Tabernacle Church, based in Washington State with branches in several other states, and Our Lady of the Woods, a coven and congregation in New Mexico. Wiccan churches are often organized with a coven or inner circle, consisting of initiated priests and priestesses, and a congregation or outer circle, for those who wish to celebrate the Sabbats and enjoy spiritual community. These may or may not seek legal status as corporations.

Atheist/humanist organizations

Hundreds of transnational organizations have emerged in recent decades with a broad aim of serving as a counterpoint to religious institutions or to claim an equal space in the public square. The broad term grouping such organizations is "humanist," though terminology has evolved over time. Secular Humanism has been used at least since the 1930s. During the 1960s and 1970s some Humanists who considered themselves anti-religious, as well as those who, although not critical of religion in its various guises, preferred a non-religious approach, embraced the term. In 1980 a secular, Humanist declaration was issued by the Council for Democratic and Secular Humanism (CODESH, now the Council for Secular Humanism). With this organization, secular Humanism has an institutional identity in the United States. The International Humanist and Ethical Union (IHEU) and the American Humanist Association prefer that the unmodified but capitalized word Humanism be used. In 2002 the IHEU General Assembly unanimously adopted the Amsterdam Declaration, which represents the official defining statement of World Humanism for Humanists. This declaration makes exclusive use of capitalized Humanist and Humanism, which is consistent with IHEU's general practice and recommendations for promoting a unified Humanist identity.

Humanist organizations are found in all parts of the world. Those calling themselves Humanists may number between 4 and 5 million people worldwide in 31 countries, but there is uncertainty because of the lack of universal definitions. Humanism is a non-theistic belief system and, as such, it could be a sub-category of "religion" only if that term is defined to mean "religion and (any) belief system." This is the case in the International Covenant on Civil and Political Rights on freedom of religion and beliefs. Many national censuses contentiously define Humanism as a further sub-category of the sub-category "no religion," which typically includes atheist, rationalist and agnostic thought. In its 2006 and 2011 census, Australia used Humanism as an example of "other religions." In the United States, the decennial census does not inquire about religious affiliation or its lack; surveys report the figure at roughly 13 percent.

The IHEU is a worldwide umbrella organization for those adhering to the Humanist life stance and seeks to represent the views of over 3 million Humanists organized in over 100 national organizations in 30 countries. Originally based in the Netherlands, the IHEU now operates from London. Some regional groups that adhere to variants of the Humanist life stance, such as the humanist subgroup of the Unitarian Universalist Association, do not belong to the IHEU. Although the European Humanist Federation is also separate from the IHEU, the two organizations work together and share an agreed protocol.

Conclusion

The global institutional map of religious institutions is deeply complex and infinitely varied. The institutions involved range from entities with tightly organized governance structures that are readily describable and comparable to non-religious global institutions, to others where lines of authority are hard to define, layered in history, religious tradition, and personalities. Competition among organizations and legitimacy are common issues. What is most important to appreciate is that the institutions exist and that they are in many instances significant actors in global politics. They are also in many instances intimately linked to cultural and ethnic identities that affect politics at national and international levels. Religious beliefs and ties are, for example, important if complicated forces shaping the ways that many diaspora communities are organized and their interactions with their "home" countries: witness the complex roles that religion played in international relations around Ireland and Sri Lanka, as well as Israel, but also the ways in which African and Hispanic communities in many countries rely on religious ties to form new communities and to maintain links with their country of origin. The chapter provided only a brief introduction to this fascinating and fast-changing world, with many simplifications and glaring omissions. Its central conclusion is that the institutions matter, that over-simplifying their roles is a pitfall to avoid, and that, in approaching global issues, taking into account the religious institutions involved is a necessary part of understanding stakeholders and looking to solutions.

3 Religious movements in a globalized world

- The Indian sub-continent: a ferment of religious and spiritual movements
- New religious movements in East Asia
- Christian-inspired movements
- Muslim movements
- Movements known for violence and terrorism
- Pilgrimage: shades of globalization
- Conclusion

Formal institutions and hierarchies often present the most visible and best-known institutional face of contemporary religion, but churches, temples, monks, and clerics are only part of the world of global religious institutions. Another complex and dynamic set of institutions may be loosely described as movements.[1] These entities range widely in size, organization, beliefs, activities, nature of adherence, and their impact on global affairs. They defy simple categorization and the descriptions applied can be sharply contested. "New religions" is one broad descriptive category, increasingly used in academic circles, but it does not do full justice to the range and complexity of what is involved. Some movements are plainly offshoots of mainstream religious traditions (Christianity, Buddhism, Hinduism, and Islam, notably), while others defy clear pedigrees; spiritual is a common self-description (used as distinct from religious). The terms cults or sects are quite commonly applied, usually in a derogatory sense, to describe some movements (see Box 2.8). Some are appropriately termed non-governmental organizations (NGOs), though a common pattern is for a movement to include both formal (NGO-like) and informal elements. Others might aptly be seen as global corporations. Some movements are vast in scope, with millions of passionate followers or members, while others are tiny, generally centered around a single individual or small group—in a sense, lonely prophets or solitary gurus. Many truly fall into the private domain, their beliefs and activities far removed from global politics, while others are active in various temporal domains, including global and local affairs and international politics.

There are movements that are quite structured entities, with clear, sometimes fairly transparent governance and hierarchies, while the organization and governance of others are far more difficult to fathom. Missions and functions vary widely, from internal peace to global advocacy for peace and justice, from community organizing to running schools or programs that care for orphans or those with HIV and AIDS. Examples of more structured movements include the Rome-based Community of Sant'Egidio; Catholic orders like the Jesuits (described by one expert as the world's oldest NGO); the Japanese lay movements Risho Kosei-kai and Soka Gakkai; the India-based Art of Living organization; the Egyptian Muslim Brotherhood; and the two enormous Indonesian organizations Nahdlatul Ulama (NU) and Muhammadiyah. The many South Asian religious and spiritual movements, inspired generally by a charismatic individual, combine religious, political, and operational dimensions, in very different formulas.

Some movements, while lacking formal institutional structures and hierarchies, have a distinctive and often large global impact. These include several transnational Buddhist movements, largely Asia-based, and the Turkish Gulen Movement. Loose coalitions of individuals or small groups may work for some common cause or causes but lack any specific institutional framework. The Liberation Theology movement is an example: it clearly originated within the Catholic Church but has roots and branches that extend far beyond it. Religiously inspired women work for peace—for example, through trauma healing or addressing violence against women—but have no common formal organization, just loose networks. Some movements promote vegetarianism as a spiritual goal and a movement of "contemplatives" urges action on the environment. Humanist and atheist communities might also view themselves as movements, working for a common cause of countering religion's excesses. Boundaries between religious, spiritual, and secular may be blurry and may shift over time. For example, Gandhian ideals and inspiration have given rise to a wide range of institutions and initiatives of many sorts that defy simple labels.[2] Another example (illustrating the sometimes evolving nature of specific religious impact) is the Oxford Movement that emerged in the 1930s, evolved into Moral Re-Armament, and is now the largely secular Initiatives of Change (with offshoots to Alcoholics Anonymous along the way) (see Box 3.1).

Box 3.1 **A movement's evolution: from the Oxford Group to Moral Re-Armament (MRA) to Initiatives of Change**

A prominent international organization or movement known for its earnest and dogged work for peace and reconciliation over 80 years goes today by the name Initiatives of Change (IofC). Its work is profoundly shaped by conscious ethical values, notably personal responsibility and the importance of apology, but it is not explicitly religious. However, its roots are very much in a religious tradition. The path the group has taken highlights the way movements can and do evolve over time and their complex influence on global affairs.

The origin was the Oxford Group, a modern, nondenominational revivalistic movement founded by an American visionary, Frank N.D. Buchman. His initial aim was to deepen the spiritual life of individuals who continued as members of their own churches. It was initially a primarily Protestant movement, and indeed some Roman Catholic authorities at first greeted the movement with suspicion (though others gave it support). Buchman, a lecturer in personal evangelism at the Hartford Seminary Foundation in Hartford, Connecticut, resigned to "live by faith" and launched a worldwide evangelistic campaign based on God's guidance, moral absolutes, and the "life changing" of individuals through personal work. Shifting operations to Princeton University, he generated controversy (and eventually left) by organizing student discussions that included public confessions on sexual matters. He moved to Oxford, UK, where the movement became known as the Oxford Group. Thousands of people attended its conferences there, and it spread to other countries. In 1938 the movement took the name Moral Re-Armament (MRA), and over time its appeal widened beyond its original, quite muscular Christian roots. Buchman hoped that the world would avoid war if individuals experienced a moral and spiritual awakening. Senator (later President) Harry Truman, chair of the Senate committee investigating war contracts, told a Washington press conference in 1943:

Suspicions, rivalries, apathy, greed lie behind most of the bottlenecks. This is where the Moral Re-Armament group comes in. Where others have stood back and criticized, they have rolled up their sleeves and gone to work. They have already achieved remarkable results in bringing teamwork into industry, on the principles not of "who's right" but of "what's right."[1]

In its peak years after World War II, MRA sent "task forces" to all corners of the free world to carry out its program, in part through plays emphasizing cooperation, honesty, and mutual respect between opposing groups. Its theology was simple and conservative: surrender to a higher power and share with others whose lives have been changed in pursuit of four moral absolutes— purity, unselfishness, honesty, and love. In Britain, MRA bought the Westminster Theatre in London as a living memorial to MRA men and women who had died in the war, and for 50 years it presented a host of plays and musicals; the pantomime *Give a Dog a Bone* ran every Christmas for many years. MRA work expanded around the globe, particularly in Africa and Asia, working to ease the transitions to independence.

MRA has since World War II focused especially on reconciliation. The organization bought a large, derelict hotel at Caux, Switzerland, and many meetings have taken place there over the decades, with thousands gathering from all over the world. In the years after 1945 an extraordinary effort centered on bringing Germany back into the international community.[2] Those who met included German Chancellor Adenauer and French Foreign Minister Robert Schuman. Hans von Herwarth (West Germany's first ambassador to Britain) observed that, "At Caux we found democracy at work, and in the light of what we saw, we faced ourselves and our nation. It was personal and national repentance. Many of us Germans who were anti-Nazi made the mistake of putting the whole blame on Hitler. We learned at Caux that we, too, were responsible."[3] MRA thus made an important contribution to "one of the greatest achievements in the entire record of modern statecraft: the astonishingly rapid Franco-German reconciliation after 1945."[4]

In 2001, the MRA movement changed its name to Initiatives of Change (IofC). Initiatives of Change International, an NGO based in Caux, Switzerland, is the legal and administrative entity that coordinates the national bodies of Initiatives of Change. It holds Special Consultative Status with the United Nations (UN) Economic and Social Council (ECOSOC), and Participatory Status at the Council of Europe. Its first president was Cornelio Sommaruga, formerly President of the International Committee of the Red Cross, succeeded by Mohamed Sahnoun, formerly Senior Advisor to UN Secretary-General Kofi Annan, Professor Rajmohan Gandhi, historian and biographer of his grandfather Mahatma Gandhi, and Dr. Omnia Marzouk. National initiatives include "Hope in the Cities" in the United States,[5] the "Caux Forum for Human Security" in Switzerland,[6] and the "IC Centre for Governance" in India.[7]

The movement has taken and continues to take many forms. One is the Caux Round Table, a business group that, meeting at Caux in 1986, formulated important principles for ethical business, termed "moral capitalism."[8] An offshoot is Alcoholics Anonymous, formed in 1935 through William Wilson and Dr Robert Smith, who recovered from their alcoholism through a combination of the Oxford Group (the forerunner of MRA) and medical treatment. Before adopting the name "Alcoholics Anonymous," AA was known as "the alcoholic squadron of the Oxford Group."

[1] Garth Lean, *Frank Buchman: A Life* (Fount PBS, 1988), 324.
[2] Michael Henderson, "The Spirit of Caux: Moral Re-Armament/ Initiatives of Change in Switzerland," 2005, www.mh.iofc.org/ node/25380.
[3] Cited in Ibid.
[4] Douglas Johnston and Cynthia Sampson, *Religion: The Missing Dimension of Statecraft*, 1994.
[5] www.hopeinthecities.org.
[6] www.cauxforum.net.
[7] www.iccfg.net.
[8] www.cauxroundtable.org.

Obviously very different in nature, organizations like Al Qaeda, Boko Haram, Hezbollah, and the Japanese Aum Shinrikyo—hybrid organizations with religious and political aspects—might be said to warrant the term movement. Their destructive agendas disproportionately shape perceptions of religion and religious movements and, since the 1970s, have focused new attention on such entities. Scientology, likewise, might be said to fall within a category of highly controversial transnational movements and organizations that evoke strong reactions and controversies.

In short, this is a complex institutional arena, imperfectly mapped and understood, yet large in scope, fluid, and often with enormous global impact. A common theme is that the spiritual and material are tightly interrelated and that spiritual and moral development can lead to material development and, more broadly, that a spiritual vision of the world is essential to understand completely the aspirations and motivations that drive many communities. There are negative and positive dimensions. As a Hindu mystic is said to have remarked, "Religion is like a cow. It kicks but it also gives milk."[3]

Religion has long played diverse roles in global affairs and few such roles are as fascinating as the ancient (and modern) practice of pilgrimage. The people who traveled far and wide, often mingling across classes and communities as they ventured to distant places, traced many of the earliest paths that linked global communities, opening new windows and opportunities and sparking ideas and change. The call to pilgrimage is generally (though not always) tied to a specific religion or part of a religion, but the impulse to travel and the actual patterns and impact of pilgrims and pilgrimages have repercussions that extend well beyond personal spiritual mission.

This chapter explores the modern phenomenon of religious movements and how some of them engage on global issues. Whether or not they may properly be termed institutions, they engage many millions of people, often across national boundaries. They shape ideas, motivate people, and undertake material as well as spiritual activities. With hundreds of thousands of groups or coalitions that might fall into the general category, the chapter illustrates different types of organizations through descriptions of a selective sample. The aim is to explore ways in which religiously inspired leaders, ideas and alliances help to shape global agendas, politics, and local action, through the lens of these movements. A section on pilgrimage focuses on that special dimension of religion's impact on globalization. The chapter concludes with a reflection on issues that arise in international policy circles with respect to these movements: what is the significance of cults? What are the roles of religious movements as political actors? When are they forces for violence, and when for peace?

The Indian sub-continent: a ferment of spiritual and religious movements

In exploring the contours of religiously or spiritually inspired movements, the richest place to start is the Indian sub-continent, where a vast number and enormous variety of movements play central roles in peoples' lives.[4] Many, though their origins are clearly rooted in South Asia, today have global scope. Several have exerted wide influence, whether purposefully or through less traditional channels (witness the influence of Maharishi Mahesh Yogi on the Beatles in the 1960s, and of

Hindu- and Buddhist-inspired yoga and meditation on thinking and health practices in the twenty-first century).

Estimates of the numbers of organizations and members are very rough (an estimate of the largest is 300 million members), but they clearly number in the tens if not hundreds of thousands; perhaps 1 million NGOs operate in India today, and many are movements that are religious or spiritual in nature.[5] Adherents range from passionately devoted followers whose entire lives are dedicated to the movement, to those who are more casually engaged. A focus on a charismatic leader is a common feature: *sampradaya* is "a tradition which has been handed down from a founder through successive religious teachers and which shapes the followers into a distinct fellowship with institutional forms."[6] A classic example is Sathya Sai Baba, a south Indian guru believed by some to be a full divine incarnation of Shiva and Shakti; his movement now involves some 1,200 centers in 130 countries worldwide.[7]

Among these many thousand entities, eight, all with global scope, today convey some idea of their widely ranging nature, and suggest the very different ways in which they engage in social, political, and economic domains. The Swaminarayan, Ramakrishna, and Svadhyay movements all grew out of Hindu traditions. The organizations created by Sri Sri Ravi Shankar, the Brahma Kumari movement, and the Isha Foundation created by Sadhguru Jaggi Vasudev characterize themselves as spiritual, rather than religious; all are very active internationally, including at the UN. Mata Amritanandamayi, or Amma, the "Hugging Saint" from Kerala, India, is self-described as purely involved in conveying love, but has a large charitable organization with increasing international scope. The Sarvodaya Movement, established by Dr A.T. Ariyaratne in Sri Lanka, also has expanded its community development activities and philosophy across several continents.[8]

The Swaminarayan Movement,[9] founded in the nineteenth century by Sahajanand Swami, is generally seen as a modern development well within the Hindu tradition, and today counts 5 million members. It emerged as a sociopolitical reform movement in the state of Gujarat during the British colonial era, sparked by famine and unrest (the Hindu Vaishnavite tradition from which it emerged holds that times of hardship call forth a great religious leader to restore peace and order). Early movement devotees were strict ascetics, refraining from sins like theft and adultery, from eating meat and drinking alcohol, and from violence. The discipline that is a characteristic of the movement aims to counter the decline of the social and moral order that is seen as the primary cause of instability. The movement today has wide-ranging practical activities, including social welfare (education and health) and infrastructure projects, run by a formal entity that is part of the movement: Bocha-sanwasi Shri Akshar Purushotam Swaminarayan Sanstha (BAPS). As an example, BAPS treats some 415,000 patients annually and is active in disaster relief and environmental action. The movement's expansion beyond India began through communities with a large Gujarathi presence. It counts today 55,000 volunteers worldwide who donate 12 million hours of service annually. Cultural festivals in India, the United States, the United Kingdom, and Africa attract 34 million visitors.[10]

The Ramakrishna Mission (also called the Vedanta movement), founded in the nineteenth century by Ramakrishna Paramahamsa, is today two legally separated but overlapping organizations: Ramakrishna Math (monastery) and Ramakrishna Mission. The first is a religious monastic order following the teachings of Sri Ramakrishna and engaging in Hindu reform efforts; the second a humanitarian, philanthropic, volunteer organization founded in 1897 by Swami Vivekananda. Like the Swaminarayan movement, the Ramakrishna movement engages in health care, disaster relief services, elementary and higher education, culture, rural programs, and tribal welfare all over India. Ramakrishna Mission runs 15 hospitals and 130 outpatient clinics, training centers for nurses, maternity clinics, tuberculosis clinics, charities, 59 mobile dispensaries, orphanages, and homes for the elderly.[11] It has a distinctive presence in education in India, with its own university, five colleges, vocational training centers, 45 high schools, primary schools, schools for the blind, and five teacher training institutes. It runs public health awareness programs in rural villages, focusing on sanitation and cleanliness, and agricultural development programs to improve cultivation methods and develop wasteland. It, too, has centers on several continents.

Svadhyay is a different style of Hindu-based movement. It emerged in the mid-1940s in Mumbai, India, as a response to frustrations about the dilemmas of modern man, materialism, liberal welfare programs and socialism, and the untapped potential to apply the teachings of the Bhagavad Gita, Vedas, and Upanishads to modern life. The Sanskrit word *Swadhyay* literally means "self-study," with connotations of divinity, austerity, and self-restraint. Swadhyay is a socioeconomic movement of social regeneration in the Indian context with a spiritual vision. Self-duty for individuals is at the core of the teachings, and it emphasizes individual and group "experiments" to develop self-esteem and human dignity in individuals. Swadhyay recognizes that alongside basic human needs (food, shelter, clothing), people also want and, in fact, require self-dignity, esteem for cultural heritage, a sense of becoming, participation in community, command of one's destiny, wholeness, and justice in society. Swadhyay is nonpolitical, operating at the grassroots level, focused on communities, and it stresses face-to-face contacts. Swadhyayees from neighboring villages come together to live on a farm (commune), working for the good of the community and strengthening relations between the villages. The leader, Pandurang Shasatri Athavale (Dada Ji), was recognized by the UN for creating innovative sociological models for change, and received the Templeton Prize for advancing the world's understanding of religion in 1997.

The followers of Sri Sri Ravi Shankar, who describes himself as a spiritual rather than a religious leader, have established a wide range of institutions, Indian and international, including the Art of Living Foundation and the International Association of Human Values.[12] The movement is active in many world regions. Art of Living, founded in 1981, in a nonprofit, humanitarian, and educational NGO focused on stress-management and service initiatives, and promotes Sudarshan Kriya, a breathing technique said to yield a number of mental and physical benefits such as decreased stress, anxiety, and depression and an improved immune system[13] (see Box 3.2). The International Association for Human Values (IAHV) works at the grassroots level on a range of social initiatives including youth outreach. Peacebuilding is seen as an essential part of the mission, and is based on principles set forth by Sri Sri Ravi Shankar, who argues that without a stress-free and thus violence-free society, world peace is impossible. The Art of Living Foundation operates as a social business on conflict resolution, disaster and trauma relief, prisoner rehabilitation, women's rights, education, human rights (preventing female feticide and child labor, for example), and environmental sustainability programs. Its Silver Jubilee celebrations drew an audience of 2.5 million people, which the organization describes as the world's largest-ever spiritual conference.[14] Sri Sri Ravi Shankar's organizations focus sharply today on their international presence and role. Accredited as a UN NGO in 1996, the Art of Living Foundation has regional centers in more than 150 countries and claims to have had an impact on 300 million people. Most of the organization's officers, staff, and teachers act in a voluntary capacity and there are close relationships among organizations of the movement. Sales of Art of Living Publications and Ayurveda products finance part of the work.

***Box 3.2* Sri Sri Ravi Shankar's international organizations**

A popular Indian spiritual leader with a wide international following, Ravi Shankar was born Ravi Shankar Ratnam in 1956. He is also frequently referred to simply by the honorific "Sri Sri" or as Guruji. He is a spiritual leader who describes himself as outside or beyond traditional religions. He founded the Art of Living Foundation in 1982. Its aim is to relieve individual stress, societal problems, and violence, which Sri Sri sees as the path to a better world. The foundation is an NGO with UN Educational, Scientific and Cultural Organization (UNESCO) consultative status. He also established the Geneva-based charity the International Association for Human Values in 1997, which engages in relief work and rural development and aims to foster shared global values. Other related organizations include Ved Vignan Maha Vidya Peeth (VVMVP), Sri Sri Ravi Shankar Vidya Mandir (SSRVM), and Vyakti Vikas Kendra India (VVKI).

Another large movement with a rather different character is the Brahma Kumaris. A spiritual movement, its focus is on meditation and a simple, pure lifestyle that it describes (and prescribes) as a path to peace. It is a rare religious movement led by and consisting largely of women. Founded in the 1930s in Sindh Hyerabad in present-day Pakistan, it is described by some as neo-Hindu, though members suggest that both Hindu beliefs and Brahma Kumari teachings trace their origins to earlier traditions

Figure 3.1 Sri Sri Ravi Shankar visiting areas in Bihar affected by floods
Source: The Art of Living Foundation

in the sub-continent. Following the partition of Pakistan and India, the movement's headquarters moved to Mount Abu in Rajasthan, India, recognized for its ancient heritage and considered by many as a sacred destination in Hindu pilgrimage. Madhuban, on Mount Abu, remains the Brahma Kumari headquarters today. The founder, Lekhraj Kripilani, originally a teacher and jeweler, was a man and—before he founded his own movement—a follower of the Vaishnavite Vallabhacharya Sect. Dada Lekhraj sent women from the community to Bombay and Delhi to establish Brahma Kumari centers that offered the partition-torn people of India spiritual reprieve and consolation. Today, there are Brahma Kumari centers in virtually all towns in India. Since the 1950s, the movement has spread beyond India and today it has centers (which focus on teaching meditation) in many countries, and an active presence at the UN. Some describe it as a global corporation. Its leader today is Janki Kripilani, known as Dadi Janki, who, aged 96 in 2012, still traveled the world as a spiritual leader. Estimates of the movement's membership vary: they include those described as "surrendered," who are fully dedicated to the movement and have no other jobs, and a larger number who study practices and teachings at the movement's many centers. The Brahma Kumaris count 825,000 students in over 8,500 centers worldwide. The lifestyle includes a strictly vegetarian diet and celibacy and there is great emphasis on purity, epitomized in the white garments its members wear. The movement describes its practices as tools for psychological healing and this, together with conferences and presentations that the movement's leaders offer, is presented as the path to peace. The movement has also entered the sphere of leadership training, focusing on what it calls "self-management leadership," and runs training programs in various countries. A "Call of Time" dialogue series draws leaders from across the global for conversation and meditation focused retreats. The movement has done pioneering work in solar energy and sustainable energy, including developing what is described as the world's largest solar cooker. An ongoing research program described as "yogic agriculture" involves entirely organic farming and channeling spiritual messages to plants; evaluation research is said to be showing promising results. Its research on diet, stress, and heart disease has been described as world class.[15] Neither their governance structure nor their finances are well understood or transparent beyond a small inner leadership circle, though the movement appears to be well financed and holds considerable property.

Another spiritual leader well known in international circles (he attends the World Economic Forum at Davos regularly and has been featured in TED talks) is Sadhguru Jaggi Vasudev.[16] He founded the

Isha Foundation, which promotes and teaches yoga in many countries. It also supports community development programs. An example is Action for Rural Rejuvenation (ARR) a "multi-pronged, multi-phased, holistic outreach program whose primary objective is to improve the overall health and quality of life of the rural poor." It supports indigenous models of health, disease prevention, and community participatory governance, and offers primary health care services and allopathic treatment.[17] The Sadhguru focuses on self-transformation, drawing on Indian traditions, on science, and on common sense. He argues that businesses need to be governed by a simple set of rules where everyone knows what can be done and what cannot. An example of his philosophy is as follows:

> What Karl Marx offered was a fantastic dream in which everybody lives by his need, not by his greed. But this was a utopian ideal. Marx had a brilliant vision for humanity, but grossly underestimated the human need to be committed to limited boundaries. Our existing society is a consequence of existing human nature. Without working to transform human nature, you cannot transform society. Communism is wonderful if it comes voluntarily, but when it is enforced, it is the ugliest way to live.[18]

A very different but also charismatic figure is Sri Mata Amritanandamayi Devi, also known as Amma, or "the Hugging Saint."[19] Born in Kerala in a fishing village to very poor parents, she has attracted millions of followers, in India and worldwide, with a message centered on love and hugs. Beyond her role as a personal spiritual icon (called by many a saint), however, Amma has developed a large charitable complex based in Kerala (but with a widening international presence), with hospital, schools, and community activities. They include programs to house the homeless, orphanages, and relief and rehabilitation in the aftermath of disasters like the 2004 Indian Ocean tsunami. She supports environmental protection groups, slum rehabilitation, facilities for the elderly, and free food and clothing for the poor. Various organizations have been established to run these projects and are known collectively as Embracing the World. They include the Mata Amritanandamayi Math (India), the Mata Amritanandamayi Center (USA), Amritanandamayi-Europe, Amritanandamayi-Japan, Amritanandamayi-Kenya, and Amritanandamayi-Australia. Amma commented in 2004: "As for the activities, there was no planning. Everything happened spontaneously. One thing led to another on seeing the plight of the poor and the distressed." Most work is done by volunteers as a form of spiritual practice: "It is Amma's wish that all of her children should dedicate their lives to spreading love and peace throughout the world. Real love and devotion for God is to have compassion for the poor and the suffering." Amma is said to hug individually over 50,000 people in a day, and it is said that she has hugged at least 21 million people in the past 20 years. In 2005, *Darshan—The Embrace*, a film based on her life, was showcased at the Cannes Film Festival. Today she heads a global spiritual empire, known as "the messiah of the poor and downtrodden," and has followers who include Hotmail founder Sabeer Bhatia, US senator Larry Pressler, and Martin Luther King, Jr's daughter Yolanda King.[20]

The Sarvodaya Shramadana movement is one of the most significant and admired religiously inspired movements in South Asia.[21] Its core principle is a return to traditional village life based on Buddhist principles as the cure for the corruption and materialism of modern urban societies. Founded in 1958 in Sri Lanka by Dr A.T. Ariyaratne, the movement receives inspiration from Gandhian as well as Buddhist principles.[22] *Sarvodaya* is Sanskrit for "Awakening of All," and *Shramadana* means "to donate effort." The movement started in a single village as an education program and local initiative, and then expanded across Sri Lanka, emerging as a movement seeking comprehensive and nonviolent social transformation. It is today the largest and most established NGO in Sri Lanka, with headquarters in Moratuwa, near Colombo.

Sarvodaya accepts little foreign aid or state support, relying on volunteer labor, mostly from the beneficiaries themselves. The movement's core principles of self-reliance, community participation, and a holistic approach to community "awakening" to appeal to communities and to other supporters. People organize in their communities and villages to meet the basic human needs that the movement defines—clean and adequate drinking-water supply, proper housing and sanitation, communications facilities, access to energy resources, education, and cultural and spiritual satisfaction. Programs include peacebuilding, conflict resolution, appropriate technology and programs for children at risk, elders, and those with disabilities. Sarvodaya has a strong youth focus, involving over 100,000 youth in peacebuilding. Sarvodaya Economic Enterprise Development Services (SEEDS) is Sri Lanka's largest micro-credit organization, with a cumulative loan portfolio of more than US$1 million. The organization's budget exceeds US$5 million and supports 1,500 full-time employees. Sarvodaya has been particularly effective in responding to emergencies like the 2004 tsunami and is involved in cutting-edge programs like early childhood education. Sarvodaya's international programs are a new and important feature of its operations.

All of these movements attract admiration and also some controversy. As an example, the Ramakrishna order has sought but was denied status as a non-Hindu minority religion because it feared that the schools it administered were going to be taken over by the local government. In striking contrast to the gentle image their adherents project in public settings, the Brahma Kumaris have been investigated by the state for "criminal" activities involving cases of murders, rapes, scapegoating and police cover ups,[23] and both the Greek and French governments have classified the group as dangerous and a cult movement. Issues often center on financial management, succession disputes, recruitment methods (requiring large financial contributions from women entering the Brahma Kumari movement, for example), and reports of abuse of members, ex-members, and critics. The exclusivity of movements is seen as breaking up families.[24] An important issue about the movements is limited knowledge about their work. Some have been researched in some detail but there are many that have not, and there is little by way of analysis of the overall phenomenon and its impact on society and politics.

New religious movements in East Asia

The term "new religions" applied to religious movements originated as a reflection of an explosion of new religious forms and institutions in the post-World War II era, and indeed Japan, for all its secularity, has given birth to several very different kinds of new religious movements. There are hundreds of officially recognized new religions in Japan alone, and total membership is said to be in the tens of millions. The largest new religion, Soka Gakkai, claims about 10 million members in Japan and is actively engaged in international and interfaith activities. Other movements with global ambitions or presence include another large, lay Buddhist-inspired movement, Risho Kosei-kai; the neo-Shinto World Mate; the spiritual World Peace Prayer Society; Happy Science; and the quintessential violent cult Aum Shinrikyo. Many have an inspiration of peace but their work is expanding in many different areas from education to advocacy of interreligious dialogue (see Box 3.3).

Box 3.3 A Japanese passion for peace

Several Japanese organizations have world peace as their central mission and these often are characterized by a spiritual ethos that may be more or less explicit. Many (though not all) have emerged following the horrors of World War II and an anti-nuclear weapon focus is a common theme. Peace is an ideal running through most Japanese new religious movements, including Soka Gakkai and Risho Kosei-kai, but there are also a number of smaller organizations.

An example is the World Peace Prayer Society, a small, private organization that focuses on specific peace-focused activities and awarding or supporting obelisk shaped "peace poles" with "May Peace Prevail on Earth" written in different languages. Its poles are visible in many corners of the world, including at the UN.

Another example is the Arigatou Foundation (Arigatou International), established in 1990 by Rev. Takeyasu Miyamoto. Its mission is to create a better environment for children the world over by promoting a lifestyle of "prayer and action" advocated by Myochikai, a Japanese Buddhist organization founded in 1950 that today claims 1 million members. Myochikai is representative of characteristics found in many of the new Japanese religious movements in its promotion of an ethic of common virtues such as endurance, repentance, and thanksgiving; its participation in local and international charitable activities; its emphasis on world peace and interreligious cooperation; and in the succession of leadership within the family of the founder.

Soka Gakkai (which means Value Creation Society) is one of the more successful of the new Japanese religions, with a particularly active international presence. It emerged within the Nichiren Buddhism tradition, a branch of Mahayana Buddhism. Founded by an educator, Tsunesaburo Makiguchi, in 1930, with education reform as its main goal, the organization was suppressed during World War II because it opposed the government-supported State Shinto, and its leaders were charged as "thought criminals." One died in prison of malnutrition in 1944, but Josei Toda was released in July 1945 and rebuilt the Soka Gakkai membership from fewer than 3,000 families in 1951 to more than 750,000 before his death in 1958. Many members came from the poorer classes in larger urban areas. Soka Gakkai took on the character of a lay religious movement dedicated to social reform. The current core organization, Soka Gakkai International (SGI), was founded in 1975 in Guam by Daisaku Ikeda. SGI characterizes itself as both a support network for practitioners of Nichiren Buddhism and as a global Buddhist movement for peace, education, and cultural exchange. Membership growth owes much to the movement's tradition of small group, neighborhood, and local community discussion meetings. Over time its political activities within Japan have expanded and it created the Komeito (clean government) Party. Today, Soka Gakkai claims a membership of 8.27 million households in Japan.

From 1960 on, Soka Gakkai has had a substantial international character and presence. This turned in part around Daisaku Ikeda, the Soka Gakkai president who became a strong advocate for disarmament and opposition to nuclear weapons. In late 2011, Soka Gakkai claimed a total membership of 12 million in 192 countries and territories· in North America, South America, Australia and parts of Asia, Africa, and Europe. Its activities are far ranging and include two universities, in Japan and in the United States. Soka Gakkai is also active in humanitarian relief. Soka Gakkai, in part because of its size and influence and its political role, has attracted considerable controversy, both in Japan and internationally.

Risho Kosei-kai, another large, lay Buddhist movement, is also a new religious entity in the Nichiren tradition of Buddhism. Founded in Japan in 1938 by Nikkyo Niwano and Myoko Naganuma, business and spiritual leaders, it centers its teachings on the lessons of the Buddha, and especially the Lotus Sutra. A core message is that everything on Earth is interconnected and that with human respect will come harmony and peace for all. All of the organization's considerable charitable activities link to this central rubric. Risho Kosei-kai has over 2 million members and 300 Dharma centers in 20 countries throughout the world.

Risho Kosei-kai is particularly known for its interfaith work and is active in several international interfaith organizations including the International Association for Religious Freedom (IARF) and Religions for Peace (WCRP), for which Risho Kosei-kai's current leader Nichiko Niwano long headed the Japan branch. The organization actively engages in UN-led discussion and initiatives, particularly on disarmament issues, and holds special consultative status. The Niwano Peace Foundation is part of Risho Kosei-kai, and since 1983 awards an annual Peace Prize to individuals or organizations worldwide that work for peace and development and promote interreligious cooperation: past recipients include Thai Engaged Buddhist leader Sulak Sivaraksa, Prince El Hassan bin Talal of Jordan, Rosalina Tuyuc Velazquez, a Guatemalan Mayan leader, and the lay Catholic Community of Sant'Egidio.

A different new Japanese religious movement, World Mate (meaning "friend of the world") draws on both Shinto and Buddhist traditions. Founded in the 1950s by Aiko Uematsu, it describes its mission as guiding young people to follow a path of virtue, and "elevating humanity to its ultimate fulfillment." Dr. Haruhisa Handa has served as spiritual leader and chairman of the organization since 1984. World Mate has about 37,000 members, in Japan and abroad. The organization, registered as a nonprofit philanthropic organization in Japan, focuses on both Japanese and international charitable ventures, with a rather extraordinary concentration of activities in Cambodia. It supports hospitals, universities, think tanks, schools, and humanitarian activities (for example, through the Red Cross). Following the March 2011 earthquake and nuclear disaster in Japan, World Mate mobilized many volunteers (equipped with Geiger counters to gauge the dangers of radiation) to come as close as possible to those affected and provide support.

Another Japanese movement is the World Peace Prayer Society, a non-sectarian, pacifist organization that exemplifies a blend of very secular and spiritually motivated ideals (see Box 3.3). Its motto is "May Peace Prevail on Earth." Founded by an idealistic leader in 1955, the organization seeks to promote world peace in large part through a worldwide network of obelisk-shaped peace poles inscribed with the prayer. These can be found in over 180 countries. The society organizes peace festivals, fairs, and events for schoolchildren.

A Buddhist-inspired organization in the Chinese tradition, the Dharma Drum Mountain organization (based in Taiwan) was founded by Buddhist monk Sheng Yen, a religious scholar and mainstream teacher of Chinese Chan Buddhism. He taught Buddhism for a modern and Western-influenced world and was one of Taiwan's four prominent modern Buddhist masters. The organization, which has activities in some 14 countries, focuses on education and culture. Among the organization's activities is one of the world's leading museums of religion. Dharma Drum's vision is to "uplift the character of humanity and build a pure land on earth." Its spirit is to "give of ourselves for the benefit of all." In its educational work, it focuses on academic education to cultivate high-caliber Buddhist talent in the fields of research, teaching, and public outreach through traditional Buddhist practices such as meditation or recitation of the Buddha's name, as well as modern cultural activities and education through caring services, which include, for example, emergency assistance in response to natural disasters. The movement also has a strong environmental focus. Its work for peace is focused on core values and ethical principles: for example, that "cultivating a peaceful mind lies in reducing desires, cultivating a peaceful body lies in hard work and thrift, and cultivating peaceful activity lies in being honest and upright."[25]

Tzu Chi Foundation, also based in Taiwan, was founded in 1966 by Cheng Yen, a Buddhist nun (*bhikkhuni*), teacher, and philanthropist often called the "Mother Teresa of Asia." Its vision is "instructing the rich and saving the poor," and Cheng Yen's work began as charitable work inspired by compassion. Today it also includes medical, educational, cultural, and social welfare activities. The foundation is deeply involved in international disaster relief, bone marrow donations, environmental protection, and community volunteering. *Tzu Chi* means "Compassionate Relief," and the foundation (which has a substantial international presence) is the largest NGO in the Chinese-speaking world. It claims some 10 million members, and has chapters in 47 countries. A feature of the organization is its extensive reliance on volunteers, mostly women—initially, almost exclusively housewives who set aside a small amount of grocery money each day to care for needy families. It provides aid to all people regardless of race, religion, or nationality. With particularly deep roots in Asia, Tzu Chi is considered one of the most effective aid agencies in the region. It is one of the rare Taiwanese and religious institutions welcome to work in China. Tzu Chi has several sub-organizations, for example the Tzu Chi International Medical Association (TIMA), composed of medical profession personnel who volunteer their services in poor communities around the world, and a youth organization.

Perhaps the most contentious of modern Asian movements is Falun Gong or Falun Dafa (literally "Dharma Wheel Practice"). A spiritual discipline first introduced in China in 1992 by founder Li Hongzhi, it combines meditation and slow-moving *qigong* exercises with a moral philosophy that emphasizes morality and the cultivation of virtue through truthfulness, compassion, and forbearance. It draws on both Buddhist and Taoist traditions (Taoism or Daoism is a more ancient indigenous Chinese faith). Some estimates (1999) placed the number of Falun Gong adherents in the tens of millions. Hundreds of thousands are believed to practice Falun Gong outside China across some 70 countries worldwide. Those who practice Falun Gong aspire to better health and, ultimately, spiritual enlightenment. Western academics have described Falun Gong as a *qigong* discipline, a "spiritual movement" based on the teachings of its founder, a "cultivation system" in the tradition of Chinese antiquity, and sometimes a religion or new religious movement.

Falun Gong practice enjoyed considerable support from Chinese officialdom until the mid- to late 1990s. Since then, the Chinese Communist Party and public security organs have increasingly viewed Falun Gong as a potential threat due to its size, independence from the state, and spiritual teachings. A nationwide crackdown and propaganda campaign launched in 1999 sought to eradicate the practice and the government declared Falun Gong a "heretical organization." Human rights groups report that Falun Gong practitioners in China are subject to a wide range of human rights abuses; hundreds of thousands are believed to have been imprisoned extra-judicially, and practitioners in detention are subject to forced labor, psychiatric abuse, torture, and other coercive methods of thought reform at the hands of Chinese authorities.[26] In the years since the suppression campaign began, Falun Gong adherents have emerged as a prominent voice in the Chinese dissident community, advocating for greater human rights and an end to Communist Party rule.

Christian-inspired movements

Within the Christian sphere, the boundaries between denominations, orders, and new movements are not easy to trace. Most orders and lay movements of the Catholic Church have deep and ancient roots, while other movements (both Christian and Catholic) are far more recent and take different shapes. Given the size and depth of Christianity, this diversity is hardly surprising. What is a new prophetic vision to some (take the Latter-Day Saints or the Jehovah's Witnesses), to others may be a deviant and dangerous sect. Given that Christianity in general tends to be a proselytizing religion, many of these movements and offshoots have an active global presence and role.

A particularly active group of Christian movements are part of the Catholic Church. There are many, representing different styles and missions, ranging from active to secluded, from left-leaning and liberal to highly conservative. They all fall under the notional authority of the Vatican administration, but often operate with considerable degrees of freedom. Six examples are the Jesuit Order, the Community of Sant'Egidio, the Focolare movement, the Missionaries of Charity, the Maryknoll organization, and Opus Dei.

The Jesuits (officially the Society of Jesus) represent the largest single Catholic order and a community and movement that is legendary for its intellectual vigor and the courage of conviction of its members. It is especially dedicated to education, and renowned world leaders as diverse as King Abdallah II of Jordan, William J. Clinton, Fidel Castro, Arthur Conan Doyle, Charles de Gaulle, and Joseph Goebbels were all educated in Jesuit schools or universities. The order also has NGO wings, notably the Jesuit Service and the Jesuit Volunteer Service. The order was founded in the fifteenth century by a Spaniard, Ignatius Loyola, who called the group the "Company of Jesus" to highlight both its spirit of leadership and its soldierly virtue. It is a body of priests organized for apostolic work, following a religious rule, and relying on alms for their support. Long and diverse multidisciplinary study is an integral part of preparing to take vows as a Jesuit. Today, the roughly 19,000 Jesuits are active in 112 countries on six continents.

Early Jesuits were sent to many countries, including India, Japan, China, Canada, and nations in Central and South America, with the initial objective of propagating and strengthening the Catholic faith. They were an important part of the Counter-Reformation, the re-conquest of southern and western Germany and Austria for the Church, and the preservation of the Catholic faith in France and other countries. They also came to respect the cultures of the countries where they worked. They are best known for the excellence of their schools, although they also play roles in the fight against war, poverty, social injustice, and violence.

The Jesuits are also familiar with controversy, both as a central actor and as a target, within and outside the Catholic Church. Conspiracy theories have long dogged the order, while Catholic conservatives criticize their independence of mind and "modern" views. The Order has been banned and disbanded at different periods, notably in the eighteenth century when Pope Clement XIV ordered it dissolved in France, Spain, Portugal, Naples and Austria; Catherine the Great of Russia refused to carry out the Pope's orders, so many Jesuits fled to Russia. When Pope Pius VII reinstated the order in 1814, it was the Russian Jesuits who rebuilt the order in all countries.

Most important, the Jesuits have the reputation for being strong, open-hearted men of faith. During the Holocaust, many Jesuits risked their lives to help the Jews. Jesuits, either as individuals or working through their NGO arms, have often been the first on the scene after terrible disasters; their active presence in Cambodia immediately after the Khmer Rouge era and continuing presence there is a prime example.

A lay Catholic movement founded amidst the tumult of student activism in 1968 by a group of young Romans, the Community of Sant'Egidio is a self-described movement dedicated to peace and friendship. Widening its scope from its work with poor, immigrant communities in Rome's suburbs, the group caught the attention of the Pope and of young people first in Europe, then in Africa and Latin America; it expanded its work, organically. Working with the most destitute and troubled communities wherever it found them, the Community was drawn progressively into mediation work in conflict situations. Its direct role in the long negotiations that led to the Mozambique Peace Accords won it praise and in turn carried it into many other conflict situations. Community members are volunteers: none are paid. They hold "regular" jobs, but are strikingly loyal to the friendship and mission of the Community. The Community's activities evolve from what they see as the imperatives for peace and justice. Thus in Mozambique, for example, a major initiative to address the HIV and AIDS challenge grew from their work for peace. In Burkina Faso and Côte d'Ivoire, they became strong advocates for the registration of citizens, as that emerged as a critical issue to implementation of peace agreements. The Community is also a leader in interfaith work (see Chapter 4), and, on behalf of the Vatican, organizes brilliantly the annual interfaith gathering termed the Prayer for Peace. The Community is loosely run and organized, with no formal structure. Each national Community has considerable autonomy: a Sant'Egidio leader once described the arrangement as a franchise. The movement has benefitted from the charismatic leadership qualities of its founder, Andrea Riccardi (who became Minister of Development and Integration in the Italian government in 2011), and others among that tight group. Though it is considered on the "left" side of the Catholic community politically, it has enjoyed and nurtured strong ties to the Roman Catholic hierarchy and a wide respect among the peacemaking community internationally.

The Focolare movement is another Roman Catholic movement, motivated by Christian unity and dedication to neighbors as brothers and sisters in Christ.[27] It is marked by leadership by women and its global outreach. *Focolare* means fireplace or hearth, representing "a home where there is a family full of warmth."[28] Members devote their lives to service, especially to the poor, the sick, and the destitute; there are many different types of membership including fully consecrated individuals (men and women), who live in communities (and hold regular jobs), and lay members. Officially approved by Pope John XXIII in 1962, the Focolare movement is inspired by the leadership of founder Chiara Lubich and has its roots in a community that ministered to those affected by World War II bombings in Italy. The movement has become highly ecumenical, spreading beyond the Catholic Church to include other Christian denominations such as Lutheran, Dutch Reform, Anglican, Orthodox, and Coptic Christians. Since the 1980s, the movement has formed tight ties with the Japanese Buddhist Risho Kosei-kai community that includes a School for Oriental Religions in Tagaytay, the Philippines. The Buddhist-Christian dialogue encouraged at the School has helped many Asian Christians overcome a mental aversion to Buddhism out of fear of diluting their personal faith. Success here inspired other such schools including the Isaiah School in New York and the Center for Dialogue with Muslims and Christians in Algeria. An Asian Inter-Religious Young Forum in 1985 encouraged Asian youth to take on pertinent issues of development and peace in Asia and small towns were established in 29 countries, following the Focolare model, complete with schools and summer schools aimed at spiritual and practical development.

The Focolare movement's response to globalization took a much more pointed approach in the early 1990s, when Lubich, on a visit to Brazil, focused on the glaring wealth disparities between the city and the surrounding slums. The Economy of Communion was born: a global Focolare network of businesses run on Christian guidelines and committed to the redistribution of wealth to the poor, to the development of infrastructure, and to further business investments.[29] This network has grown to include about 800 companies worldwide that provide a share of their profits for redistribution to the poor through Focolare. The idea is that the market takes on a new meaning and function, serving not only its practical purpose as a place for the exchange of goods, but also a social, spiritual purpose, connecting people through a Christian spirit of giving. Offshoot programs include a social cooperatives' consortium in Italy that manages homes and communities for the elderly, the mentally ill, and those with special needs. The movement promotes microfinance programs, sustaining small, individual businesses in African countries, such as Kenya and Nigeria.[30] Focolare advocates sacrifice not for the sake of sacrifice, but to weed out material and physical encroachments on individual spiritual development and, thus, to experience properly God's influence in daily life.

The Missionaries of Charity, a religious order, was established in 1950 by Mother Teresa, a Roman Catholic nun (and winner of the Nobel Peace Prize) born in Macedonia of Albanian origin.[31] She went to India as a teacher with an Irish order. In 1950, she received Vatican permission to start her own order in India[32]; in 1965, the Pope approved Mother Teresa's request to expand the congregation beyond India and houses were established in Venezuela, Rome, and Tanzania. Today the order operates worldwide in some 133 countries with about 520 missions. The order comprises both Contemplative and Active branches of Brothers and Sisters; the order's more than 4,500 sisters all take vows of chastity, poverty, obedience, and give wholehearted service to the poorest of the poor. Among those for whom the congregation cares are refugees, ex-prostitutes, mentally disabled, sick or abandoned children, lepers, AIDS victims, the elderly, and the convalescent. The congregation has 19 homes for women, orphaned children, and for the dying in Calcutta alone, as well as a hospice for AIDS victims, a school for street children, and a leper colony. They charge nothing for any service they provide and do not discriminate on the basis of religion or caste. Groups affiliated with the Missionaries of Charity include the Co-Workers of Mother Teresa, the Sick and Suffering Co-Workers, the Lay Missionaries of Charity, and the Corpus Christi Movement for priests.

As the founder of the congregation, Mother Teresa wrote the constitution and gathered the first group of sisters. Since 1961, the position of Superior General has been elected by the Chapter General, which meets every six years and comprises both elected and appointed members. The Chapter General discusses the life and work of the community and, in addition to electing the Superior General, elects the Councilors General. Members of the Chapter General include an appointed Superior General, Ex-Superiors General, Councilors General, and Regional Superiors; and two elected representatives from each region and elected representatives of sisters in charge of formation. In 1990 Mother Teresa resigned as the head of the Missionaries but was soon voted back in as Superior General. Six months before her death in September of 1997, Sister Mary Nirmala Joshi was selected as Superior General of the Missionaries of Charity. In 2009, Sister Mary Prema was elected to succeed Sister Mary Nirmala Joshi.

While the Missionaries of Charity enjoy a remarkable global reputation for selfless service, as with virtually all religious institutions it has faced some controversy. The most significant involves the quality of care offered to terminally ill patients in the Homes for the Dying as well as to patients in various hospitals—for example, concerns over sanitation. Two medical journals, *The Lancet* and the *British Medical Journal*, reported re-use of hypodermic needles, inadequate living conditions, and failure to adhere to tenets of modern medicine by insisting on cold baths for all patients and failing to engage in systematic diagnosis.[33] In Sri Lanka a sister was suspected of child-trafficking, among other offenses.[34] However, these are rare critiques of a widely admired organization.

Maryknoll is a name shared by three organizations that are part of the Roman Catholic Church, the joint focus of which is on the overseas mission activity of the United States Catholic Church. They include a society of apostolic life for men, a religious institute for woman, and a lay group: respectively, the Maryknoll Fathers and Brothers (The Catholic Foreign Mission Society of America); the Maryknoll Sisters (The Maryknoll Sisters of St Dominic); and the Maryknoll Lay Missioners. The organizations are independent entities that work closely together in many of their missionary endeavors. Over a more than 100-year history Maryknoll has focused on ministry and missionary work, especially in East Asia, China, Japan and South Korea. It also engages in advocacy for the poor in the United States.

The Opus Dei ("work of God" in Latin) movement originated in Spain, and today is considered by many the most controversial and conservative forces within the Roman Catholic world. Formally known as the Prelature of the Holy Cross and Opus Dei, it is a mixed priestly and lay movement, founded in Spain by Catholic priest St Josemaría

Escrivá in 1928. Its central teaching is that ordinary life is the path to sanctity and holiness. Most members are laypeople, with secular priests under the governance of a prelate (bishop) elected by specific members and appointed by the Pope. In 2010 there were over 90,000 members— men and women—worldwide in over 90 countries. About 70 percent of Opus Dei members live in their private homes, leading traditional Catholic family lives with secular careers. The other 30 percent are celibate and live in centers. Aside from personal charity and social work, Opus Dei members are involved in running universities, university residences, schools, publishing houses, and technical and agricultural training centers.

Controversies about Opus Dei have centered on its perceived secretiveness, its recruiting methods, its strict rules governing members, the practice by celibate members of mortification of the flesh, its reputation for elitism and misogyny, the right-leaning politics of most of its members, and links of some members to authoritarian or extreme right-wing governments, especially the Franco government of Spain before 1978. It is viewed as a powerful, if often shadowy force in many governments, especially in Latin America. Within the Catholic Church, Opus Dei is criticized for seeking independence and more influence, even as it is admired for its discipline and commitment to ethical principles in life.

Muslim movements

There are also important Muslim movements. These take many very different forms and the very definition of a "movement" presents particular difficulties as the boundaries between religious body, loosely knit grouping, and purposeful organization are far from precise. To illustrate the varying character of different types of entity, five examples are introduced: the two vast Indonesian organizations Muhammadiyah and NU; the Turkish Gulen Movement; the Egyptian Muslim Brotherhood; and the West African Tijanniyah movement. Box 3.4 presents a modern phenomenon, perhaps appropriately termed a movement also: the influential Egyptian televangelist Amr Khaled.

Box 3.4 Modern religious figures: the case of Amr Khaled[1]

I also have a message of reform and development, which I call "development through faith." Faith is the motor of development and one can't do without it. I am not a Mufti, and I don't deliver legal judgments on what's permitted or forbidden under Islamic law. What I want to do is to move Arab youth.[2]

Attracting comparisons to Billy Graham, Joel Osteen, and even Oprah Winfrey, Amr Khaled is one of the Arab world's most popular and influential Muslim preachers; his sermons reach millions daily through the internet and satellite television. Born into an upper middle-class family in Alexandria, Egypt, in 1967, Khaled was originally trained as an accountant before leaving that profession to pursue preaching full time in the late 1990s. Today, he is recognized as one of the world's most important Muslim spiritual leaders, despite his lack of formal religious training. His message of tolerance, dialogue, and grassroots community development based in Islamic principles earns both praise and criticism. His following is particularly strong amongst young, middle-class Muslims.

Amr Khaled's preaching style is based in the tradition of Taswīr, a method pioneered by Sayyid Qutb, which seeks to "bring the lessons of the Quran to life" through the use of sensory descriptions and illustrative examples, as opposed to the more traditional styles of memorization and recitation. His message focuses on Islam's everyday applicability as well as practical lessons to be drawn from its teachings, like manners, respect, tolerance, and avoiding drugs. Followers see this as meeting the needs of the modern world, while detractors call it simplistic, "air-conditioned Islam." Because he advocates peaceful dialogue and coexistence with the West some have dubbed him the "anti-bin Laden." His immense popularity itself draws anxiety from some authorities, and from 2002 to 2005 Khaled lived in self-imposed exile in the UK. Khaled works through two faith-inspired networks: The Lifemakers and the Right Start Foundation. The first, with thousands of local branches, primarily throughout the Arab world, involves youth in service and community development projects in the name of Islam; it is especially popular on university campuses in the Middle East. The Right Start Foundation, based in the UK, reaches out to Muslim youths living in the West to engage them in service and dialogue projects. Khaled argues that rising unemployment, poor economic conditions, and authoritarian rule have created a situation in which Muslim youths are prime targets for extremist groups like Al Qaeda, but that transforming current realities must be internally driven, with Islamic principles as a guide.

Khaled's charismatic personality and Western style allow him to appear at home in the often-conflicting worlds of religion, business, and politics. Many conservative Muslim scholars, for instance, argued that a 2006 conference between Muslim and Danish youth in Copenhagen to discuss the controversial cartoons depicting the Prophet Mohammed placed Western values of free speech above religious tradition. Others deride his lack of traditional religious education, asserting that he has no formal legal authority—a charge Khaled does not deny. Others worry about Khaled's conservative stances on issues like head coverings for women. However, Amr Khaled's masterful use of new technology to reach a transnational audience with a modern message and immense influence, particularly among young Arabs, certainly attracts attention.

[1] Sources include, for example, David Hardaker, "Amr Khaled: Islam's Billy Graham: More Popular Than Oprah Winfrey, the World's first Islamic Television Evangelist Commands an Army of Millions of Followers," *The Independent*, 4 January 2006, www.independent.co.uk/news/world/middle-east/amr-khaled-islams-billy-graham-521561.html.

[2] Amr Khaled cited in Mona Naggar, "I Want to Move Arab Youth: Amr Khaled," *The American Muslim*, www.theamericanmuslim.org/tam.php/features/articles/i_want_to_move_arab_youth_amr_khaled.

The initial vision of the large Indonesian movement Muhammadiyah (established in 1912) was to adapt Islam to modern Indonesian life. Inspired in part by an Egyptian reform movement and also concerned about the inroads being made by Christian missionaries, Muhammadiyah advocated the abolition of all superstitious customs, mostly relics of pre-Islamic times, and the loosening of the stiff traditional bonds that tended to strangle modern cultural life. It employed many methods of the Christian missionaries, notably establishing schools that operated along modern lines. Today it has some 29 million members and has a wide range of activities, though its central focus continues to be education: it operates some 5,800 schools and several major universities. It also runs hospitals and several hundred medical clinics. It has both women's and youth organizations.

Muhammadiyah's central doctrine is Sunni Islam, but the movement's focus is mainly on heightening people's sense of moral responsibility, thus purifying their faith in a true Islam. It emphasizes the authority of the Qur'an and the Hadiths as supreme Islamic law that serves as the legitimate basis of the interpretation of religious belief and practices. It opposes syncretism, where Islam in Indonesia has coalesced with spirit worship and with Hindu-Buddhist values that were spread among the villagers, including the upper classes, from the pre-Islamic period. It also opposes the tradition of Sufism, where Sufi leaders act as the formal authority of Muslims. Though Muhammadiyah refrained from direct political activity during its early years, it was an important actor during the tumultuous period after 1998 and is clearly influential in shaping national agendas and ethos. Muhammadiyah is largely focused on Indonesia but has an increasing international presence, both as a voice for Muslims worldwide and in interfaith circles.

Muhammadiyah's governance structure involves a central committee structure that consists of five advisors, a chairman, a vice-chairman, a secretary-general and deputies, a treasurer and deputies, as well as several deputies of the chairman. The current leader is Professor Din Syamsuddin. The movement's women's and youth groups operate as largely autonomous organizations.

Nahdlatul Ulama, or NU (the name means "Awakening of Religious Scholars"), was established in 1926 in reaction to the more modernist Muhammadiyah organization. It presents itself as a traditionalist Sunni Muslim movement and is probably the largest independent Islamic organization in the world, with a membership estimated at 30 million. Its main function today is to spread Islamic teaching through preaching and a vast network of educational institutions: some 6,830 Islamic boarding schools, or *pesantren*, and 44 universities. It is also involved in economic and agricultural work and a range of social services. NU's positive work on family planning has earned it wide international respect.[35] It functions as a charitable body that *de facto* addresses many shortcomings in government services. NU is involved in other activities including running a system of rural banks.

NU's governance is well structured and quite transparent. It is governed by a supreme council and, under it, an executive council. An advisory council provides input to both. Sahal Mahfudz, elected chairman of the Executive Council in 2010, also serves as executive chief. There are provincial-level regional boards, as well as autonomous bodies, institutes, and committees, with the structure extending down to sub-branch representative council boards in villages.

NU has a long and complex history of political involvement. During the Indonesian war of independence, it declared that the fight against the Dutch colonial forces was a holy war, obligatory for all Muslims.

At the time of independence, the NU argued that Indonesia should become an Islamic state, which the nation rejected in favor of *Pancasila*, a philosophy and ideology that blended monotheism (but not Islam), socialism, and "guided democracy." In 1965 it sided with the General Suharto-led army and was heavily involved in the mass-killings of Indonesian communists. In 1984 it began to oppose Suharto's regime and its leader from that date, Abdurrahman Wahid (Gus Dur), was elected President of Indonesia in 1999 as leader of the National Awakening Party (PKB). Gus Dur has supported *Pancasila*, calling it a "noble compromise." Generally, though, since around 1987 NU has been less directly involved in electoral politics.

The Gulen Movement, named for its founder, Turkish Imam Fethullah Gulen, has recently emerged as one of the world's more visible and influential faith-inspired movements. It consists of an extensive decentralized and individually funded network that includes business, journalism, and interfaith organizations, charities, a newspaper, and television and radio stations, as well as over 1,000 schools in 140 countries around the world.[36] Hard statistics are difficult to obtain, and membership estimates range from 200,000 to 10 million—although there is no formal membership process or status (this explains the wide range of estimates).[37] The Gulen Movement describes itself as "a faith-inspired, non-political, cultural and educational movement whose basic principles stem from Islam's universal values, such as love of creation, sympathy for fellow humans, compassion, and altruism."[38] Heavily inspired by the pluralistic legacy of Ottoman-era Turkey, as well as the teachings of Sufi scholar Said Nursi's *Nur* ("light") movement, Fethullah Gulen and his followers teach that moderation, tolerance, interfaith dialogue, science and mathematics, and democracy are not only compatible with Islam—they are central to it.[39]

Born in Erzurum, Turkey in 1938, Fethullah Gulen moved to Izmir in 1962 as a government preacher and the Gulen Movement (in Turkish, *Hizmet*, or "service," Movement) was born there. It was initially simply a network of teaching centers that largely prepared religious students for university. As the movement grew, secular Turkish authorities grew concerned and Gulen served seven months in prison in the 1970s for "clandestine religious activities" and entered a self-imposed exile to Pennsylvania in 1999 following accusations of an attempt to subvert the Turkish government—charges that were dismissed in 2008. While its size, influence, and opaque structure have garnered suspicion, Gulen's teachings, including the separation of religion and state, religious tolerance and interfaith dialogue, and a belief that liberal concepts of democracy and free enterprise and the teachings of Islam are compatible, have led many to see the Gulen Movement as a moderate influence in an era of growing religious extremism and tensions between East and West.

The Gulen Movement is best known for its extensive network of schools with a reputation for high academic standards and an emphasis on math, science, and Turkish- and English-language instruction. While most Gulen-affiliated schools are located in Turkey and other Central Asian states with ethnic Turkic populations, they are also present in much of Africa, Asia, Europe, and Australia. With some 130 schools operating in 26 states, Gulen schools make up the largest public charter school network in the United States.[40] The schools do not discriminate based on faith or nationality and abide by national curricula, strictly avoiding religious instruction where prohibited. Religious instruction, when it does occur, is performed in small group and mentorship settings outside of school hours. The goal, supporters say, is not to proselytize, but to form individuals "who are adept in their professional fields but who are, more importantly, complete human beings who strive to improve the conditions of their collective societies."[41] Their reputation for academic excellence has attracted large numbers of students, including many from Turkey and Central Asia's elite political and economic classes, as well as thousands in the United States.[42]

The Gulen Movement, including its network of schools, has provoked controversy in various places, perhaps most notably in Central Asia, where it has a large presence. Much of the region's political establishment remains vehemently secular and suspicious of any religious organization—particularly one with as much influence as the Gulen Movement. Its schools, meanwhile, have come under attack by some Central Asian governments for fostering a pan-Turkic identity through Turkish language and cultural instruction—a practice supporters argue enables students to "continue their education in the most distinguished universities of Turkey, Europe, and [the] USA."[43] The group's opaque leadership structure and growing network in the United States have also led to some suspicions, as well as charges of nepotism in hiring and contracting practices. Notwithstanding, the Gulen Movement is one of the most influential faith-inspired voices for education, tolerance, and moderation today.

The Muslim Brotherhood is an Egyptian Islamist organization and at least the inspiration, if not the practical bond, for similar socio-political-religious organizations in many other countries. Founded by Hassan al-Banna in the 1920s, the movement initially had spread Muslim morals and good works as its central goal, but it soon became involved in anti-colonial politics that extended from governance to ways of life. The movement had youth groups and at some points a paramilitary wing. Long banned as a dangerous political force in Egypt, it was nonetheless a pervasive presence, over the years, taking many different forms: contributing social support in communities via schools and clinics, providing economic support, and engaging in advocacy for political change. The Muslim Brotherhood from its early days worked to build a transnational organization, founding groups in Lebanon (1936), Syria (1937), and Jordan (1946). It recruited foreign students in Cairo. A prominent intellectual, Sayyid Qutb, spoke of *jihad* (struggle) against *jahili* (ignorant) societies, both Western and Islamic, seeking transformation. His 1964 work, *Milestones*, exercises influence to this day to citizens across society, but also to groups like Al Qaeda. The Brotherhood's most famous slogan, used worldwide, is: "Islam is the solution." Following the Arab uprisings of 2011, the Brotherhood swiftly reemerged as an open political force. A leading continuing issue is how the Brotherhood, as both a political and social force, views the role of Islam in modern Egyptian society. Adhering more closely to Islamic Sharia law has widespread popular appeal among Egyptians, but the question is what that translates into in practice. Over its lifetime the Muslim Brotherhood's leaders have committed themselves to an enhanced role for Islam in Egyptian public life. Now that they are in power, what this signifies in practice and how the ideal will be translated into reality is a central policy question for Egypt.

Sufism is at least in part marked by its mysticism, and its role within the Muslim world presents its own mysteries. Some term the common elements that mark Sufi traditions within Islam as something close to a movement: a thread that binds different, far-flung communities through shared practice that involves the common five pillars of prayer, charity, and so forth, but even more through music, poetry, and elements of the love of God and man. For others, these threads are either simple attributes of cultures or even a distortion of Islamic faith. Some look to the beauties of Sufi culture and its supple linkage of intellectual and artistic as a hopeful opposite to the harsh thinking and rigidities of Salafist Islam and a path towards a more peaceful way to link Muslim and non-Muslim communities. Sufism is not a single denomination or even a tradition akin to Shi'a communities and the durable influence of a common love. The Sufi Persian poet Rumi, for example, does not find clear expression in institutional terms. Nonetheless, different Sufi brotherhoods do, like other faith communities, exhibit remarkable strength across international borders and offer followers an important practical, cultural, and spiritual bond that can at times even translate into politics and policy.

One example is the Tijaniyyah Order, a Sufi *tariqa*, or order, that was born in North Africa but today is expanding rapidly and represents the largest order in West Africa, especially Senegal. West African immigrants all over the world include Tijaniyyah and this faith tradition as a backbone of their community—mutual support in times of trouble, shifting cultural identity, and changes in practice. Among distinctive characteristics of Tijaniyyah are its history as a brotherhood of the poor with a focus on social reform and a commitment to education.

Movements known for violence and terrorism

A wide variety of movements have objectives and operating styles that may articulate visions of justice and social reform, as well as apocalyptic visions, but also use violent means in purposeful ways towards their ends. These ends may be explicitly political or cast in more general terms, for example creation of a specific form of social order. Extremist organizations can be found in most world religious traditions, as well as in newer religious movements (and of course in secular organizations also). Two well-known examples are the Japanese Aum Shinrikyo and the Lebanese organization Hezbollah.

The Japanese apocalyptic sect Aum Shinrikyo—also known as Aum and Aleph—combines tenets from Buddhism and Hinduism.[44] Its 1995 chemical attack on the Tokyo subway system catapulted it to international fame and appearances on international terrorist lists. Twelve people were killed and an estimated 6,000 people sought medical attention. The group split into two factions in 2007, the result of internal friction over attempts to moderate the cult's religious beliefs and improve its public image. It has been largely inactive since then, but the groups remain under surveillance by Japanese authorities. Most of Aum's current 1,500 members live in Japan, while about 300 are in Russia.

At the center of the group's belief is reverence for Shoko Asahara, Aum's founder and spiritual leader, whom adherents consider the first "enlightened one" since Buddha. He preached that the end of the world was near and Aum followers would be the only people to survive. Asahara had claimed that the United States would hasten Armageddon by starting World War III with Japan. He accumulated great wealth from electronic businesses and restaurants; he also required members to sign their estates over to the group. Aum recruited young, smart university students and graduates, often from elite families, who sought a more meaningful existence. At the time of the 1995 subway attack, the group claimed to have an estimated 40,000 members worldwide, with offices in the United States, Russia, and Japan. Shoko Asahara is awaiting execution for his role in planning the 1995 attack.

Hezbollah (meaning "Party of God") is an example of a political party, a socio-political religious movement, and a military organization. Founded in Lebanon in the early 1980s by a group of Muslim clerics, it includes mainly Shi'a Muslims and has become a powerful force across the region. Support from Iran is another continuing feature of its ethos and work. Hostility to Israel is its defining platform and it has a strong military arm. However, its efficient organization of social services and advocacy for the poor are also important dimensions of its organization and public persona. Its initial stated aim was to transform Lebanon's multi-religious state into an Islamic state, though today its platform looks to a more inclusive model. The United States and other countries list Hezbollah as a terrorist organization.

Pilgrimage: shades of globalization

Cultural interaction has been the rule throughout history, though today globalization has sharply increased the tempo while engaging far larger shares of the world's population. Pilgrimage routes and traditions have always been, and remain, an important part of this global cultural interchange. Pilgrimage traditions of great world religions offers a distinctive and informative picture of globalizing flows and dynamics that reach much farther back than the more widely understood beginnings of the contemporary "era of globalization." The mixing of gender, class, and background in Chaucer's fourteenth-century *Canterbury Tales*—which is, of course, a collection of tales told by "medieval" pilgrims as they travel to a pilgrim shrine at Canterbury—brings to mind the sort of polyphonic social dynamics thought to characterize the "globalized" present more than the supposedly hierarchical and segmented medieval past.

Pilgrimage traditions vary widely from religion to religion, but there are common threads. They represent specific spaces, considered as sacred, where people of different backgrounds, classes, and sometimes cultures, mix and mingle. Pilgrimage routes often parallel social and economic flows; the paths and flows are often as significant as the destination in exerting influence on pilgrims and their societies. In early and medieval Christian Europe, pilgrim trails cut across boundaries of provinces, realms, and even empires. The Church claimed a universality that encouraged pilgrims from far-flung areas "to take up staff and scrip" to travel to the great shrines in other Christian lands. Over time this international religious tourist traffic became increasingly organized.[45]

While monastic and mystical traditions were being built up in Christendom, pilgrimage, as they described it, offered an outlet for laypersons to reckon with their own understandings of religious doctrine. The voyages that pilgrimages involved were often the only opportunity for long-distance travel, economic opportunity, and social mobility. Pilgrimage was (and is) not just a matter of religion, but is marked by a certain kind of comradeship. The Crusades, frequently thought of as arenas of cultural and military battle, were originally tied to pilgrimage and capitalized on the widespread popularity that pilgrimage-based travel to the Middle East enjoyed. When Pope Urban first preached the First Crusade, he combined the idea of the Palestine pilgrimage with that of holy war.[46]

In Japan, popular pilgrimage practices have long encompassed a diverse range of traditions that span social class and blur the lines between what we might assume are "religious" and "secular" motivations for pilgrimage. At least four Japanese pilgrimage traditions can claim a vast, national, and nonsectarian clientele from all classes of society.[47] While Japanese citizens today might claim they are on pilgrimage because of a particular temple's artwork or cherry blossoms rather than piety or religious devotion, "such entertainment motives ... do not cut these tourists off from their pilgrim predecessors."[48] Tourism and pilgrimage have always been mixed, and a coinciding of artistic, social, tourist, and religious functions of pilgrimages is a key dynamic of pilgrimage traditions worldwide. India also has many pilgrimage traditions; its sacred sites are often firmly rooted to notions of place—often informed by the confluence or sources of rivers, which are accorded their own particular import in Hindu cosmology.[49] The virtue of pilgrimage is often connected to a notion of travel as a force of moral and social good that dates back to Vedic times.[50] Through pilgrimage, spiritual, social, cultural, and economic geographies come to overlap.

Pilgrimages today are on the increase, and they are organized, bureaucratized, and subjected to the influence of the modern forms of mass transportation and communication, involving full-time travel agencies.[51] The pilgrimage to Lourdes in France and the romance of the demanding Camino de Santiago ("Way of Saint James") in France and Spain are important symbols of both the spiritual and material aspects of modern pilgrimage. The significance of pilgrimage as a globalizing force, however, is nowhere more evident than in the case of the *Hajj*, the pilgrimage to Mecca that is a religious duty for any Muslim able to complete the journey.

The *Hajj* originated through a confluence of pre-Islamic rituals and pre-existing trade routes. Muslims believe that the Kaaba, the sacred stone at the heart of the *Hajj* rituals, was part of a shrine built by Abraham and his son Ishmael and rebuilt by Mohammed himself. Before the rise of Islam, probably no more than 10,000 pilgrims a year visited the site; by the 1970s, the numbers had climbed to nearly 1 million annual visitors in some years, with over 120 flights a day bringing pilgrims to nearby Jeddah during the three weeks running up to the pilgrimage season, which occurs during a pre-appointed time on the lunar Islamic calendar. The over-lapping of trade, travel, and pilgrimage routes suggests what was true of the *Hajj* in the past as well as now: that the ritual, deeply religious for many, is also intertwined with social, economic, political, and educational goals and activities. The *Hajj* was and is a major unifying factor in the Islamic world. A glance at the biography of nearly any North African scholar of the Middle Ages, for example, will bring to light an astounding set of itineraries: it was quite commonplace for scholars to leave their North African homes for their pilgrimage to Mecca and spend a decade or more before or after studying with the great scholars of Damascus, Cairo, or Baghdad. Today's equivalent unifying measures are many; the post-industrial (and post-oil boom) Saudi economy has given rise to numerous expansions and modernizations of the pilgrimage sites, and *Hajj* rituals and Qur'anic readings are broadcast via satellite television around the world so that even those Muslims unable to make the journey are direct witness to it through technology. The *Hajj* is now a highly regulated and, it could be argued, thoroughly modern event, with the Saudi government overseeing a quota system to allow a certain number of pilgrims per country to complete the rituals each year, erecting a series of modern complexes and transit systems to house and cater to the influx of pilgrims, and even purifying and pumping the holy water of Zamzam through modern pipes so that pilgrims may access it safely and conveniently.[52]

For many Muslims, the *Hajj* is a pivotal life event. One scholar, study-ing populations of West African Hausa Muslims who were delayed en route to Mecca in the Sudan, essentially settling there, contends that the *Hajj* actually constitutes a "paradigm for life," defining social structures as well as individual identity.[53] Flows of people and ideas across Europe, Africa, and Asia are deeply embedded in the history of the *Hajj* itself. The experience is felt not only by the individuals taking part in the pilgrimage, but by their communities back home. Hausa women, who have only recently been able to participate in the *Hajj* in significant numbers, recount their journeys in the form of poetry and song, performing it after the return home.[54] Countless individuals have chronicled the transformational effect of the *Hajj*, including Malcolm X, for whom it was a watershed moment. "Each hour here in the Holy Land," he wrote from Saudi Arabia in 1964, "enables me to have greater spiritual insights into what is happening in America between black and white."[55] He emphasized the intercultural and interracial mixing that occurred over the process of the pilgrimage rituals, and how the event exemplified the Islamic principle of equality of all races and people—in stark contrast to the experiences of his day-to-day life in the United States. One study suggests that the *Hajj* indeed increases participation in traditional, universal Muslim practices (such as prayer and fasting, which along with pilgrimage form three of the five "pillars" of the faith); decreases pilgrims' likelihood to participate in more "localized" practices connected to traditional or folk cosmologies; and rather than creating antipathy towards non-Muslims, fosters greater belief in equality (including gender equality), ethnic and sectarian harmony, and interreligious peace in general.[56]

The *Hajj* has also emerged as a major focus for events outside of the world of Islam. In 1979, militants occupied the Grand Mosque in Mecca as a way of protesting what they perceived to be an extravagant and corrupt Saudi regime; after two weeks, many deaths of hostages and militants alike, and a team of French commandos brought in and swiftly converted to Islam (the holy places in Mecca and Medina are off-limits to non-Muslims), the situation was resolved and the holiest pilgrimage sites in Islam were thrust onto the world stage. The pilgrimage's significance as a security target has paralleled its rise as a major economic event: a pilgrim opting for the more luxurious accommodations offered in Mecca may spend as much as US$40,000 on the trip, and overall the revenue created by the *Hajj* reaches US$30 billion annually. The event has become a site for "networking and deal-making" that can quite reasonably be expected when people from the far corners of the Islamic world converge on one spot at the same time.[57] The *Hajj*, in other words, epitomizes the way that pilgrimages can embody "a capacious arena capable of accommodating many competing religious and secular discourses."[58] A pilgrimage site and its attendant flows can be read as a microcosm of a particular historical or cultural world and the globalizing forces that constitute it.

Conclusion

Religious movements play as widely different roles in global affairs as they do in people's lives. They satisfy hungers for spiritual meaning, for community, for charismatic leadership, and for services for hundreds of millions across the board. The "new movements" that we witness today have these ancient roots and are one of the marvels of human civilization, but with the transformation of technology, their mystical and pragmatic dimensions are more apparent and the movements themselves can move with great rapidity across borders. As this chapter illustrates, the diversity of religiously inspired movements is enormous, with perhaps the only common distinguishing feature being their capacity to appeal to imagination. Their force, capacity to spread, and impact on believers generate both admiration and adulation and fear, especially when a religiously inspired movement exhibits a power to incite violence and foster divisions within societies. The policy implications for national and international leaders are murky, as by their nature most movements operate outside the framework of state institutions and thinking. A first imperative is understanding. Too little is known about most of these leaders and organizations and about their impact. A second is engagement. Many movements offer potential new avenues to engage on issues like protection of the environment, fighting corruption, and social welfare. In sum, beyond formal religious institutions representing the hierarchies and governance structures of different world religious traditions are a host of very different, influential, and often powerful bodies that shape societies, economies and, in many instances, political thought and action.

4 Interfaith encounters
Institutions, approaches, and questions

- Interfaith work: the rationale and the issues
- Interfaith history: a sketch
- The contemporary interfaith landscape
- "Bilateral" dialogue and cooperation
- The Unification Church and the Universal Peace Foundation
- Religion and the United Nations
- Faith-secular engagement: some examples
- Conclusion

Since the 2006 meeting of the G8 (Group of Eight leading nations) in St Petersburg, Russia, groups of senior religious figures, organized by interreligious leaders from the nation hosting the respective heads of state summit, have gathered shortly before the event to reflect on priority issues on the global agenda and to prepare a declaration to present to the heads of state. Similarly, one of the largest and most diverse groups of religious leaders ever assembled met at the United Nations (UN) in New York just before the historic Millennium General Assembly in 2000. These and other global interfaith meetings reflect two different currents of thought and ideals. The first is the sense within faith circles that the world's religious institutions and their followers have deeply relevant ideas and counsel for the world's secular leadership because of their ancient wisdom and spiritual insight, and thus should be part of setting agendas and taking decisions. They see their advice as reflecting the hopes and wishes of the members of their religious communities, which number overall in the billions. They also seek to offer an ethical, moral perspective that they perceive as missing in many global deliberations. The second current is the effort to bring about more harmony among religious communities in all their diversity. Tensions among religious communities have an ancient pedigree, but with globalization new religious trends have emerged. They include, besides the historic strife, new and different tensions and conflicts linked to religion. Interfaith gatherings aim to identify, establish, and build on common values and interests that link different religious traditions and thus work for peace.

This chapter focuses on inter- and intra-faith movements and organizations that have emerged in recent decades, with an emphasis on their respective mandates, organization, and governance. Interfaith initiatives come in many forms and sizes. They range from those with visions that are truly global and universal to far more modest, often local and time-bound endeavors. Some are inspired by a broad vision of what is needed to achieve peace and harmony, while others have arisen in response to specific issues or crises. They seek to address relationships among religious communities and particularly to address tensions among them. Many also aim to build on interfaces with the non-religious, secular world, bringing the voice of religions into a wide range of issues. As in the case of the religious leader summits for the G8 and G20 (the Group of Twenty finance ministers and central bank governors), there is a sense among various religious communities that the historic displacement of faith leadership in human affairs by secular leadership has left a moral void that begs to be filled. Illustrative of this impulse are long-standing efforts to introduce some form of formal religious voice within the UN system, with some groups going so far as to advocate for a "spiritual council" that would work parallel to the Security Council. Most often, however, interreligious work responds to specific problems or, too often, crises, often within a specific setting—for example, responses to religiously fueled violence in India or to terrorist threats in Europe and the United States. A recent trend is for interfaith groups to seek to address a widening range of socio-economic challenges. A prominent example is a growing movement to promote interfaith responses to the problem of climate change.

The chapter begins with a brief history of interfaith efforts and movements, and then describes the major contemporary interfaith institutions and efforts, focusing on those that have a global dimension. It comments, more briefly, on "bilateral" interfaith dialogue and cooperation (that is, efforts that involve specific groups—for example, Catholic and Jews) and on intra-faith engagement (for example, among Christian denominations or between Sunni and Shi'a Muslims). The next section focuses specifically on the roles of religious institutions in the UN and other global bodies. These are significant both in highlighting various visions of what religious institutions might bring to global debates and in pointing to both tensions and assets emerging from religious engagement in international affairs. The chapter concludes with an introduction of various engagement efforts that focus on religious roles in global affairs. These include the Earth Charter (linked to the 1982 Rio Environmental Summit), a much newer UN interagency effort led by the UN Population Fund (UNFPA) that parallels a network of religiously linked non-governmental organizations (NGOs) engaged with UN programs, the World Bank venture with a dialogue with faith institutions, and the multi-year dialogue process involving the World Council of Churches (WCC), the World Bank, and the International Monetary Fund (IMF).

Interfaith work: the rationale and the issues

Interreligious (or interfaith—the terms are generally used interchangeably) efforts tend to elicit quite divergent responses. For some observers, especially those with a religious orientation, few topics are as important as the need to address the deep tensions that divide different religious traditions, tensions that cleave societies and contribute to wars and other painful and often violent conflicts. Dialogue and common action are seen as the only path to true peace and social harmony. Swiss theologian Hans Küng puts it this way in an often-quoted, pithy summary that links religion, peace, and global ethical norms: "There will not, indeed, be peace among nations without peace among religions, no peace among religions without dialogue between them, and no serious dialogue without common ethical standards."[1] Governmental and intergovernmental efforts to engage with the wide diversity of religious traditions through interfaith approaches are often motivated by what is perceived as an additional advantage (particularly for nations that emphasize religious freedom). Dealing with institutions that gather and represent different religious traditions may help to assure equitable, fair treatment of different faiths, to avoid the pitfalls inherent in favoring one over another and, more positively, to hold out the hope of encouraging broadly acceptable avenues towards common action with multi-religious "buy-in." In moments of high tension—for example after 11 September 2001, or the 2005 crisis that swirled about the cartoons of the Muslim prophet—the symbolism of assembling leaders from different religious traditions and the personal leadership of religious figures calling for calm are vital elements in crisis management. Interreligious encounters, however, tend to involve a complex balancing act, on the one hand emphasizing common ground, values, and shared symbolism, while also seeking substantive engagement on what are commonly intensely sensitive matters. Different faith traditions take a very different stance on interreligious dialogue: the Bahá'í and Zoroastrian[2] communities, for example, see interfaith dialogue as deeply embedded in their history and traditions, while Christian and Jewish (especially Ortho-dox) leaders often have taken a more wary view. The rhythm of inter-faith discussions can be slow and many statements smack of inoffensive generalities. While dialogue within many religious traditions is a valued, honored approach that implies an openness to transformation and a commitment to listening and sharing, in more secular circles dialogue may be code for talk without action, and interfaith gatherings can be viewed by worldly critics as anodyne events where symbolism trumps substance and only those who are already convinced are prepared to participate.

There is plenty of truth in these varying perspectives. The often dia-metrically opposed interpretations of the impacts of interfaith work are complicated by the particular difficulties inherent in evaluating the impact of efforts that have such broadly defined and generally long-term goals. Evaluation work has generally been rather limited and restricted to limited facets or specific events or measures. There is growing recogni-tion that more rigorous metrics of assessment and, more importantly, clearer goals are needed in today's results-and-outcomes-focused world. The challenge is nonetheless large, even more so as benefits that are often ascribed to interfaith work commonly involve either "counter-factuals" (crises that did not occur) or secondary benefits—for example, when leaders who meet each other through a broad interfaith gathering later collaborate to solve a specific problem. Notwithstanding the debates and the general fuzziness of tangible outcomes, the stakes of religious tension are too high to treat interfaith efforts lightly. Many courageous initiatives and dogged conflict management efforts are involved in the complex interfaith world and they merit both attention and support.

Interfaith history: a sketch

Neither religious tensions nor efforts to rally different religious leaders and their followers to a common end are new—the Indian emperor Ashoka is one of several icons from the past who sought actively to promote interfaith harmony. Various religious communities cherish and celebrate ancient traditions of outreach or at least attitudes of religious tolerance towards others. The history of interfaith harmony in pre-1492 Spain, where practical tolerance among Muslims, Jews, and Christians was unmatched elsewhere for centuries, has an element of Camelot idealism but also important elements of truth. However, rivalry among religious communities and leaders and a desire to bring all to a passionately held belief have been more common threads in history.

Interfaith activist Marcus Braybrooke summarizes interreligious relations thus: "The history of religions has been marked, on the whole, by hostility and rivalry. Religions and indeed rival groups within religions have claimed possession of the truth. Those who disagreed with them were wrong and to be refuted and perhaps physically repressed or persecuted."[3] His narrative of the interfaith movement highlights the modern trend towards an agreement (and an often-stated ideal) among leading world religions that this kind of hostility betrays the true teachings of their various faiths. Even so, the path to interfaith dialogue has been rather tortured, characterized by stops and starts and a wide diversity of approach. At one extreme are perspectives that see unity of religions as an ultimate goal, and at the other a genuine celebration of religious pluralism and diversity as part of the essence of the human condition. Some approaches focus on theology while others, in contrast, hold that approaches that tackle concrete, pragmatic challenges offer far better promise of building relationships that are conducive to social harmony and common purpose. Intra-faith reconciliation—between Catholics and Protestants or different strands of Islam, for example, can be as demanding, at least, as interfaith efforts. Efforts to bridge religious and secular worldviews also present difficult challenges. Specific interfaith (and intra-faith) institutions and meetings parallel knowledge-based initiatives that see a basic understanding of different religious traditions in the society at large as a *sine qua non* for harmony within and among today's increasingly plural communities.

An historic meeting in 1893 in Chicago—the World's Parliament of Religions—is usually seen as marking the start of the complex modern tradition of formal interreligious dialogue. Part of the euphoric celebrations of the Chicago World's Fair, the parliament was a Christian-led and very largely male-organized event, but in its openness to the public and spotlight on several Asian traditions, it opened American eyes to a broader religious world than many had even imagined. Peace and brotherhood were the common themes. As organizer Charles Bonney put it in his opening speech:

> In this Congress the word "religion" means the love and worship of God and love and service of man ... When the religious faiths of the world recognize each other as brothers, children of one Father, whom all profess to love and serve, then, and not till then, will the nations of the earth yield to the Spirit of concord and learn to war no more.[4]

The lead-up to the parliament and its aftermath foreshadowed many later debates about interfaith work, prominently including a long list of worried observers concerned that interfaith work undermined Christianity. The Archbishop of Canterbury refused even to bless the event, and in 1895 Pope Leo XIII censored Catholic participation in any "future promiscuous conventions."[5] It was 100 years before a further Parliament of the World's Religions was organized in Chicago (in 1993).

The historic 1883 parliament was followed by a bewildering set of interfaith meetings and new institutions that reflected the complex evolution of what can loosely be termed the interfaith movement. The successive initiatives were influenced by the history of the era and international as well as religious events, and notably by the two world wars that shook the world. The religious dynamics of the time included, for example, the emergence of evangelical churches, missionary work as part of colonization, the religious turmoil around the communist revolutions, and then the upheavals of decolonization. Among the many organizations with an interfaith character that emerged were the International Association for Religious Freedom and the World Congress of Faiths, both of which function still today. On balance, the roles of religious institutions in world affairs and in forging interfaith links were at best a patchwork of individual efforts. Their main achievements may have been a gradual process of education about religious diversity that took both academic and social forms. Generally, parochial attitudes were beginning to shift. Illustrating this change in thinking was a 1986 reflection on the history of interfaith relations by then Archbishop of Canterbury Robert Runcie: " ... dialogue can help us to recognize that other faiths than our own are genuine mansions of the Spirit with many rooms to be discovered, rather than solitary fortresses to be attacked."[6] Among the major milestones were the opening of Vatican attitudes towards different religions and notably Judaism, reflected in the 1964 creation of a special department of the Roman Curia for relations with people of other religions by Pope Paul VI, initially known as the Secretariat for Non Christians and renamed the Pontifical Council for Interreligious Dialogue in 1988, and the important milestone of Nostra Aetate in 1965, which marked a new Vatican opening to relationships with Jews. Within the Protestant world, intensive meetings and negotiations on the eve of World War II led to an agreement to form the World Council of Churches, which was formally established in 1948.

The contemporary interfaith landscape

Today, the major interfaith and intra-faith institutions in North America and Europe trace at least some of their origins to this long period of quest, pursuit of ideals for world peace, and tentative openings among different religious traditions. Initially the momentum to institutionalize and advance interfaith work was largely driven by Christian churches and leaders, but the period was also marked by new approaches to Jews and Judaism in the wake of the Holocaust and the creation of Israel and by efforts to address the mounting tensions with Muslim communities in the Middle East. Over the years, the interfaith movement has progressively seen a broadening in its conception of religious pluralism with engagement with Eastern religions, increasing openness to a range of newer religious movements, and an opening to inclusion of traditional, primarily indigenous beliefs and believers (largely neglected in the early years), to a variety of self-defined "spiritual but not religious" groups (that do not see themselves as religious *per se*), and to non-believers ("people of all faiths or none" is a common formulation).

The various global interfaith organizations work at different levels and have quite different styles. The initial character of interfaith events and institutions has tended to be set by individual charismatic leaders, by members who are not necessarily leaders of specific denominations or traditions, by local communities, and by public intellectuals. At issue has always been the degree of "representativity" of the organizations: how far do they represent the authentic and authorized voice of religious traditions, and beyond that, how far do formal religious structures truly represent the believers they claim? As a general trend, formal bodies of religion have become more directly engaged with the various interfaith institutions over time, though there are still complex reservations and webs of relationships. With a rather diverse set of institutions with overlapping objectives and often membership, cooperation among interfaith bodies and ideas is a continuing challenge. To a degree, the various institutions seek to work together in their endeavors, and most have carved out reasonably clear definitions of objectives and "turf." However, there is considerable overlap and, especially in terms of funding and influence, competition and sometimes tension remain an important feature of the interfaith worlds.

This discussion focuses on six interfaith organizations and platforms, both because they are the most prominent, and as examples of different styles and approaches. Taking them in the order of their establishment, they are:

- the Council for a Parliament of the World's Religions;
- Religions for Peace (formerly—and formally—known as the World Conference of Religions for Peace, or WCRP), established in 1970;
- the annual Prayer for Peace, initiated by Pope John Paul II with an interreligious gathering in 1986 in Assisi and organized each year as

a continuing "pilgrimage for peace" by the lay Catholic Community of Sant'Egidio;
* the United Religions Initiative (URI), founded with the inspiration of the 50th anniversary of the UN in 1996;
* interreligious gatherings organized by the Government of Kazakhstan; and
* Interfaith Action for Peace in Africa (IFAPA), which exemplifies a regional approach to dialogue and action.

There are other organizations tied to a specific religious tradition: Pax Christi, a global Catholic organization, comes to mind.[7] The initiatives of the Unificationist Church also bear mention as a distinct and often contentious approach to interreligious engagement.

The Council for a Parliament of the World's Religions

The Council for a Parliament of the World's Religions emerged as part of the effort to organize a Parliament event in Chicago in 1993, exactly 100 years after the seminal interreligious event there in 1893. Formally launched in 1988, the parliament worked from that point on as an established interfaith organization from a base in Chicago. Its focus has been on the organization, at roughly five-year intervals, of large interreligious gatherings that are termed parliaments. These take place in different cities, in cooperation with interreligious movements in the respective countries. Thus, parliaments were held in Chicago in 1993, in Cape Town, South Africa in 1999, in Barcelona, Spain in 2004, and in Melbourne, Australia in 2009. The date and location of the next parliament was unclear at the time of writing.

The parliament defines its objective in ambitious terms: "cultivating harmony among the world's religious and spiritual communities and fostering their engagement with the world and its guiding institutions in order to achieve a just, peaceful and sustainable world." Its vision is bold and idealistic: a peaceful and sustainable world in which religious and spiritual communities live in harmony and contribute to a better world from their riches of wisdom and compassion, religious and cultural fears and hatreds are replaced with understanding and respect, people everywhere come to know and care for their neighbors, the richness of human and religious diversity is woven into the fabric of communal, civil, societal and global life, and the earth and all life are cherished, protected, healed, and restored. The parliament articulates its roles in relation to the world's powerful and influential institutions (guiding institutions, it calls them)—this includes the major global institutions, including the UN, as well as states, leading academic institutions, philanthropic organizations, and private companies. Since the 1993 re-launch of the parliament, it has focused on defining and refining a common global ethical foundation, grounded in shared values "to realize the common good." The much-discussed Global Ethic, which seeks common ethical principles drawn from the major religious traditions, was launched in 1993 and has echoed as an important theme of interreligious dialogue ever since.[8]

In practice, the parliament has operated as a small interfaith organization for most of the time, necessarily gearing up to a far larger organization as five-year parliament events (which are large and complex) approach. It has worked over the years to develop a continuing set of activities, to date largely focused on city-to-city contacts. It has a rather complex governance structure (as do all the formal interfaith organizations), with a board of trustees with members from major world faiths (though they do not purport to represent their own faith traditions in any formal way) and an international advisory council that includes such distinguished religious figures as the Dalai Lama. Finances are somewhat precarious and, to a significant extent, drive the capacity of the parliament to attain its broad and continuing objectives.

The parliament prides itself on its commitment to interfaith harmony and to the breadth of its reach. Parliament events are large (up to 10,000 people) with an astonishing set of events that reflects the diversity of those who attend. The world's smaller faith traditions have tended to see the parliament as a rare opportunity to find a forum and voice and the principle of inclusion extends to atheists and Pagan groups, as well as a growing commitment to including indigenous traditions. At the 2009 Melbourne Parliament, the focus on relations with indigenous communities was front and center. The parliament has also been particularly sensitive to the critiques of religious institutions for exclusion of women and youth and its sessions have deliberately engaged quite large numbers of women and young people.

Religions for Peace

The World Conference of Religions for Peace, founded in 1970, is in many respects the most formally constituted and ambitious of the global interfaith institutions. It dates its origins to the early 1960s, when a small group of religious leaders from various traditions began to explore the idea of a "religious summit" that would bring the energies and talents of religious communities more directly into work for peace, especially at the national and regional level.[9] Religions for Peace describes itself as the largest international coalition of representatives from the world's great religions who are dedicated to achieving peace. As is the case for the Parliament of the World's Religions, Religions for Peace is insistent that it does not seek religious unity, but respects cultural and religious differences "while celebrating our common humanity." "Representativity" is a term it has coined, reflecting a careful, continuing effort to ensure that its ties to formal religious institutions are clearly defined and balanced, but with a broader religious representation (thus reaching out to those outside formal religious institutions). This balance is reflected in both governance and programmatic focus. Religions for Peace is active on every continent and in some of the most troubled places on earth. The primary means by which it operates is through a variety of geographically defined multi-religious partnerships that "mobilize the moral and social resources of religious people to address their shared problems." These consist of regional conferences and some 75 national and local affiliates.

Religions for Peace has an international secretariat whose headquarters are across the street from the UN buildings in New York City. It prides itself on enjoying consultative status with the UN Economic and Social Council (ECOSOC), UN Educational, Scientific and Cultural Organization (UNESCO), and UN Children's Fund (UNICEF). In its legal form, it is an NGO, the governance (also complex) of which consists of a world council of senior religious leaders, who are elected at its global assembly every four years, and a board of trustees responsible for oversight of the organization. Financial support has come from various foundations, governments, intergovernmental organizations, religious communities, religiously affiliated development agencies, and individuals.

Religions for Peace is about partnerships with different religious bodies and secular organizations, especially UN organizations. An example is its longstanding connection with Japan's newer religious movements, and especially with the lay Buddhist organization Risho Kosei-kai. Its first meeting was, in large measure because of this connection, held in Kyoto, Japan, in October 1970. Subsequent world assemblies have been held in different world regions, including in Leuven, Belgium, in 1974; Princeton, New Jersey, in 1978; Nairobi, Kenya, in 1984; Melbourne, Australia, in 1989; Riva del Garda, Italy, in 1994; Amman, Jordan, in 1999; and Kyoto, Japan, in 2006. Morocco is the likely location for a 2013 assembly.

Like the Parliament of the World's Religions, Religions for Peace has made special efforts almost from its inception to engage two groups so often marginalized in formal religious institutions: women and youth. In recent years, each global assembly has been preceded by youth and women's assemblies, which deliberate independently and report to the broader assembly. The governing structures include both women and younger representatives.

The core of Religions for Peace's work, historically and also at present, centers on its efforts to contribute to peace, and specifically to address religious conflicts and tensions. It counts some important successes, especially in soothing tensions through the work of interfaith groups of religious leaders in West Africa and other regions. It also claims significant success in forging a climate conducive to reconciliation in Iraq. Religions for Peace has also sought to broaden both its understanding of peace and its work to a broader range of issues, with a theme of "shared security," a concept that suggests that there is no real security, physical or otherwise, unless it is broad, and thus shared across nations and communities. This implies both action to address poverty and equity issues and environmental sustainability. This focus has brought the organization into partnerships: to support the Millennium Development Goals with the UN Development Programme (UNDP),[10] to work on HIV and AIDS through the Hope for Africa's Children program in Africa, and to promote action on the environment through a partnership with the United Kingdom-based Alliance of Religions for Conservation. Still, Religions for Peace is more focused on building the capacity of regional religious leader councils to advocate for and work towards peace. It is engaged here in many countries, including Ethiopia, Eritrea, Sierra Leone, Bosnia and Herzegovina, Liberia, Indonesia, and Sri Lanka. Religions for Peace Secretary-General William Vendley, a theologian and scholar, has served on the US White House Interreligious Dialogue and Cooperation Task Force (among numerous challenges).

The Prayer for Peace

In October 1986, Pope John Paul II convened an unprecedented gathering of some 160 leading religious figures in Assisi, Italy (the symbolic birthplace of St Francis of Assisi). The gathering was prompted by the unsettled global situation at the time. As the Pope declared at the meeting's closing, "If there are many and important differences among us, there is also a common ground, whence to operate together in the solution of this dramatic challenge of our age: true peace or catastrophic war?"[11] The meeting was heavy with the symbolism of religious leaders standing side by side, their diversity as apparent as their willingness to come together. With his initiative, the Pope was moving the Catholic Church in new directions; these were openly contested, especially by those within the Catholic Church who saw a risk in suggesting equity among religions in the symbolism of standing side by side. However, what the meeting made abundantly clear was the unique convening power of the Roman Catholic Church within the religious world: both by size and tradition, no other figure could have brought together the group that assembled in Assisi.

The "spirit of Assisi," as it has been termed, gave rise to what has become one of the most significant and creative interfaith initiatives today. The lay Catholic Community of Sant'Egidio, a movement that grew from the 1968 student uprisings and the spirit of change inspired by Vatican II, took on the task of organizing an annual "Prayer for Peace." This gathering takes place each year in a different city, to date almost always in Europe, and it constitutes what Sant'Egidio terms a Pilgrimage of Peace.[12] The event is highly respected as an interfaith gathering, and brings together some of the leading figures from the Christian, Jewish, and Muslim faiths especially, but also representatives from other major world religions, always including substantial delegations of Shinto and Buddhist leaders from Japan. Participation by heads of state (with a special focus on Africa) is the norm. At the 2011 Munich Prayer for Peace, Germany's chancellor, president, and finance minister spoke, as well as regional authorities from Bavaria and leading religious figures. The event each year involves a grand opening ceremony with statements by major political and religious leaders and public intellectuals, followed by two days of a rich menu of seminar-style presentations and discussions. These normally address the live conflict issues of the day and other major global issues (for example, water, children's rights, and HIV and AIDS). The event culminates in a "pageant of peace" that symbolizes the power of image that interfaith gatherings can bring. Each faith group first worships separately as a group (Christians, Jews, Muslims, Buddhists, etc.) to reflect the spirit that interfaith gatherings deepen and do not dilute one's faith heritage and tradition. Each community then processes towards the city's central square, with the groups meeting (like tributaries of a river), embracing as they gather. The faith leaders sit together on a platform (a colorful sight, though the dominance of older men is unmistakable). During the concluding ceremony, witnesses describe the horrors of war and a moving declaration calling for peace is read, signed by the religious leaders on the platform, and then handed to children who pass the declarations on to diplomats and other leaders in the audience. The religious leaders light candles symbolizing their commitment to peace. Music, color, and a host of enthusiastic volunteers attest to a spirit and excitement in the spirit of peace. Remarkably for such events, media coverage tends to be intense and is focused on the specifics of faith engagement on conflict resolution as well as on the

Figure 4.1 Sant'Egidio at Georgetown University. The Annual Prayer for Peace interreligious gathering took place at Georgetown University in September 2006
Source: Photo: Georgetown University

hope for harmony that the event symbolizes. The September 2012 Prayer for Peace took place for the first time in the Balkans, in Sarajevo, Bosnia and Herzegovina.

The United Religions Initiative

The idea for the United Religions Initiative (URI) came to California Episcopal Bishop William Swing in 1993 after the UN invited him to host a large interfaith service in San Francisco marking the 50th anniversary of the signing of the UN Charter. He questioned why, if there was a UN working for peace, there could not also be a united forum for the world's religions. After a protracted period of consultations, a charter was defined, and in 2000 the global organization—URI—was born, with its headquarters in San Francisco. Its governance structure involves a global council and regional bodies, as well as a board of trustees. URI sees itself as working to promote enduring daily interfaith cooperation, and thus to end religiously motivated violence and to create cultures of peace, justice, and healing "for the Earth and all living beings."[13] URI's vision centers on a network of engaged and interconnected communities, committed to respect for diversity, nonviolent resolution of conflict, and social, political, economic and environmental justice. It is thus, at its core, a grassroots organization and its network of local groups are called cooperation circles (CCs). It counts some 525 member groups and organizations with a common theme of community action, including not only direct conflict resolution work, but also reconciliation, environmental sustainability, education, women's and youth programs, and advocacy for human rights. Inclusion is an important principle and, even more than other interfaith organizations, URI is open to a wide range of indigenous religious communities and new religious and spiritual traditions.

URI's work focuses on peace, and highlights the common quest for peace among people of different faiths. URI CCs are active in 22 of 30 regions where there are ongoing religiously motivated conflicts. URI runs a traveling "peace academy" that teaches grassroots leaders to build multi-stakeholder partnerships for peace and community development. It also focuses squarely on youth, and many CCs are youth-led and youth-oriented. URI's Young Leaders Program provides training and connectivity for this next generation of leaders. Since its launch in 2008, it has grown from 100 to 500 members who do what is often innovative work all over the world. Many URI CCs are today organized around environmental issues, including pollution, resource depletion and global warming, which cut across religious, cultural, and geographic boundaries and underlie many of the social and economic issues they face. An "environmental satellite" is a network of environmental experts and environment-oriented CCs. URI's Global Council issued a Climate Change Call to Action in 2010. URI also prides itself on its support for women through activities like domestic violence counseling in Angola and job and skills training in Mozambique, Pakistan, and Panama. The URI Women's Coalition, a crosscutting CC, advocates for women and girls across URI's geographic regions.

Kazakhstan interreligious dialogue

A different interfaith dialogue entity is sponsored by a national government. It represents the initiative of President of Kazakhstan Nursultan A. Nazarbayev, and involves triennial meetings convened in Astana, Kazakhstan, which are described as a Congress of Leaders of World and Traditional Religions. Kazakhstan presents these meetings as its tangible contribution to interfaith and intercultural understanding, harmony, and cooperation, with the goal of maintaining regional and global stability. The vision is of Kazakhstan at the crossroads of Europe and Asia and Islamic, Christian, and Buddhist cultures with its over 130 ethnic groups and 46 religious denominations—thus, as a meeting place of different religions and civilizations. The interfaith initiative is seen as part of the government's policy priority for interfaith and interethnic accord and tolerance. A secular state with religion separated from government that guarantees freedom of belief and religion, Kazakhstan states its goal as creating "conditions for spiritual revival." The official interfaith gathering is presented as a central foreign policy goal. The generous financing attracts a mix of often senior religious leaders, politicians, and representatives of international organizations. World religious leaders from Islam, Christianity, Judaism, Buddhism, Hinduism, Taoism, Shintoism, and Zoroastrianism all attend. Outcomes are difficult to measure but networking and contributions to a common awareness of challenges are undoubtedly among them.

Interfaith Action for Peace in Africa

Interfaith Action for Peace in Africa (IFAPA) was largely the creation of Lutheran pastor Ishmael Noko and stresses its African, "home grown" character. It is a pan-African nonprofit that works to unify religious communities across Africa to cooperate and work together to seed peace. It involves the seven distinguishable faith traditions in Africa: African traditional religions, Judaism, Christianity, Islam, Hinduism, Buddhism and the Bahá'í faith. Registered in Kenya and Senegal, it is overseen by a representative commission made up of 30 members. It works through existing religious structures mobilized by established IFAPA chapters in over 30 countries in all regions of Africa. Through the same structures, IFAPA has established a secretariat, Women's Desk, and Youth Desk.

"Bilateral" dialogue and cooperation

Not all interreligious dialogue and cooperation involves a wide range of faith traditions. There are many more sharply focused encounters that are structured and formalized to varying degrees and involve two or more traditions. These include a range of specific and continuing dialogues—for example, involving Anglicans and Orthodox Christians, Catholics and Jews, and others that are organized as the result of specific events or crises. These events, ranging in their focus from scholarly theological engagements (an example is a series of challenging meetings organized by the Elijah Institute based in Jerusalem), to highly practical, problem solving initiatives, are too numerous to list but form part of the interfaith landscape. Among the most significant in recent years is the Common Word initiative, which involves a group of leading Muslim clerics and scholars, addressing a broad Christian leadership (see Box 4.1). Box 4.2 summarizes a quite different, more specific example of a US evangelical group meeting with Moroccan Muslims on the topic of climate change.

Box 4.1 A Common Word Between Us and You[1]

A special concern of interfaith work is the tension between Muslim communities and what is frequently if inexactly termed "the West." Reasons for this focus are all too obvious: the 11 September 2001 attacks on the United States; terrorist bombings in London, Madrid, and elsewhere; and the eruption of violent protests after specific incidents like the Pope's Regensburg speech that was understood to criticize Islam, and a Danish newspaper's competition for cartoons portraying the Muslim prophet. Numerous initiatives have emerged in response, including the World Economic Forum's Council of 100 Leaders (from different sectors, shared between the "West" and "Islam"), the Brookings Institution annual gathering of the United States and the Muslim world, and the Archbishop of Canterbury's annual Building Bridges Dialogue. Among these many efforts, the Common Word initiative is both exemplary and has special significance because of its strong support among Muslim religious and secular leaders.

The Common Word initiative began with an open letter dated 13 October 2007, signed by a group of senior Muslim faith scholars and clerics, and addressed to leaders of the Christian faith. The letter calls for peace between Muslims and Christians and emphasizes the common ground between the two faiths. It cites the Qur'anic commandment, "Say: O People of the Scripture! come to a common word as between us and you: that we worship none but God," which echoes the biblical commandment to love God and one's neighbor. Since the letter was sent, a number of meetings have taken place to discuss the principles, including at the Vatican. Several universities support the effort, building on the overture to probe the intellectual basis for the "common ground" and to address differences. Many additional signatories have joined the original group.

[1] The official Common Word website is at www.acommonword. com. Yale University is among academic institutions supporting the exchange.

Box 4.2 **Creation care and Christian-Muslim understanding**

The terrorist attacks of 11 September 2001 highlighted sharply negative views within various American Christian communities towards Muslims and the Muslim faith. Harsh statements, including those by evangelical leaders, fanned the flames. At the same time, tensions arose in Morocco that centered on concerns that Christian groups were seeking to convert Muslims, whether by direct, religiously focused outreach or in the context of social works, especially orphanages. Several Christians were obliged abruptly to leave Morocco. Seeking better understanding and dialogue, a group of American evangelical leaders and theologians, under the aegis of the National Evangelical Alliance, reached out to Moroccan leaders and proposed a meeting centered on global climate change as a topic that promised to offer common ground focused on shared interests in the future. A day-long meeting took place in June 2008, organized by the World Bank and the World Faiths Development Dialogue.[1] Establishing shared interest in climate proved relatively easy, though identifying practical common action was more difficult. However, the objective of opening a frank dialogue was largely achieved and discussions moved back and forth between the impetus behind proselytizing, Morocco's concerns about upsetting a delicate social balance with visible Christian evangelical work, and the concerns of young people about the looming threat of climate change. The meeting has seen some follow-up in establishment of an institute in Morocco and continuing discussions about the practical significance of religious freedom in the context of US-Moroccan relationships.

[1] Description of the event can be found at berkleycenter.georgeto wn.edu/blogs/faith-in-action/posts/climate-change-meeting-with-religious-and-civic-leaders-from-morocco.

One of the more interesting, challenging interfaith endeavors has involved a World Congress of Imams and Rabbis for Peace.[14] The effort, inspired by several idealistic individuals and supported by visionary foundations, is essentially based on building better understanding among the Muslim and Jewish communities that have, at least in recent decades, found themselves alienated one from another. Fraught with financial challenges and leadership issues, the effort has nonetheless succeeded in organizing several large and ambitious gatherings, with leaders coming from some 43 countries. The first was in Brussels in January 2005, the second in Seville in March 2006, and the third in Paris (at UNESCO headquarters) in December 2008. For many of those involved in the gatherings and dialogue, they represented a new window on religious and global affairs and opened channels to dialogue.

Another avenue towards engaging religious institutions and bolstering their interfaith work is a growing number of prizes and honors that celebrate constructive work, from global to local level. Among notable prizes are the Niwano Peace Prize, seen as an Asian Nobel Peace Prize counterpart, with a spiritual dimension, the Carus Prize, administered by the Parliament of the World's Religions, the Tanenbaum Prize, which honors religiously inspired peacemakers, the Guru Nanek Prize for interfaith work, and the Templeton Prize. What these quite diverse efforts have in common is their conscious effort to counter negative images of religion as contributing to friction and conflict with tangible examples of courageous and prophetic work that contributes to peace and justice.

The Unification Church and the Universal Peace Foundation

Interfaith work takes many forms and it includes both widely respected efforts (most of those outlined above fall within this category) and others that are more controversial. Among the most complex and contested players in the interfaith world are the organizations sponsored by the Reverend Sun Myung Moon and his Unification Church. The Church, founded in South Korea in 1954 and with a widely disputed membership (estimates vary between 100,000 and 7 million), has given rise to a network of very different organizations, some of which have interfaith dialogue as a central focus. As early as 1980, Moon sponsored the creation of the Global Congress of World Religions, which supported a long line of interreligious conferences.[15] The International Peace Foundation, founded in 2005, is a contemporary organization that is part of the network, with the stated objective of building "a world of peace in which everyone can live in freedom, harmony, cooperation, and prosperity." Among its causes are support for the family as the "school of love and peace." Transcending racial, religious and ethnic barriers is "an imperative of our time," as faith "can give people the power to forgive, and the love to overcome even generations of hatred, resentment and violence."[16] The foundation sees the renewal of the UN as a central objective, and thus has pursued for some years the formation of an interreligious council at the UN.

Generous financial support and appealing vision statements have opened doors but, especially among interfaith organizations, reservations about Rev. Moon's theology, his avowed desire to achieve interfaith harmony through unification under his leadership (a goal that is contrary to the commitment to diversity and respect that most interfaith organizations espouse), and complex and often questionable financial dealings of the organizations often raise flags. Beliefs include faith in a universal god and the idea that Rev. Moon has received instructions from Jesus to be realized as the second coming of the Messiah.[17] The Unification Church stresses the idea that "God's ideal is realized through the family," and this underpins the mass marriages that are a hallmark of the church, as well as opposition to homosexuality and same-sex marriage. As an example of the conservative stance of the church, Rev. Moon has been quoted as calling homosexuals "dung-eating dogs," and has argued that the Holocaust was retribution for Jews' role in Jesus' crucifixion.[18] The Church is strongly associated with politically and religiously conservative causes and media outlets.

Religion and the United Nations

Religious institutions and religious voices have been part of the UN from its creation. However, an explicit "role" for religion has never been clearly established, hardly surprising given the widely differing approaches to religion among the member nations that constitute the UN. The history of religious engagement in the UN context illustrates both contestation and changes that have taken place over the years, and it can be viewed as a continuing dialogue and drama. From the UN's earliest years, the role that religion should play was an issue, figuring in the debates about both the UN Charter and Universal Declaration of Human Rights (reference to God was omitted in large measure because of firm objections from the Soviet Union). The role of religion reemerged especially around the Cairo Conference on Population in 1994 and the Beijing Conference on Women the following year, as an unanticipated and often startling coalition of religiously motivated groups made common cause in raising questions about the meaning of women's and reproductive rights. Active debates around the question of how religious groups should properly engage with global institutions and especially those of the UN system, continue to this day, taking place in a variety of settings and involving a wide spectrum of religious groups.[19]

In practice, only one religious body has a formal status as part of the UN itself: the Holy See. As the website puts it, "The Holy See enjoys *by its own choice* the status of Permanent Observer at the United Nations, rather than of a full Member. This is due primarily to the desire of the Holy See to maintain absolute neutrality in specific political problems." Thus, the Vatican participates in all debates and in conferences run by the UN, but without a vote.[20] It has offices both in New York and Geneva. This role has a long history (it was formalized in 1964) and is not without contest (a coalition of largely Catholic groups, See Change, seeks to strip the Vatican of this status). Notwithstanding this important and distinctive exception, the primary place where religious institutions participate in the work of the UN is as civil society organizations. One estimate puts the number of NGOs that have a religious affiliation at 10 percent of the total of civil society groups accredited to the various UN bodies.[21] A religious NGOs organization has existed as a modest body, organizing various events and fulfilling a coordinating role. What is striking in looking at the roughly 350 NGOs with an explicitly religious identification is their wide variety. The largest group is Christian; the number of Muslim groups is increasing, but is still small in relation to the world's Muslim population.

Religious groups engage on virtually all matters before the UN and, given their diversity, their engagement is as often marked by dissension among religious groups as in any distinctive pattern or "position." On one set of topics, however, their activism has been especially marked and tensions around it most acute: issues involving gender and reproductive health. To a large extent, these color and shape the ways many governments and civil society organizations view religion's roles today, for good and ill, in the UN.

There has been a long history of efforts, varying in intensity and in effectiveness, to see a more active engagement of religious voices within the formal UN structure. There has also been a long series of proposals for more formal councils or membership. The arguments for such religious engagement include expressed concerns that the UN operates on excessively secular principles and misses a solid ethical voice and a broader suggestion that religious bodies, given their size, the trust that people have in them, and their global scope that differs from the nation-state configuration, should be part of the system of global institutions in a formal way. Interfaith organizations, including Religions for Peace, the United Religions Initiative (created on the UN's 50th anniversary with a parallel mandate in mind), and the Parliament of the World's Religions, take inspiration in significant ways from the UN and see themselves in significant global governance roles, especially as peacemakers and, to an increasing degree, in advocacy for and implementation of both the Millennium Development Goals and human rights. The UN Alliance of Civilizations (UNAOC) was born of concerns about fears of civilizational clash; religion, and especially Muslim communities, are central to its vision and its activities. However, even UNESCO (the organization charged with working with culture, generally defined as encompassing religion) and the UNAOC find member states at odds as to how directly they should engage religion.

Interestingly, the most significant leadership among UN agencies has come from UNFPA, where deliberate efforts to engage religious institutions at many levels and in many ways resulted from the contentious politics that surround reproductive health issues and gender roles, UNFPA's core mandate. UNFPA's leadership role on taking religions seriously into account is also to the credit of Thoraya Obaid, Executive Director from 2000 to 2010.

In sum, religious issues are constantly on the political and social agendas of UN agencies. However, they entail particular sensitivities and are colored by divisions among and within religions and by the specific policies and approaches to engagement with religious institutions among member states. The result is a disharmony in approaches and positions. There are many examples of cooperation among UN leaders and with different bodies and specialized agencies (see Chapter 5), as well as a host of instances of friction and missed opportunity. At the level of the UN headquarters, the most recent instance of an explicit effort to enhance relations with the interreligious world was agreed upon by the UN General Assembly in December 2010 at the proposal of King Abdallah II of Jordan. As a UN observance event, the importance of interfaith work will be marked annually in February, with a week devoted to interfaith harmony. The idea is to broaden the goal of faith-driven world harmony by extending King Abdallah's call beyond the Muslim and Christian community to include people of all beliefs, including those with no set religious beliefs. This agreement represented, for some, a compromise with proposals to focus UN attention on religion with a decade of interfaith harmony, and those who would rather see religion kept separate from the official agenda and institutions.

Overall, the special complexity and sensitivity of state-religion links and the diverse approaches to dealing with concerns about religion's roles both among member states and within religious communities have resulted in an often uneasy engagement at an aggregate level and a diversity of views across and within member states.

Faith-secular engagement: some examples

Dialogue among religious communities and institutions presents specific challenges but often benefits from a shared sense of common ethos.

When secular institutions are involved different challenges emerge, though obviously these take very different forms. Some examples of purposeful efforts along these lines follow.

Earth Charter

The Earth Charter is built on a global consultation process that began in 1987, and was propelled by the 1992 Rio Summit on the Environment. Maurice Strong and Mikhail Gorbachev were instrumental in the vision, but it has also drawn on spiritual leaders. Over the years, it has secured the endorsement of organizations representing millions of people. It "seeks to inspire in all peoples a sense of global interdependence and shared responsibility for the well-being of the human family, the greater community of life, and future generations." The Earth Charter Initiative Organization, based in the Netherlands, promotes the Charter.

The Earth Charter[22] exemplifies an effort to bring to bear a statement drawing on fundamental values and principles, many specifically inspired by religious traditions, with the goal of working towards a just, sustainable, and peaceful global twenty-first-century society through a global partnership. It has, from the outset and throughout its life, involved a spiritual dimension.[23] Environmental protection is the primary focus, but it also highlights the links to human rights, equitable human development, and peace.

UNFPA interagency task force and religious institutions network

The UN Population Fund (UNFPA) finds itself frequently at the vortex of the most contentious issues around religion within the UN system: women and especially reproductive health and their links to human rights. The agency comes under criticism and even threats of violence from groups that contest abortion and family planning—described as the feminist agenda—and also from women's advocacy groups concerned that the agency does not press for women's equal rights with sufficient force. It thus took both courage and foresight for Thoraya Obaid, as executive director, to make engagement with religion a centerpiece of her mandate. She argued repeatedly that social change in such highly personal and culture-specific areas as family planning and women's rights was tightly tied to religion, and engagement with religious leadership and communities was therefore essential.[24] UNFPA has engaged actively and creatively at many levels and in many countries following this mandate.

UNFPA took this leadership role two steps further in 2009 with the establishment of an interagency task force focused on engagement with religious institutions (at many levels, of many kinds). The task force meets periodically under UNFPA's lead, and with the secretary-general's blessing, to compare notes. Active participants have included the World Health Organization (WHO), UNESCO, UNICEF, the UNDP, the Joint UN Programme on HIV/AIDS (UNAIDS), the World Bank, the Alliance of Civilizations, and the UN Department of Economic and Social Affairs (DESA). To date, the primary activities have involved information exchange, but an example of more concrete engagement was discussion of the UNAIDS strategic framework for working with religion.

A second initiative involved a series of regional meetings of religiously linked civil society organizations to discuss issues and agendas, culminating in a gathering in Istanbul and the establishment of a global network of the organizations to facilitate interaction and cooperation.

Dialogue with world faiths: a World Bank experience

An active (and controversial) initiative to engage in an effective and purposeful dialogue with world religious leaders was launched in 1998 by James D. Wolfensohn, president of the World Bank, an institution that might be considered the least probable among global institutions to embark on such an effort. Wolfensohn's initiative, a continuing partnership with then-Archbishop of Canterbury George Carey, was stimulated by both defensive and more positive impulses. The times were contentious, with active civil society protests and questioning of the World Bank (among other global bodies), and religious leaders were prominent among the critics. Survey evidence highlighting popular trust in religious leaders (above most other categories) and growing appreciation of faith roles in two high-priority sectors—education and health—caught Wolfensohn's attention, as did the weight of ethical challenges emanating from respected religious figures around, for example, the environmental impact of dam construction and community displacement. With development and religious institutions preaching poverty alleviation and equity, the discordance and tension jarred. A succession of meetings of senior religious figures and development institution leaders between 1998 and 2005[25] produced sparks and discord, but above all new insights for all concerned. As singer Bono, an active participant, pleaded, "God is on his knees to you all, telling you to get off your behinds," and to act, together.[26] The leaders agreed that the dialogue needed an institutional form, and the small NGO the World Faiths Development Dialogue (WFDD) was born, in 2000.

However, there were surprises ahead and although the proposal was solely about dialogue, not programs or finance, intense opposition to the proposal emerged from virtually all the World Bank's executive directors, and the response among World Bank managers was at best tepid. Wolfensohn proceeded, more cautiously than initially envisaged and WFDD continues its work, but the experience suggested insights and lessons. The insights focused above all on the intense sensitivity of governments, unequal but nonetheless widespread, to direct engagement with virtually any religious actors at a global level. Concerns about bias, the contentious nature of interreligious relationships, links between religious institutions and political parties, and a general sense that religion was patriarchal and probably fading with modernization and did not deserve priority, dominated the discourse. The lessons include the difficulty of engaging with religious institutions, generically; a case-by-case approach (for example, on HIV and AIDS) yields better results. The special sensitivities for many states of religious relationships and partnerships were highlighted, as were large gaps in knowledge and research, amounting in many places to a religious illiteracy. If anyone thought that interfaith dialogue was an anodyne pursuit, their illusions were swiftly dispelled.

Unlikely sparring partners: the International Monetary Fund, the World Bank, and the World Council of Churches[27]

At a sensitive moment in negotiations of global pacts among several UN agencies, including the IMF and the World Bank, an unexpected broadside came from the WCC. This ecumenical body, based in Geneva, Switzerland, claims to represent some 525 million Christians. The critique was harsh, focusing on what the WCC described as unjust governance and disastrous policies that harmed rather than helped the poor. Following a protracted set of largely unproductive exchanges, the WCC, the IMF, and the World Bank agreed to engage in a structured dialogue process. The starting points were quite graphically illustrated in the title of WCC's preparatory document: *Lead Us Not Into Temptation*. The IMF and World Bank hoped to "explain" their positions and constraints to what they perceived as an ill-informed audience. The atmosphere was not propitious.

The dialogue process extended over almost three years, with successive meetings and many papers, and culminated in a meeting of leaders in Geneva. The formal outcomes were sketchy: some agreement on what constituted common ground (commitment to fighting poverty, good governance) and areas of disagreement aimed at further dialogue.

As is often the case in such engagements, strong personal connections were forged which have yielded significant, if unintended benefits. Above all, though, the encounters highlighted the complexity of engaging even with an institution purporting to represent a single religious tradition (Christianity, minus the Catholic Church) because of widely divergent views within the community and also the different perceptions of reality on the ground that came from the various experiences. The IMF and World Bank came away with an enhanced appreciation of how their policies and communications were perceived (not favorably) and an inkling of why. The conclusion of a substantial investment in time and energy was a sober awareness of gaps in perceptions and worldviews that would require far more extensive engagement to bridge.

Conclusion

A complex web of global interfaith institutions and initiatives has taken form, largely in the past 40 years. Their somewhat overlapping and worthy mandates are primarily focused on addressing the threat and reality of religious conflicts and tensions within increasingly plural societies. Initial mandates centered on peace have broadened over the years to encompass a far broader social justice agenda, with the ideal of common action to address the world's central problems, including inequity, poverty, and threats to the environment. The interreligious world includes— besides global interfaith institutions—initiatives and institutions in different regions, bilateral dialogues and cooperative efforts, and intra-faith dialogue and common efforts. Again, some focus on religious issues and institutions *per se*, while others aim to contribute to or alter global agendas and policies. The major interfaith organizations have engaged in complex and diverse ways with the formal global institutions, including the UN, but a clear-cut, cross-cutting approach is notably missing and tensions within these institutions around how to engage with the world of religion present a significant and continuing challenge.

5   Faith-inspired organizations at work

- Categorizing, defining, and setting in context
- Transnational faith-inspired organizations
- Major areas of action
- Regional perspectives
- Conflict resolution and religious peacemaking
- Conclusion

In the Democratic Republic of the Congo most schools, universities, and health facilities were founded by and today are run by religious institutions. This is also the case in many of the world's most tumultuous, conflict-ridden societies. In Cambodia, faith-linked institutions from most Christian denominations are at work across an extraordinarily wide range of social and economic activities, even though 95 percent of the population is Buddhist. In Bangladesh, imams are important partners in programs to prevent HIV transmission and to care for people with AIDS. Successful family planning programs in Iran are credited to government and mosque cooperation. Microcredit, forest planting and protection, advocacy against destructive mining practices, provision of water and sanitation, and shelters to rehabilitate trafficked women and children: faith-inspired organizations (FIOs) are deeply engaged in these and many other fields—providing services, advocating with governments and society on priorities, and critiquing policy and implementation. Action crosses borders, linking communities from different world regions. Sometimes the geography of cooperation is driven by historical missionary roots, sometimes by diaspora community ties, and sometimes (as in programs launched following the 2004 tsunami or the 2010 Haitian earthquake) by a universal human compassion that fires a religious community to reach out to help.

The chapter begins with a discussion of what is known and what is not, various categorization efforts, and regional and denominational patterns. Major categories of work and activism are explored, largely as illustrations of the kinds of activities that different groups undertake. Among the constellation of organizations, the focus is on the major global players but their interrelationships with national and community entities are also important to an understanding of their work and roles. Several boxes introduce some of the largest and most "global" institutions. A final section explores evolving roles of religious institutions in conflict, conflict resolution, and peacebuilding, as a long-neglected dimension of global affairs. It reflects both on religion as a source of conflict and on global, organized efforts to bring religious approaches and leaders more directly into work for peace.

Categorizing, defining, and setting in context

Religious work on health, education, and care of society's most vulnerable members (for example, orphans) generally draws on deep historic and philosophical roots, part of what religious communities see as their core business and ethic. A prime example is the Catholic Church's commitment to providing health care: one Cardinal, asked whether the Church would continue in the contemporary era to run hospitals, replied: "the hospital is our cathedral," and went on to emphasize the inspiration of Jesus' healing mission.[1] The Jewish faith highlights *tikkun olam*, "healing the world," as a central duty. Muslims stress that learning is emphasized in the Qur'an's first *sura*, and that giving charity (*zakat*) is one of Islam's five pillars. In modern times, religious institutions have often been at society's frontlines, pressing for social action, whether running soup kitchens or supporting the homeless, running an ever-expanding gamut of social and economic programs, and fighting slavery and racial discrimination. Systematic efforts by a wide range of religious institutions to engage proactively in conflict resolution, conflict prevention, and peacebuilding are on the increase. Thus the work that FIOs do is inspired both by their religious beliefs and teachings and by the pragmatic demands of communities.

This chapter focuses on what are, within international circles, often the most visible institutions associated with religion: the vast array of operational and advocacy institutions with specific, widely diverse areas of action that extend well beyond rituals and pastoral care. Often termed faith-based organizations, or FBOs, these institutions are central players in the non-governmental world. However, the term FBO leaves aside a host of institutions that eschew the labels "faith-based" or "organizations." Institutions that are in varying ways inspired by faith (even if they are not formally affiliated with religious bodies) take widely different forms in different world regions. They range from global giants like Caritas Internationalis, World Vision, and Islamic Relief, to emerging networks of Muslim women's organizations, religious orders with specific program priorities, informal groups working for peace, and myriad organizations working at community level, like youth groups and cooperatives. Some are integral parts of religious institutions and hierarchies, while others claim an inspiration that is religious or spiritual but whose ties to any formal religious body are loose or tenuous (Habitat for Humanity International, the giant housing organization, is an example). The discussion here overlaps in many cases with the earlier chapter that focused on religiously inspired movements, as many (for example Sarvodaya in Sri Lanka, other sub-continent movements, and most Catholic orders) are also actively involved in social and economic programs and advocacy. Likewise interfaith organizations look increasingly to "dialogue through praxis," with programs ranging from work for children to fighting malaria and tuberculosis.

There are literally hundreds of thousands if not millions of such organizations, and many of them are transnational—that is, working across national boundaries. FIOs are among the roughly 3,000 plus non-governmental organizations (NGOs) with formal credentials at the United Nations (UN) (an estimated 20 percent have faith links). However, given, *inter alia*, definitional challenges, the institutional map is sketchy. There is no agreed upon set of definitions, much less anything resembling a global census of organizations. Financial flows are poorly captured in most data sets, for many reasons, including the important reality that much takes place in kind or relies on volunteer labor. Many groups prefer to work outside official channels, fearing interference and skeptical of government approaches. Even at a country level it is common to find that there is no reliable database or coordinating or monitoring framework that captures the bulk of work by faith-linked entities.[2] The various actors often do not know one another and many fall off government radar screens.

In "mapping" the work of FIOs, the Millennium Development Goals (MDGs) offer a useful set of compass points in exploring the significance and impact of faith-inspired programs in the areas of humanitarian relief and development. Established following the 2000 UN Millennium Summit to offer inspiration and disciplined focus on priority goals, the MDGs represent the closest proxy that exists to a global agenda of needs and priorities. While they are far from comprehensive in their coverage of social and economic topics, they zero in on priority issues like health and child welfare and opportunity. FIOs are active across the board on MDGs, whether the topic is hunger or extreme poverty, water and sanitation, child and maternal survival, major communicable diseases, and perhaps most significant, education. They contribute ideas, advocacy, practical programs, critiques, and finance. Engaging and harnessing the contributions of faith-inspired development actors towards achieving the MDGs has been, admittedly, challenging. Much of their work has been poorly known and appreciated and the mechanisms to bring their voice to policy debates are fragmented and weak. Nonetheless both actually and potentially FIOs are major actors in achieving MDG targets and in identifying issues that might stall or accelerate progress towards ending world poverty.

Transnational faith-inspired organizations[3]

The activities and organizations involved in the universe of FIOs are remarkable for their diversity. To a large (and probably growing) degree, the major global transnational organizations share common characteristics with one another and with other global NGOs. However, each is shaped by its history, leadership, and religious affiliation. These in turn influence where they work and in what sectors, and their relationships both to public and private organizations. Each organization has its story and a narrative it presents that outlines its mission and the way it sees its strengths. The boxes that describe a selected group of organizations illustrate their diversity and the complexity of their evolution and relationships with other faith institutions, with governments, and often with the communities where they were born.

Catholic Relief Services (CRS) offers an example of progression in its focus. It began as a humanitarian organization, part of the US Catholic Church, and has changed over time. Today it is broadly engaged in development with a focus on peacebuilding. CRS is the United States affiliate of the Rome-based, Catholic Church Caritas Internationalis (introduced in Box 5.1), and thus has links with other similar bodies—for example, CAFOD in the UK, Cordaid in the Netherlands, and Misereor in Germany. CRS was born after World War II as an emergency relief organization focused on Europe. Like many similar organizations, the humanitarian goal and focus on disaster relief gave way to a broader understanding and desire to expand its focus to longer-term, sustainable programs that would improve people's lives. CRS was jolted by the 1994 Rwanda genocide and the failure of Catholic churches and communities to stand up to the brutality around them. As a result, CRS has since shifted focus again to a central preoccupation with peacebuilding. World Vision (the giant among FIOs with some 44,000 staff worldwide) had a quite different origin and history (see Box 5.2). It began as a virtually one-man show, then evolved into an evangelical organization focused on child sponsorship, before it assumed its contemporary worldwide array of development programs. Over the years, it has become more ecumenical, though staff are still required to affirm a declaration of faith, and its focus has broadened. Islamic Relief began from a base in Birmingham, UK (where Hany El Banna, its founder, was practicing medicine) as a response to horrific famine in the Horn of Africa. It, too, evolved from a primary humanitarian focus towards broader development programs (see Box 5.3). The American Jewish World Service supports a wide range of largely community-based programs, without regard to religious affiliation. It is in its appeal to Jewish communities as donors that its religious affiliation is most obvious (see Box 5.4). The Aga Khan Development Network is the remarkable creation of the Aga Khan, spiritual leader of Ismaili Muslims. The network includes seven different organizations, ranging from education (its special focus) and private-sector investment, to culture and historic preservation. Respected worldwide for the excellence of its programs, the network wears its rather obvious faith link warily, preferring to emphasize its technical rigor and commitment to core values (see Box 5.5). ChildFund International began as a Christian organization but as its mandate and strategic vision shifted, and as it came under criticism for its perceived secular ethic, it went so far as to change its name, dropping the word Christian (see Box 5.6). A final short tale focuses on an unusually successful and often overlooked child support and advocacy group, Compassion International (Box 5.7).

Box 5.1 Caritas: a global confederation within the Catholic Church

Caritas Internationalis is the umbrella organization for 165 Roman Catholic relief, development, and social service entities that operate in more than 200 countries and territories. These entities include Catholic Relief Services and Catholic Charities (the US organizations working, respectively, internationally and domestically), CAFOD (UK), and Misereor (Germany). The missions, both collectively and individually, are essentially the same: to work to build a better world, especially for the poor and oppressed. They share similar governance structures. Caritas Internationalis, overseen by the Pontifical Council Cor Unum, is based in the Vatican City with a Cardinal as its governor.

The federation began (informally at first) in the 1920s as a voluntary coordination effort, and more formal structures emerged after 1947, responding to a sharp increase in the demands for humanitarian work. The Church entrusted the emerging coordinating body with an official representation function for all Catholic welfare organizations at the international level, especially at the UN. This took formal shape following a 1950 gathering in Rome where the decision was made to set up an international conference of Roman Catholic charities. The first General Assembly of Caritas Internationalis took place in 1951 with 13 countries represented. The name Caritas Internationalis came in 1957. Today, the Confederation is one of the world's largest humanitarian networks.

The governance structures are quite light, with most responsibility centered in national organizations. Representatives from all member countries meet every four years in the Vatican City to review work carried out and approve a budget. The General Assembly elects a smaller group, the Executive Committee, to serve four-year rotating terms to govern the confederation's activities. The General Assembly also elects a Caritas Internationalis president, secretary-general, treasurer, and seven regional presidents. This group plus observers comes together as the Bureau with overall responsibility for governance.

The Caritas organizations are widely respected, with high standards on all operational fronts. They attract outstanding staff and few financial management issues have surfaced over the years. Their financing comes from many sources, public and private. In any humanitarian crisis the Caritas organizations are likely to be the first on the scene and they are key development partners in many domains. Caritas has generally avoided controversy but issues do arise. For example, lively debates arose in 2011 when the Zimbabwean secretary-general was not endorsed for reelection by the Vatican. The issues at stake appeared to turn largely on how faithfully Caritas followed Catholic teachings and on a Vatican wish to assert its Catholic identity, though issues of attitudes towards women also surfaced. Questions about the approach to reproductive health, most dramatically in relation to policies to promote condom use to combat HIV and AIDS, are raised constantly. The Caritas response is to affirm its commitment to Catholic social teaching and stress the remarkably wide and loving work that the institutions perform.

The opening passage of the 2004 Canonical Legal Status note on Caritas from Pope John Paul II[1] conveys the faith ethos of the organizations:

During the Last Supper, on the eve of his Passion, the Lord Jesus made a specific request to his Apostles: "A new command I give you: Love one another. As I have loved you, so you must love one another" (John 13:34). Sustained by this mission, the Church has proclaimed the Gospel and bestowed the grace of the sacraments, always making sure to accompany its action with the witness of love.

Therefore, since the beginning, the life of the Christian community has been characterised by the active exercise of charity, expressed in particular through attention to the poor and vulnerable (see Acts 2:42–47). For almost two hundred years, diocesan and parish groups emerged and subsequently took on the name of Caritas, with the purpose of helping those in need. As time went by, they also began to organise themselves at national and international levels.

[1] Caritas, "Canonical Legal Status," www.caritas.org/about/CanonicalLegalStatus.html.

Box 5.2 The growth of World Vision, a faith-inspired Colossus

Almost anywhere you care to name—and in places you probably can't—World Vision is there … It's huge. It's impressive. It plays on an international field like no other Christian organization. Nevertheless, World Vision usually flies under the radar. The organization takes few controversial positions. Much of its funding comes in small monthly gifts that sponsor 2.2 million individual children. Who would question the value of linking Western donors to poor children in the developing world?[1]

World Vision International, one of the world's the most active and largest FIOs, was born with one man's vision. The Reverend Bob Pierce was traveling in China, met a teacher and an abandoned child, and agreed to send five dollars a month to help the woman care for her. From this foundation he launched an effort to help the world's children. World Vision was established in 1950 and grew into a large and complex child sponsorship organization, helping hundreds of thousands of orphans at the end of the Korean War. The year 1970 was a watershed, marking the transformation of World Vision into a global partnership with a widening range of programs (humanitarian relief, community development, and microfinance among them). Adaptation as well as growth are constant themes, and World Vision is known for its capacity to innovate and learn.[2]

One major shift is away from the unabashedly evangelical, American, evangelizing focus in its earlier years. World Vision served as the organizational backbone of the Lausanne Committee for World Evangelization in the 1960s and collected and published data about "unreached people." It put out the *Mission Handbook: North American Protestant Ministries Overseas.* However, the organization today has a broader, larger ecumenical tent. It responded to reactions and to realities it met on the ground. World Vision declares a Statement of Faith that corresponds to the Statement of Faith put forward by the National Association of Evangelicals (NAE) as the standard for their evangelical convictions and this serves as the theological frame within which the organization as a whole operates. Staff must still sign a Christian declaration of belief, but World Vision US President Richard Stearns stated that World Vision has a strict policy against proselytizing, which he describes as " ... using any kind of coercion or inducement to listen to a religious message before helping someone."

The organization has grown remarkably fast and its character, programs, and very purpose have evolved over the years. In 2011 it employed some 44,000 people and operated worldwide in over 100 countries in a wide range of sectors with total revenues of over US$2.8 billion. Almost 80 percent of World Vision's funding comes from private sources, including individuals, corporations, and foundations, with the remainder from governments and multilateral agencies. About half of World Vision's programs are funded through a child sponsorship arrangement where individuals, families, churches, and groups are linked with specific children or specific community projects in their own country or abroad, pledging a monthly amount to support community-led programs that benefit children. World Vision uses a leading third-party provider of ethical reporting services to support a "whistleblower" mechanism.

World Vision consists of national entities around the world, grouped in what is informally referred to as the World Vision "partnership." World Vision International (WVI), established as the international coordinating body in 1977, works to ensure that global standards and policies are pursued. WVI has offices in

London, Geneva, Bangkok, Nairobi, Lusaka, Dakar, Cyprus, New York, Los Angeles, and San José, Costa Rica. The board of directors (the International Board) oversees the partnership, and its body of members (the Council) is the highest governing authority for certain fundamental decisions. WVI is incorporated as a non-profit corporation under the laws of the US State of California. National offices, many governed by their own boards, are linked through a common mission statement and shared core values and each office signs the Covenant of Partnership, agreeing to abide by common policies and standards. Accountability is assured through a system of peer review. The International Board (24 members) meets in full twice a year, and appoints senior officers, approves strategic plans and budgets, and determines international policy. The Council of Members meets every three years. National Boards, composed of business professionals and church and social service leaders, govern many national offices, where as many operational decisions are made as possible. National directors approve more than 90 percent of projects within previously approved budgets.

Not surprisingly for a giant of its size, World Vision meets criticism. Both its evangelizing focus and reliance on child sponsorship (which is quite controversial in contemporary development thinking) are continuing issues. Leadership issues dogged the institution at different points and more than one leader left under a cloud, but the dedication of staff and its determined creativity mark it to this day.

[1] Tim Stafford, "The Colossus of Care: World Vision has Become an International Force—and a Partner with the Poor," *Christian Century* 49 (24 February 2005), www.christianitytoday.com/ct/2005/march/18.50.html.

[2] Alan Whaites, "Pursuing Partnership: World Vision and the Ideology of Development: A Case Study," *Development in Practice* 9 (August 1999): 410–23.

Box 5.3 Islamic Relief: balancing faith traditions and international standards

Dr Hany El Banna, the Egyptian founder of Islamic Relief, says of its origins that he was inspired and provoked by seeing so many Christian organizations working in the Horn of Africa during the terrible drought of the 1970s. A physician beginning his practice in Birmingham, UK, he called on Muslim traditions of charity in demanding a comparable but distinctive Muslim response. His initiative has grown into the largest Muslim humanitarian organization operating internationally.

Islamic Relief Worldwide (IRW) calls itself a family of 15 aid agencies that aims to alleviate the suffering of the world's poorest people, inspired by their Islamic values, and aspiring to a world where communities are empowered, social obligations are fulfilled, and people respond as one to the suffering of others. Founded in the UK in 1984 by Dr El Banna, IRW is increasingly active in UN organizations, and is a signatory to the Code of Conduct for the International Red Cross and Red Crescent Movement and NGOs in Disaster Relief and of the Disasters Emergency Committee. Islamic Relief supports the global Make Poverty History coalition that campaigns to end extreme poverty, and it was part of the Jubilee Debt campaign. Islamic Relief works in over 25 countries, promoting sustainable economic and social development and working with local communities to eradicate poverty, illiteracy and disease. It responds actively to disasters and emergencies, including drought and conflict, in Muslim majority countries like Pakistan, but also in non-Muslim countries, like South Sudan. Islamic Relief works in six main sectors: sustainable livelihoods; education; health and nutrition; orphans and child welfare; water and sanitation; and emergency relief and disaster preparedness.

Islamic Relief focuses both on direct assistance to vulnerable people (clothing, food parcels) and on the causes of poverty, such as conflicts, exclusion and environmental degradation. Its microcredit programs involve interest-free loans. IR has taken important steps to ensure a coherent and positive response to the HIV and AIDS pandemic, and in 2007 it organized a consultative conference on Islam and HIV/AIDS in South Africa to formulate and promote an Islamic approach on contributing to the international effort to fight the disease. IR has responded to and made efforts to contribute to the work outlined in the UN Convention against Corruption.

Faith is a major factor that shapes IRW's identity and its values and choices. In seeking to be both true to its faith and to adhere to international humanitarian and accountability standards, it intentionally and explicitly integrates Islamic perspectives with professional relief and development. It builds on the core principle of Islam, that each individual has a duty to care for the poor and is accountable for his or her deeds on earth. IR's fundraising on the one hand, and projects on the other hand, demonstrate the spirit of its Islamic humanitarian work. In seeking funds, it calls on the Muslim obligation to provide for the poor, marginalized, and vulnerable through *zakat*, or almsgiving. Muslims are also encouraged to make voluntary contributions, or *sadaqah*, to help the poor and needy, or to contribute to other social welfare purposes such as sponsorship of orphans. *Waqf*, or charitable endowments, are another vehicle. IR receives donations from multilateral and bilateral institutions and individual donors (Muslim and non-Muslim). Partnerships are an important dimension of its operations, and partners include Christian organizations like CAFOD, as well as secular organizations like UNICEF. IR works with Muslim and non-Muslim beneficiaries. *Da'wa*, or inviting others to Islam, is obligatory for each Muslim, and is supposed to occur through reasoning rather than luring and coercion. Islamic Relief stresses that *da'wa* has little to do with international development and should remain a separate activity from humanitarian work. The institution has developed specific processes and systems to cater to Muslim traditions of giving. For example, during Ramadan IR undertakes specific feeding programs (as do many Islamic FIOs), and it ensures that donations are used according to Islamic guidance, but also that it abides by the standards of the international humanitarian sector in the way it delivers the service to its beneficiaries.

Box 5.4 The American Jewish World Service

The American Jewish World Service (AJWS) is a widely respected organization that focuses on grants to grassroots, community-driven projects. Its Jewish origins and identity are apparent in its name, but its religious links are primarily its conscious effort to reach out to Jewish donors, calling on their religious beliefs and obligations to "repair the world" (*tikkun olam*). Founded in 1985, in Boston, Massachusetts, AJWS was the first and remains the only American Jewish organization the primary focus of which is to alleviate poverty, hunger and disease and expand human rights for people across the globe. AJWS became involved almost immediately in responding to the 1986 Armaro, Colombia volcano disaster and has continued to respond to world crises, helping communities move from disaster to development. Since 1995, AJWS has organized international service trips, including the International Jewish College Corps (now Volunteer Summer) and takes several hundred young adults and skilled professionals to the global South for periods from a week to a year. AJWS is also actively involved in advocacy for causes, Darfur notable among them, and is currently working extensively as a leader in the fight against world hunger. The organization funds some 400 grassroots organizations that work in many areas, from health promotion, to education, economic development, sexual and reproductive rights, land and water access, and social and political change. AJWS works with women, youth, ethnic, religious and sexual minorities, indigenous peoples, refugees and internally displaced persons, and people living with HIV and AIDS.

Box 5.5 **A faith-inspired human development complex: the Aga Khan Development Network**

The Aga Khan Development Network (AKDN) was established by the Aga Khan (spiritual leader of the Ismaili community worldwide) over 50 years ago, and its various entities are engaged today in more than 30 countries. The AKDN comprises an "independent self-governing system of agencies, institutions, and programmes" which work under the leadership of the Ismaili Imamat—that is, the highest religious authority of the Ismaili faith. AKDN has broad social and economic objectives, inspired by Islamic principles and explicitly directed to serving all communities worldwide. Among its areas of sharp focus are excellence in education and volunteerism. Each organization in the network works on a distinctive mandate, under the Aga Khan's overall leadership and inspiration. The AKDN includes financial institutions, a private investment arm, an institution devoted to culture, and the Aga Khan Foundation, the organization's principle development arm (based in Geneva, Switzerland).

The AKDN's highly successful programs include the establishment of global universities and excellent schools, early childhood education, and rural livelihood interventions. Among its distinguishing features are its non-sectarian character and its broad conception of development, which includes private and public sectors and social, economic, and cultural dimensions. AKDN's annual budget in 2010 was approximately US$625 million; Aga Khan Fund for Economic Development companies generated revenues of US$2.3 billion in 2010, with surpluses reinvested in development activities.

Box 5.6 From Christian Children's Fund to ChildFund International

Founded in 1938 by Presbyterian minister Dr J. Calvitt Clarke, China's Children Fund's purpose was to help Chinese children displaced by the Second Sino–Japanese War. As the mission expanded to other countries, the name was changed in 1951 to Christian Children's Fund. Today it is ChildFund International and operates as an international child sponsorship group, based in Richmond, Virginia, focusing on deprived, excluded, and vulnerable children in 30 countries, including the United States. Besides sponsorships, ChildFund supports wide-ranging programs that benefit children and their families. Among its distinguishing features is the skillful use of television advertising to evoke strong emotions on behalf of deprived children.

ChildFund's evolution from its Christian genesis to today's non-sectarian ethos was the result of controversy. In 2004, Christian charity watchdog group Wall Watchers sent a "donor alert" via e-mail to about 2,500 subscribers, informing them that the name of the charity—Christian Children's Fund—was designed, intentionally, to mislead its donors into thinking it was a faith-based missionary group. Wall Watchers executive Howard Leonard commented: "It isn't Christian in the way we look at it. If you're going to be bringing help to these children, you should be bringing the Gospel." The organization responded that indeed the organization did not proselytize any person to a faith, but linked its name to its founder's Christian principle to "love thy neighbor as thyself." In 2009 the organization changed its name.

Box 5.7 Secrets to success? Compassion International

Compassion International is the only nonprofit in the child development category to have received Charity Navigator's coveted four-star rating eight consecutive years in a row. The American Institute of Philanthropy awarded Compassion its highest rating and *Worth* magazine placed Compassion on its list of the top 10 most fiscally responsible charities. Compassion operates as a self-contained, explicitly Christian organization, refusing to seek public funding as it fears it would undermine its mission. What is its secret to success?

Founded by Rev. Everett Swanson in 1952, Compassion, like several of its fellow organizations, began out of compassion for children. The founder was inspired by Matthew 15:32 where Jesus says, "I have compassion for these people … I do not want to send them away hungry." In Compassion's case it was the orphans who were left after the Korean War that inspired compassion and called its founders to provide them with food, shelter, education and health care, as well as Christian training. Today, Compassion provides support to over 1 million children in more than 25 countries. Compassion International is an advocate for children, "releasing them from spiritual, economic, social and physical poverty and enabling them to become responsible, fulfilled Christian adults." Its programs are rooted in Christian child development and child advocacy with a commitment to long-term support, from prenatal care through university support and leadership development for qualified young adults. The main structures for its work are church-to-church partnership and child sponsorship programs.

Compassion's secrets for success seem to lie in the straightforward quality of its mission and in its sharp attention to quality of management. If there is a criticism, it is that it hides its light under a bushel, rarely engaging in global policy debates about children's causes and thus missing opportunities to inspire and teach others and to coordinate in a common effort.

These and several hundred other organizations thus bring both their history and the nature of their relationships with different religious communities to their international work. Each has a story and ethos: take the Salvation Army, the Adventist Development and Relief Association (ADRA), and Habitat for Humanity, three vast and distinctive organizations that are significant players in the international arena. The Salvation Army was founded in 1865 in the United Kingdom as a Christian mission and today describes itself as a church with a mainstream Protestant theology, operating in over 120 countries. It is distinguished by its quasi-military structure, its use of music as a call to action, and its ubiquitous presence. ADRA is the development arm of the Seventh-Day Adventist Church, an active agency in many world regions, and linked in pragmatic ways to the Church's parallel and dynamic hospital and health network. Habitat for Humanity is not and never has had an affiliation with a church but follows a Christian mission in its passionate advocacy and programs that put decent housing at the center of its work. Each of these respected organizations adheres, increasingly, to the core standards of international NGOs and, quite frequently, echoes similar strategic statements that can at times mask the nature and above all the fervor of their faith inspiration. Most pride themselves on their commitment to service and the poor, stress that they take on board evidence of performance and monitor their work with a view to assuring excellence and learning from experience, and profess their commitment to serve all without regard to religion or ethnic group. There are exceptions. Several Christian NGOs deliberately do not seek or accept government funding because it would restrict their activities, for example requiring them to separate development and faith work. Two such organizations are Compassion International, the Nebraska-based Christian organization which does remarkable work for vulnerable children, and Samaritan's Purse. Muslim Aid, in contrast to Islamic Relief (which stresses that it serves all in need), largely focuses on Muslim communities.

The majority of international faith-inspired organizations are Christian in their origin and affiliation. History is a major explanation: the NGO form and then its transnational character largely emerged in the United States and Europe, where such organizations fit legal and social norms. Many grew from the large missionary networks that were a part of most Christian denominations from the nineteenth century. Jewish philanthropy also emerged in a European and American context, and several Muslim organizations, especially those that had roots in Europe and the United States, are to a degree modeled on similar patterns. Box 5.8 summarizes the underlying religious traditions of the three Abrahamic faiths.

> ### *Box 5.8* Charity and humanitarian work: religious roots in the Abrahamic faiths
>
> Charity has deep historical and spiritual roots in many faith traditions: indeed one of the strongest common threads is the principle, expressed in remarkably similar ways, to do unto others as you would have them do unto you (the Golden Rule). In practice

such teachings inspire many religious bodies and institutions, as well as families, and individuals, to service and giving.

As faith-based charitable services and religious tithes became commonplace in the Middle Ages, giving to the needy was a pious act for the three Abrahamic faiths (Judaism, Christianity, and Islam); however, it was the spiritual welfare of the giver as much as benefit to the receiver that was the focus.[1] Over time religious charitable obligations merged with the philanthropic efforts of secular society and state.[2]

Jewish beliefs in *tzedakah* and *tikkun olam*, when interpreted as ethical *mizvot* (commands), highlight the responsibilities of Jewish individuals, families, and philanthropic institutions. *Tzedakah*—which means "righteousness" but is interpreted as "philanthropy"—refers to the religious obligation to offer up charity and good works. Though charity suggests voluntary giving, *tzedakah* traditionally must be performed regardless of financial standing. Beyond these philanthropic duties, the Hebrew phrase *tikkun olam* emphasizes humanity's shared responsibility "to heal, repair, and transform the world." Interpretations of *tikkun olam* in the Mishnah indicate that the practice should be followed not because it is required by biblical law, but because it helps avoid social chaos. Traditionally, the "world" to be repaired was limited to Jewish society, especially as persecution, displacement, and eventual Zionism focused priorities "in helping Jewish communities in need around the world."[3]

Christianity inherited a legacy of philanthropy from Jewish scripture, with Old Testament references teaching to "open your hand to the poor and needy kinsman in your land" (Deuteronomy 15:11), paralleled in the Gospel's reminders that "the poor are always with you" (Matthew 26:11).[4] This teaching shaped the overlapping but distinct virtues of "charity" and "mercy," with the former between equals and the latter "between the strong and the weak, the prosperous and the poor."[5] Catholic institutions and hierarchal structures in Europe established in antiquity and the Middle Ages were designed to ensure that Christians systematically performed good deeds. "Coercive" charity was arranged in medieval towns through tithes but unconditional almsgiving was also taught as doctrine.[6] Notable among the funds and services arranged for the poor by Catholic governing systems is the Christian hospital, which emerged in the fourth century as a means for providing health services to the poor. The tradition of Christian medical services, especially for the Catholic Church, continues to play a major role in global health care systems.

Protestant accusations later claimed that Catholic doctrines and services "encouraged dependence, palliated poverty, and probably fostered a class of professional beggars who traded on the belief that almsgiving was vital to salvation."[7] Protestant charity discarded the concept of unconditional charity in favor of more sustained philanthropic systems. Catholic charity would later embrace this critique and adjust their services, though their approach remained distinct. While Protestant poor relief created a disciplined society in which overt sinfulness was repressed, Catholic approaches were more willing to accommodate sin and bring it to the surface with the processes of redemptive charity.[8] As Christianity spread globally through rising proselytization, these modes of charity increasingly merged with international Christian missionary and evangelizing work.

Charity and almsgiving have been central tenants of Islam since its inception. Although they are interpreted differently among countries, cultures, and Islamic schools, two terms, *zakat* and *waqf*, define how Islamic charity is practiced. *Zakat* is an Islamic institution with the primary objective to eradicate poverty among Muslims. The Qur'an links *zakat* to other primary acts of belief, stating, "Piety does not consist of merely turning your face to the east or to the west. Rather, the pious person is someone who believes in God, the last day, the angels, the book, and the prophets and who out of his love gives his property to his relatives, orphans, the needy, travelers, supplicants, and slaves; and who performs the required prayers and pays the *zakat*" (Qur'an 2:177).[9] *Zakat* is the third pillar of Islam and is commonly known as "almsgiving," although the word has much deeper religious connotations. Several countries have developed non-state financial agencies to manage donations. In Pakistan, Saudi Arabia, Sudan, and Yemen, legislation was created to include *zakat* as part of the state fiscal practice and exists as a mandatory tax. *Waqf* refers to the endowment of personal property towards charity and the faith and it is an integral part of property rights in the Islamic legal code. *Waqf* played important roles in the provision of education, health centers, mosques, shrines, and public goods like roads and bridges.

[1] *The Journal of Interdisciplinary History* 35, no. 3 (2005), dedicated an issue to the history of charitable traditions.
[2] Rachel M. McCleary, *Global Compassion: Private Voluntary Organizations and U.S. Foreign Policy Since 1939* (New York: Oxford University Press, 2009), 53.

3 Ruth Messinger, "Practitioners, Faith Inspired Organizations, and Global Development Work: A Discussion with Ruth Messinger, President, American Jewish World Service," interview by Katherine Marshall and Thomas Bohnett, 8 April 2009, berkleycenter.georgetown.edu/interviews/a-discussion-with-ruth-messinger-president-american-jewish-world-service.

4 Mark R. Cohen, "Introduction: Poverty and Charity in Past Times," *The Journal of Interdisciplinary History*, Vol. 35, No. 3 (Winter 2005): 347–60.

5 Ibid., 354, 347.

6 Ibid.

7 Ibid., 354.

8 Ibid., 355.

9 Azim Nanji, "Zakāt," in *Encyclopedia of Religion*, ed. Lindsay Jones, second edn, vol. 14 (Detroit: Macmillan Reference USA, 2005), 9924–26. See Gale Virtual Reference Library.

A large and growing number of transnational, faith-inspired organizations are, however, linked to other world regions and faith traditions. Notable is the explosion of new foundations and organizations in the Arab Middle East and especially the Persian Gulf.[4] These are active in humanitarian, emergency relief work but also provide far wider social services. The Qatar Foundation is a prominent example. The Red Crescent organizations are part of the non-religious Red Cross movement but do frequently invoke religious values in their humanitarian work. Relatively small faith traditions, for example the Bahá'í and Sikh faiths, run ambitious social programs that belie their small size and often inward focus on their community. Also well known are Hamas and Hezbollah, Islamist organizations notorious for their remarkable social work but also for their involvement in politics and terrorist activities (see Chapter 3). In Japan, the growing number of Buddhist and Shinto organizations are working internationally, on programs that extend well beyond their core spiritual missions (also elaborated in Chapter 3).

Disaster relief is commonly the main entry point for direct engagement in social action. In the world of international organizations, the larger faith-inspired organizations have earned a clear and respected seat at the table in humanitarian coordination bodies, notably the UN Office for the Coordination of Humanitarian Affairs (OCHA). They are very much part of the humanitarian community, in its positive dimensions, but also carrying the freight of the critiques and less positive dimensions of international humanitarianism today (for example in the dilemma of adhering to principles of neutrality). Norms of behavior are accepted by the traditional players. Nonetheless, some issues around humanitarian aid have particular pertinence for faith-inspired organizations. Some are among the "new players," for example from the Middle East, which feel that they are shut out from the established humanitarian world. The question of defining the limits of proselytizing also arises. The degree to which the large international disaster relief organizations work effectively among themselves or with local partners who have deep roots into communities is open to question. There are some noteworthy examples of effective cooperation among the large organizations. For example, following the 2004 tsunami in Aceh, World Vision, Mohammadiya, Catholic Relief Services, and others worked together well in active partnerships, and an effective if somewhat unexpected alliance was forged between the Salvation Army and Islamic Relief in Haiti. Meaningful evaluations of the lasting impact of much humanitarian work are missing, including where faith is a central element inspiring an organization's mission.[5]

Many organizations began with a relief and humanitarian mission but, as the various institutional biographies make clear, tended to expand their work and see their missions evolve to take on increasing roles in addressing the full panoply of challenges of development. Here, the institutional map is far less clearly traced and coordination mechanisms are less effective and transparent (Chapter 6). The diversity of organizations in size, ethos, practical approach, and geographic location militate against clear codes of conduct and harmonization of effort.

In short, notwithstanding the Christian dominance of the faith-inspired organizations in the past, diversity is significant and growing and few transnational faith traditions today do not engage in some form of international programs and activities in the humanitarian and development fields. Another increasing pattern is a growing array of partnerships among different faith-inspired organizations and with secular groups, public and private. This move to partnership is in keeping with MDG number eight and yields important benefits in many cases. However, there is also considerable dissatisfaction with partnership arrangements, especially when there are wide disparities in resources and effective power among partners.

Apart from the organizations that explicitly link their global social programs and religious outreach, it is legitimate to ask how significant is the "faith-inspired" dimension. What does the "inspiration" by faith involve? There is no ready answer and indeed many programs, for example for HIV and AIDS, malaria, or community development, carry few faith "markers" or distinctions. Some organizations attract staff and volunteers from religious specific communities or even require that their staff hiring take faith into account. Most organizations, however, do not, and it is questionable to argue, generically, that staff who work for a faith-inspired organization are more or differently motivated from their committed secular counterparts (though such arguments are not uncommon).

Three distinctive characteristics are claimed. The first is that the faith "link" to local religious institutions and communities helps to assure that programs are far more deeply grounded in local culture and society than what are disparagingly called "brief-case" or "cowboy" NGOs, which are seen to arrive on the humanitarian or development scene without a solid community anchor. An example of the importance given to these roots is the celebration in Uganda and other African countries of the 100th anniversaries of many health facilities and schools. Second, such institutions are often able to mobilize financing from their adherents, thus also helping to forge links across national boundaries and to enhance commitment to a "right to development" as well as at least some financial sustainability. Many faith-inspired organizations provide a channel for diaspora communities, generally for positive purposes, by bolstering investments in communities and advocating for public support. There are, however, notorious exceptions where communities have contributed to divisive political activity through their favoring of specific groups or fueling violence (Sri Lanka and Ireland are examples). Third, the argument is made that faith-linked groups, because of their long-standing ties and community links, are more likely to develop sustainable and culturally sensitive programs and programs that more explicitly and effectively target the very poor. Given the diversity of institutions and programs and a near total absence of assessments along the lines suggested by these assertions, clear evidence for any of these assertions is not available, though common sense and anecdotal evidence suggest at least elements of truth.

In the universe of faith-inspired organizations, the larger, transnational organizations have important complements and partners in more regional, national, or local organizations. While some regional and sectoral patterns emerge in the form that these organizations take and their relationships, local history, culture, and politics generally shape the context, especially at the country level. The roles that religious institutions play in health or education, for example, vary widely even between neighboring countries with similar histories or within countries. Gabon and Cameroon, Malawi and Mozambique, Indonesia and Singapore, Honduras and Cuba have very different institutional arrangements and schools and health facilities run by faith institutions vary widely in their scope and responsibilities as well as their relationship with government networks and policy oversight. As a general rule, faith-inspired actors are most active in providing social services where government or private-sector actors are weakest or absent, and they meet important gaps. This applies also, for example, to meeting the needs of disabled children and populations and those who are marginalized or excluded even in more prosperous societies. Faith-provided services are particularly (but not exclusively) present in rural areas. Faith-inspired actors often play important roles in advocacy for policy change and political focus, building on faith networks and drawing upon their grassroots experience.

Major areas of action

A common (and pertinent) critique by faith-linked observers targets the tendency of the professional development community towards sectoral, siloed approaches. A poor community or person, the argument goes, lives life as an integrated whole. Further, technocratic approaches distort realities on the ground which tend to be rather messier than theoretical models suggest. Thus many faith-inspired institutions seek to frame their programs as broad approaches, and a rather organic program development is characteristic, where, for example, an initial focus on water may lead to a concern with children's health or organizing women's groups to market their produce. Even so, faith-inspired organizations are involved in virtually every conceivable area and many specialize in certain niches, which may reflect their philosophy or "theory of change." Islamic Relief, for example, focuses on water given its central importance for the Islamic faith, and children and orphans are a common entry point for programs. The Brahma Kumaris, whose focus is on relieving stress and who are vegetarians, support research on links between diet and stress. Groups may also avoid certain types of intervention— family planning, for example. Some programs grow out of specific local needs—the explanation for the Church of Latter-Day Saints' neo-natal resuscitation program in Cambodia or a variety of faith-inspired programs there that serve victims of land-mines. In common with current development thinking, the stress is on community needs and voice.

The extent to which services and programs are linked to spiritual or religious teachings and practice varies widely, from direct links (support to church groups in Bible classes), to little-to-none, where groups explain their program focus as sorely dictated by the needs of those they seek to help. Availability of funding or appeal to donor communities is, for obvious, practical reasons, often a driver of program focus.

Notwithstanding this tendency towards integrated and locally driven action, the sectors where FIO contributions are most prominent are education, health, and youth and orphan care. Income-generating activities, for example supporting cooperative-type structures and microfinance programs, are increasingly important.

Engagement with HIV and AIDS is an example of FIO work. This has entailed a long journey and many different paths. The overall picture epitomizes the common comment, that "religion is part of the problem, and part of the solution." When the HIV/AIDS pandemic emerged as a public health crisis in many communities and congregations, faith leaders were swift to condemn those who suffered from the disease, and even their families. Yet it was faith communities and individuals who carried much of the brunt of care, advocacy, counseling, and direct assistance. Efforts to make sense of this complex picture and to act to mobilize, train, and support faith communities in their care date at least to the early 1990s. An extraordinary range of programs today support every dimension of the response to HIV and AIDS, from prevention, education, research on prophylactic techniques, and creative television sitcoms to encourage abstinence, to bold health programs offering ARVs and mother-to-child transmission programs, care of the sick and dying, and (notably) care of AIDS orphans. The Joint UN Programme on HIV/AIDS (UNAIDS) estimates that one in five organizations working on HIV/AIDS issues today is characterized as faith-inspired. Well-publicized controversies complicate the roles of FIOs in this area. They include appropriate condom use, the perception of a tension between priority to prevention or care, "secular," pragmatic approaches to changing behavior (condoms, work with high-risk groups) versus preaching faithfulness and abstinence, and a focus on treating those affected versus social change.

Religious communities have long taken special interest in and responsibility for the care of orphans and vulnerable children and this continues today. The practical instruments entail *inter alia* institution-based care (orphanages and boarding schools), community-based care systems (granny care system in Swaziland), and support for adoption and sponsorship programs. In all major faith traditions there is a clear calling to care for orphans (the Prophet Mohammed was an orphan). This emphasis is both a strength and a source of tension, because norms and approaches to care of orphans have undergone change since the times when orphanages were generally the optimal or only available solution. Orphanages are seen today as open to abuse, separating children from their community and roots, so alternative approaches are preferred. These include the child sponsorship programs that are also controversial, criticized for imposing large bureaucratic burdens and singling out specific children rather than dealing with the community at large. These debates offer telling examples both of how widely approaches differ even within a single religious tradition, of the depth of the impetus to compassion, and how these approaches and theologies can have practical manifestations. The challenge is to adapt practice to best international knowledge and norms while preserving the integrity of belief and to value and build on the impetus to compassion and respect for tradition.

Regional perspectives

The major transnational faith-inspired organizations are truly global institutions. Operating in many if not most world regions, through different forms of federal organization, with national chapters with local governance structures, is the norm. International norms shape both organizations and governance and explain a certain common language in descriptions of mission and strategic focus. Many run regional hubs. This plus the pattern of national affiliates makes it possible both to adapt programs to local realities and to respond to local legal requirements and frequent preferences by funders and governments to support organizations with local roots. In contrast, there are cases where an international organization is preferred because (positively) it brings cross-country experience or (more negatively) because it can shield local actors from arbitrary government pressures and, in some cases, takeover.

Even so, there are some distinctive features for different regions. In Europe, for example, the secular context in which faith-inspired organizations must operate calls on organizations that combine faith and secular goals constantly to legitimize themselves as development actors, respecting a more or less strict separation of religion and state. Buddhist organizations are far more active in Asia than in other regions. In the Muslim world, many organizations present their work in terms of Islamic values. Further, given great sensitivities about Islamist identity, which in some settings can call down harsh sanctions and financial difficulties, some groups that have a clear faith inspiration hesitate to put that front and center. In Africa, where religiosity is a central part of life, the boundaries between secular and religious are often blurred. Africa presents an extraordinarily varied tapestry of organizations working on development and many of them are inspired, indeed often founded, by faith traditions.

Conflict resolution and religious peacemaking

Religious dimensions of conflict and in peacebuilding are complex, varied, and often the subject of controversy. Is religion part of the problem or part of the solution? Are religious factors and actors sufficiently or even intelligently taken into account? The answer to the latter question is often no, while the response to the first is often yes, both. In the professional and academic theories and practical guidance materials that tend to shape perceptions of expected roles of various categories of players in difficult conflict situations, religious actors are often demonized or omitted entirely from the picture. This historical neglect of positive religious roles complicates the analysis of institutional roles and approaches.

The fuzzy boundaries that separate conflict and social and economic development further complicate the roles that religious institutions play. While there are some faith-inspired organizations that focus specifically on conflict resolution or on peacebuilding, most approach their conflict resolution roles as integral parts of their social and pastoral work and, in some instances, their political roles. Conflict prevention as well as conflict resolution and post-conflict rebuilding are parts of a complex whole that entails discernment of latent tensions, action to address them, advocacy at local and international levels, and direct mediation among actors, armed or unarmed. Reconciliation and healing bitter memories of past injustices and violence are critical if old conflicts are not to recur. The roles of the religious institutions and actors who are part of communities take on special importance. When a crisis jolts the situation and violent conflict erupts, development partners, public and private, leave the scene, returning only after long and painful conflict has inflicted terrible damage on institutions, communities, and infrastructure. Often religious institutions are the only ones left behind to offer what help they can as conflict flares.

Where amidst latent or flaming conflicts, juxtaposing conflict management and development actors, do religious dimensions enter the picture? Conflicts in reality rarely follow neat stages and different phases intermingle at each turn. Religious dimensions are almost invariably significant at each and every stage. Religious actors may run the most lasting, sustainable of the development efforts and keep schools and clinics operating in tense times. Religious actors may incite violence or, more commonly, respond to provocations with violent words. They may work actively to negotiate peace settlements, bring parties together, or work to reconcile aggrieved parties. They help to build resilience in society and are central to everyday life—from birth, adolescence, and marriage, to death. Common understandings of the causes and course of conflict provide little space for the critical roles that culture, faith-inspired actors, women, and other civil society groups may play. Aggravating the problem, religious actors and women share a common stereotype of backwardness and innate conservatism, but still more important are the habits of mind within diplomatic and governmental circles that simply tend not to see them as central and competent.

Each conflict situation tends (like unhappy families) to offer highly distinctive features that make generalization difficult. Each narrative is imbued with the complex history of the groups involved, complicated by multiple sources of conflict from religion, ethnicity, economics, and politics interwoven in complex ways. Take the case of Sri Lanka as an example: the clashing Sinhalese and Tamil contenders often framed their differences in terms of ethnic and religious identities. The long struggle inflamed tensions among religious communities that had long lived in peace, side by side. Many attempts, secular and religious, to reconcile parties and broker peace failed. The raw conflict was halted with a 2009 military operation that excluded the peacemakers, religious and secular, Sri Lankan and international. Where does religion fit? Clearly it was not the sole or even primary cause, yet religion was plainly part of the mix. The failures of religious peacemaking suggest lessons but not despair. Looking ahead, work by religious communities on the ground must surely play a critical part in rebuilding social cohesion and bringing about reconciliation. Box 5.9 highlights one positive story of interreligious cooperation that perhaps offers an avenue in the direction of peace.

Box 5.9 Religious tensions and interfaith response in Sri Lanka

Sri Lanka's religious tensions overlap with ethnic divisions. With deep historic roots in the colonial era, they are today magnified and distorted by politics, national and international. It is a complex scenario. One of the world's most bitter and prolonged conflicts pitted the Hindu Tamil Tigers against the Sinhalese Buddhist-led government, but the war's violent end in 2009 did not lead to a resolution of the tensions, religious and otherwise, that had fueled the conflict. Formal interfaith dialogue has largely failed to bring peace and reconciliation, in part because positions are deeply entrenched, in part because suspicions, starting with the government, make the challenges to dialogue and reconciliation nigh insurmountable. Some of the more promising paths to peace involve practical work on the ground, and improbable partnerships. The joint work of international NGOs linked to two different faiths—Muslim and Christian—offers an example of this kind of "interfaith by praxis."

The irony is that Sri Lanka's four major religious communities—Buddhist, Hindu, Muslim, and Christian—have histories and beliefs that are intertwined, exemplified in images displayed in many shops with symbols of the four faiths side by side. It is not uncommon for Sri Lankans to seek spiritual support from all four faiths. However, interfaith relations were poisoned by the conflict that, *inter alia*, segmented the population physically and politically. It led to at least the perception that religious leaders and communities were taking sides in the conflict. For Buddhists and Tamils, direct parties to the conflict, the perceptions reflected reality. However, the other two major faiths were also drawn into the vortex. While Muslims (some 8 percent of the population) were not the primary actors, they suffered acutely because of the conflict, with hundreds of thousands spending over 20 years in camps for the internally displaced. The fact that many NGOs working in Sri Lanka were Christian and concentrated their work in conflict, and thus Tamil/Hindu areas, created the impression that they had taken sides. In short, the four communities found themselves sharply polarized. The disaster of the 2004 tsunami added layers of complexity, as faith-linked groups tended to help their own, and cowboy NGOs, most with good will, some chasing the sudden largesse, often did more harm than good.

An unusual interfaith partnership formed after the tsunami shed light on the complex relationships but also pointed to paths that could bring peace and reconciliation. Muslim Aid, a British-based charity, teamed up with the United Methodist Committee on Relief (UMCOR) in 2005. Both organizations faced a range of suspicions on all fronts. They had to listen to angry accusations and the fears of communities. Buddhist leaders, for example, took a strident approach and made it clear that they viewed Muslims and Christians with equal suspicion. However, the witness of partnership and willingness to listen and to respond to specific requests for aid, quickly and effectively, helped to ease tensions. The partnership resulted in a series of programs that delivered effective aid and that offered the promise of healing bitter intergroup tensions in the areas they served.[1]

[1] For further information see Amjad Saleem, "Going Beyond the Rhetoric: The Muslim Aid/UMCOR Partnership in Sri Lanka," *Interreligious Dialogue* (21 December 2010), irdialogue.org/wp-content/uploads/2010/12/Going-beyond-the-Rhetoric-The-Muslim-Aid_UMCOR-Partnership-in-Sri-Lanka-by-Amjad-Saleem-.pdf.

An increasingly active theme among international policymakers and scholars is purposeful, experience-grounded peacebuilding and, increasingly, the roles of religious actors is coming into focus. The starting point is the common association of religion with violence; in many analyses religion ranks high among the causes of conflict. Because religious beliefs speak to deep reservoirs of motivation and identity, faith can fuel deep and lasting anger. Yet religious traditions, almost all of them, preach a message of peace, even as they offer inspiration and persistence in the face of overwhelming odds.

Religious institutions that work for peace vary widely, some through dedicated, named efforts, others as integral parts of their broader work. Institutions renowned for their active work for peace include the Community of Sant'Egidio (which is involved in negotiations at any moment in many corners of the world), Pax Christi, and Religions for Peace. Quaker and Mennonite institutions are advocates for disarmament, an end to land-mines and cluster munitions, and controlling the trade in small arms. Increasingly they define their roles as working for "positive peace" (a lasting peace with justice), and to prevent conflicts by addressing the causes of social injustice and tensions.

Religious actors may thus be directly involved in conflict resolution, peace negotiations, monitoring peace settlements, conflict prevention, and organizing humanitarian relief. Yet their roles are rarely well known. Why? Because religious elements have been, historically, neglected, especially in formal diplomacy.

Many scholars and diplomats today deplore the fact that religious actors are so rarely considered[6] and there is far greater recognition today than two decades ago that religious actors play active and central roles in conflict resolution. Even so, religious actors are often excluded from negotiations as well as from the broader work of preventing conflict and post-conflict reconciliation and rebuilding. This is especially true in the world's most complex conflict situations, where religious peacemaking is still far from being "mainstreamed" in the academic and diplomatic fields. Research and literature on Christian, especially Catholic and the so-called "Peace Churches," approaches to peace has tended to probe this work most deeply, and there are important university centers where peace studies take religion very much into account (these include prominently Notre Dame University, Georgetown University, Eastern Mennonite University, and the University of Bradford, UK). Islamic peacebuilding is increasingly important, albeit less well known, in different world regions. The approaches and practical experience of other faiths, including Judaism and Buddhism, are also coming into sharper focus. Religious communities play multiple roles in particular phases of a conflict and there is a richer and more sophisticated identification and integration of religiously inspired dimensions in the broader mainstream evolution of conflict resolution.

Religion has a special importance in fragile states and in addressing their high propensity to conflict (though here also most mainstream analysis takes little account of religion's roles). Religion is a central focus in contemporary debates about whether or not the world faces a "clash of civilizations," one that is linked to extremism and terrorism.[7] The role of women whose work for peace is inspired by their religious beliefs and religious institutions (or proceeds despite the latter) is a much-neglected topic.[8] The significance of women's roles is amplified by the intertwining of religion with gender issues in policy debates and on-the-ground action. Examples of religious actors include priests, rabbis, imams, gurus, Buddhist monks, women's and youth groups, informal mediators, as well as international religious organizations like Pax Christi, Lutheran World Federation, The Mennonites, World Council of Churches, and the Muslim World Congress.

The tendency to overlook or stereotype religious factors in both conflict and development raises some basic questions as to how far conflict specialists (and their development counterparts) appreciate the fundamental complexities that characterize virtually all conflicts. Especially in fragile or failing states and in protracted conflict situations, peacebuilding is the central challenge and conflict analysis, conflict resolution, development, governance, community stability, and politics are symbiotically linked. A priority, therefore, is to work towards better integration both of intellectual frameworks and institutional practice. Social, economic, and political development are neither top-down nor economics-driven processes and conflict resolution is about far more than negotiations and building community capacity. Both dimensions of peacebuilding need to be grounded in an appreciation of the need to engage with and support local institutions, empower communities, and meet people's needs and aspirations. In this fundamentally interdisciplinary endeavor, bringing the role of religion more consciously into the picture can help in a needed migration towards more robust understandings of social change that offer the promise of engaging more effectively the strengths of both the conflict resolution and development fields. Conflict resolution theory and practice need to address the question of how peacebuilding and development are linked and this includes understanding what religion has to do with both fields, individually and when they are (as they must be) looked at together.

Conclusion

A vast array of institutions, tied in varying ways to religious traditions and religious institutions, are central actors in humanitarian and development work worldwide. They count among them some of the world's NGO giants, notably World Vision and the Caritas Internationalis institutions, which sit at high-level international policy tables and help to shape global strategies, especially for humanitarian relief. These organizations are almost invariably among the first responders to catastrophes like earthquakes and floods. Many engage actively in providing support to victims of conflict. They are far more active in conflict resolution, prevention, and reconciliation than is commonly recognized. Their development portfolios are diverse and ambitious. The institutional map also includes a constellation of smaller organizations that work transnationally. These global and regional organizations, in turn, work with and often support national and local faith-inspired organizations. Some of these organizations are considered part of global civil society networks and organizations, and thus are part of aid coordination efforts, for example. Many others, however, operate largely outside these formal networks. Overall, the complex picture of their work is poorly mapped and understood. Experience is rarely captured fully, in part because of a tendency of many organizations to work independently of one another and, often, of governments. The work they do varies widely, both in scope and in quality. They offer outstanding programs,

Figure 5.1 The Dhammayietra. The mural, by artist Channa, shows the peace
march led by Buddhist monk Maha Ghosananda from 1992
onwards. It features the Dhamma wheel pushed by Buddhist monks,
peace-loving men and women, including people in wheelchairs,
farmers, Catholic priests, nuns, and soldiers
Source: Metta Karuna Reflection Centre, Jesuit Service Cambodia

noteworthy for intense dedication by staff and mobilization of large numbers of volunteers. Some break new ground, both in understanding the dynamics of communities and their culture and in innovation. Other organizations and their programs are of more questionable quality. Thus an important issue that arises in reviewing the contributions made and their quality and impact is the large gaps of knowledge that make it difficult to assess both their effects and their fit with national and international strategies.

Faith-inspired actors are major players in international humanitarian and relief work, and the leading institutions are well recognized and form part of the international humanitarian community. The roles of faith-inspired actors in the broader development field are also important, but the mechanisms and intellectual frameworks to engage all institutions and to draw on their experience are patchy. In some countries and sectors faith-inspired organizations are recognized as important contributors to development strategies and to achievement of the Millennium Development Goals and other international targets. In other settings, in the constellation of diverse organizations active in the development field, they are not fully perceived and their experience is largely shunted to the side. This has also applied in the areas of conflict prevention, conflict resolution, and peacebuilding. Religious actors vary widely, ranging from large, international organizations with an explicit mandate for peace (Pax Christi, for example), to individual groups, for example the Liberian women in white who "Prayed the devil back to Hell." The complex roles that religion, in all its forms, plays as a source of conflict and tension and its equally complex potential for contributing to peace are critical areas that call for greater scholarship and policy attention.

6   Emerging issues and future directions

- The landscape
- Taking practical issues
- Global institutions approach religion

The contemporary global religious picture is remarkable for its dynamism. Age-old beliefs and loyalties are challenged by forces of globalization that are creating societies where pluralism and change are the norm and every precept is open to challenge. Fundamentalist beliefs and movements are on the rise, in large part, it is believed, because long-held, often overlapping identities are stirred by social change, producing various forms of reaction and backlash. Some demographic changes are linked to specific religious traditions or to their changing hold on the behavior of both women and men. The processes of modernization that unleash both energy for change and new forms of conflict and tension often involve religious elements. Understanding religion as a central force in global politics, finding effective and modern ways to engage with religious communities and actors, and appreciating their many dimensions are all vitally important. For all these reasons, the religious mistrust or illiteracy that has characterized approaches of many international affairs actors to religion, together with an often restive unease of many religious players vis-à-vis intergovernmental institutions (as well as multinational private companies and many transnational non-governmental organizations (NGOs)) call for attention and action.

This concluding chapter focuses on emerging trends and issues. Thus it revisits the reasons for gulfs in understanding among various secular and religious actors. Five topics illustrate these issues: differing perspectives on women's roles in family and society; specific controls on financial flows to some religiously linked development and humanitarian institutions; new elements in approaches to various human rights issues; concerns about coordination and information that sheds light on the roles and work of faith institutions; and the need to define more clearly norms on religious freedom, especially where proselytizing or evangelizing is concerned. It then explores how various global inter-governmental organizations, notably the United Nations (UN), the multilateral finance institutions, and the European Union (EU), and institutions like the World Economic Forum have grappled with their relationships with both institutions and issues involving religion, and some religious institution approaches to global institutions. Taking the Millennium Development Goals and the Millennium Declaration as beacons of international agreement that underpin global institutional ideals and structures, the concluding section reflects on how religious partnerships and actors fit within these frameworks.

The landscape

The implications of the general, if shifting, pattern of disconnect among religious and secular actors is a theme that runs throughout this discussion because it results in important ways, with real-life consequences, in misinformation, miscommunication, and misperceptions. The disconnects are inspired and fueled in large part by an ideal of separation of "church" and "state," with religion supposedly relegated largely to private roles in society and, above all, governance. This notional ideal is far from universal in reality. Indeed, in parts of the world where theocratic or quasi-theocratic norms and institutions prevail, religion and governance are intertwined. In some societies relationships among different religious ideas and institutions are quite clearly and explicitly defined. That may be in a positive manner, where a religious tradition or traditions have official status, or negatively, as in various communist regimes that, at least in the past, set out to banish or root out religious influences entirely. What is most common today, however, is an uneasy and often unclear set of relationships, where religious voices and beliefs (as in the case of the United States) are influential in shaping many policies and ideas, but in a contested and often rather ambiguous manner. The combination of changing patterns and norms with often opaque relationships has contributed to the "religious illiteracy" that has resulted as education about religion dwindled in many curricula and as many professions acted on the assumption that religion was no longer a force to be reckoned with.

Global events that are forcing or encouraging different approaches to and understandings of religion's roles in global politics are still unfolding. Thus the current policy and academic pictures are decidedly mixed. Notwithstanding the clear messages of global leaders like Madeleine Albright, Tony Blair, and King Abdallah II of Jordan that religion must be taken seriously and looked at with new eyes, attention is still rather spotty and sporadic. It is notably tied to the personal views of leaders and public intellectuals. For all the messages of a David Brooks or Nicholas Kristof urging sharper attention to religious forces and actors, others question the relevance of religion in the modern, public square, or more often simple ignore it. The religious elements in longstanding conflicts, notably in the Middle East, the continuing force and influence of Islamism, and the pentecostal revolution in many parts of the world are still not systematically and thoughtfully explored. Likewise, the negative and positive effects of religious ideas on social changes in areas like family size and of religiously inspired institutions and movements are poorly understood. These gaps in understanding speak first and foremost to a need for better education and more research. They also suggest a need for review within both intergovernmental and religious institutions of their respective roles and relationships.

Taking practical issues

The practical implications of this rather broad and somewhat theoretical divide are best illustrated through specific examples, the more so when the pitfalls of overgeneralizing and oversimplifying either religious or secular are borne in mind. There is, to recall, vast diversity within each religious tradition, not to speak of global religion, such as that exists. Simplistic approaches, however common in rhetoric and even analysis, are to be avoided. The aim is informed, thoughtful, and probing reflection both on rather ancient questions about how public and private dimensions of religion affect global affairs and how these are changing.

The issue that perhaps best highlights problems and potential, as well as different perceptions and misperceptions, is gender, and specifically the role of women in modern societies. At one level, many religious institutions are virtually the last bastions of formal (as well as informal) glass ceilings that prevent women from exercising public religious roles within many, though definitely not all, religious institutions. Religious and cultural beliefs are part of the reason why practices like child marriage and female genital cutting persist. There are many religious leaders (including within the United States) who still believe in and argue for a hierarchical relationship between men and women where the man is superior and entitled to leadership roles. These visible realities explain a good part of the often-met unease among global leaders and institutions about respecting religion and according to religious institutions a recognized place within national and global institutions. A flip side is that many religious figures are uneasy about what they describe as

"Western feminism," which they equate with degradation and challenges to traditional cultures and beliefs and especially to the institution that everyone agrees is the basic social cell, upon which all is built: the family.

The complication is that many, if not most, religious actors believe that they indeed stand for a truer and deeper appreciation of the common dignity of all persons than their secular counterparts. They argue that casting out all recognition of differences between men and women is foolish and impossible. They point to their teachings on women's vital roles. Many denominations and traditions have indeed adapted their teachings and practice to the modern understanding of full male and female equality.

The challenge, therefore, is to deepen understandings and dialogue about where the problems indeed reside. How far is there a misperception? How far are the basic human rights norms of equality called into question, in theory and above all in practice? Most important, at the level of families and individual lived realities, how are religious beliefs and teachings influencing behavior? Is the evidence of benefits of women's equal rights insufficiently understood? Are the perils of modern women's roles underestimated? Given the critical and growing importance of male–female relationships in international affairs, addressing these issues deserves priority.

A second practical issue has arisen because of governmental and intergovernmental concerns about flows of finance to organizations that support or are seen to support terrorist activities. The Patriot Act in the United States and its equivalent in other countries have in practice been a serious constraint to organizations that are for the most part Islam-inspired. There are several consequences. A first is that good work by some institutions has been brought to a halt. Another is the resentment of the countries behind the controls, especially when they are seen as arbitrary or unjust. A third is the encouragement of cash transfers, outside official channels, that exacerbate the already serious problems of corruption and misappropriation of funds.

Solutions need to be sought in the first instance in more highly tuned processes of identifying truly problematic flows. It is especially important to ensure that broad-brush application of controls to virtually any organization with a Muslim character is avoided. Various initiatives, in the United Kingdom and in Switzerland in particular, aim to bring such rationality into the system and thus to ensure that the combination of efforts to avoid terrorist attacks and a broader fear of clash of civilizations does not result in widening divides and increasing mutual distrust and resentment.

A third issue that threatens to widen divides between religious and secular institutions are underlying concerns around human rights: are they truly accepted by religious bodies as a common ideal and standard? Are human rights taken to extremes that challenge deeply held religious and cultural beliefs? Is a common path traced and possible or is there an unspoken, undeclared clash? The Universal Declaration of Human Rights is described (only somewhat tongue in cheek) as the religion of the UN system. It represents a common set of beliefs that were articulated in the late 1940s, admittedly with American and European actors in the lead. Valiant efforts were made to reflect a set of values that were truly universal. The fact that there were and still are very different values and ethical norms was acknowledged, famously in philosopher Jacques Maritain's comment that, "We all agree on the rights, as long as no one asks us why."[1]

This is to underscore both the importance of the human rights framework as a foundation for the international system, its progressive refinement over the past 65 years, and the continuing nagging questions about its universality.

In this context, a tendency that appears to be on the increase is a questioning of human rights, especially in various religious circles. Some groups (for example, some US evangelical groups) go so far as to describe a UN conspiracy to undermine American and religious values. Efforts to broaden definitions of rights, for example to apply to LGBT (lesbian, gay, bisexual, and transgender) groups and to the disabled, fuel these perceptions, as do less clearly articulated doubts about women's rights, and especially reproductive rights. Once again, compromising on core human rights principles should not be seen as an option. However, engaging the doubters and understanding the sources of their doubts is important if further erosion of religious support for human rights is to be avoided.

The fourth eminently practical issue surrounds aid coordination and harmonization, a central pillar of the eighth and final Millennium Development Goal, which calls for strategic focus in achieving goals and for partnerships. Given the important and often creative faith-linked service delivery networks and approaches, many focused on what are widely viewed as global, moral priorities for action, it is striking that limited systematic effort has gone to engage with them in the context of aid effectiveness and harmonization at country and international levels. Gaps in knowledge, weak networks, and negative preconceptions (going both ways) are the likely explanations. International organizations and donor agencies may seek to "instrumentalize" the engagement of faith communities (meaning that they are tempted to want to "use" faith institutions to further already defined policies); not surprisingly, this is viewed askance by the faith institutions concerned, which hold the view that their knowledge and deep roots suggest leadership rather than executing roles. More nuanced and respectful approaches to partnership might better capture the complex contributions and assets of faith actors and enhance their contributions to what are common ends.

Finally, an issue that arises in virtually every world region concerns how and whether religious organizations exercise their right to freedom of religion through efforts to convert others, thus proselytizing or—as many prefer to term it—evangelizing, or sharing their faith. The issue concerns both the practical application of freedom of religion in different societies and legal systems and how such activities relate to the practical humanitarian and development work that organizations undertake. Within international humanitarian law, the rules of the game and codes of conduct are, at least in theory, quite well established. Anything that involves conditionality or a *quid pro quo* is counter to international norms of neutrality and to human caring for those in a vulnerable position. However, questions linger about the proper extent to which development workers can bring an explicit focus on their religious beliefs into their development work. The more established of the faith-inspired organizations differ in the nuances of their approach, but many argue that the effects of aggressive proselytizing, tied to development, particularly by evangelical organizations working in areas where Christians are a minority, are profoundly alienating and can exacerbate social tensions, with spillover effects that extend to all development work. The contrasting argument is that spiritual and material dimensions of development work cannot and should not be separated in artificial ways. In this debate, tensions between Christian and Muslim communities are the primary concern (and the most bitter divisions are often within these religious communities), but in largely Buddhist Sri Lanka and Hindu regions in India this remains a highly contentious and explosive issue. Working to define boundaries and to agree on clear and meaningful codes of conduct are possible avenues towards solutions.

Global institutions approach religion

Until the late 1990s, few global institutions (with the exception of the Organization of Islamic Cooperation (OIC) and other Islamic institutions) had articulated positions on how they understood their relationships with religious bodies. The UN Educational, Scientific and Cultural Organization (UNESCO) was the organization within the UN system with a mandate to deal with culture and religion, but religion was (and remains) essentially subordinate to culture. Religiously inspired NGOs were accredited to the UN and the special role of the Vatican/Holy See gave a visibility—sometimes unwelcome—to religious perspectives (see Chapter 4). The European Community debated whether Christianity was part of Europe's heritage and various initiatives endeavored to broaden the understanding of ethical issues to encompass religious elements. However, in general, a search for religious references within the UN system turns up very little. The major exception was the experience during the Cairo 1994 Conference on Population and Development and the 1995 Beijing Conference on Women. Both highlighted the growing intellectual and policy consensus on the vital importance of changing women's roles ("women's rights are human rights," Hillary Clinton famously declared).[2] They also brought home clearly the religious doubts about these changing roles and especially notions of human rights around reproductive health. The alliance of Vatican and Muslim nations, and later evangelical groups, for the first time made clear the challenges they presented on the human rights front.

The 1979 Iranian Revolution and the rise of terrorism in the late 1990s and early 2000s changed this picture and at the least put religion onto global agendas in a negative sense. In different ways and at differing tempos, various institutions of the UN system came to reflect on how they should engage with religious institutions and the implications of doing so. The UN Children's Fund (UNICEF) and the UN Population Agency (UNFPA) were among the leaders at a practical field level because their programs addressing respectively the needs of children, including mounting vaccination campaigns in contested areas, and women's reproductive health brought them into direct and continuous contact with religious actors and institutions.

At the leadership level in different institutions, the stance of individual leaders played significant roles in shaping approaches to the particularly sensitive topic of religion. Thus it was significant that four Washington, DC, international institutions were among those that pressed for a more dynamic and active stance on religion. Michel Camdessus, then managing director of the International Monetary Fund, and his successor, Horst Koehler, both reached out to religious leaders, especially— in Camdessus's case—the Vatican, and European intellectuals like Hans Küng. From his position in the Inter-American Development Bank, Enrique Iglesias was convinced that systematic relationships with the different religious institutions and leaders were critical to making breakthroughs in Latin America. James D. Wolfensohn, as president of the World Bank, took the most active stance on the topic. He was convinced that the criticism of development institutions coming from religious institutions needed to be addressed because there were strong common interests in fighting poverty. He also saw religious bodies as the world's largest distribution system, key actors in every dimension of the humanitarian and development fields.

Wolfensohn's initiative, launched in 1998 jointly with the then-Archbishop of Canterbury George Carey was in fact quite modest, involving high-level meetings centered on dialogue with no meaningful financial commitment at stake. It envisaged a continuing dialogue around topics like the Millennium Development Goals and country strategic priorities for poverty alleviation. Yet the effort encountered strong opposition. Table 6.1 summarizes the various critiques that were put forward by the World Bank's executive directors, then representing over 180 countries. In sum, they perceived the dialogue effort as entering into dangerous political waters given the controversies around religion. They were also concerned by the patriarchal approaches that characterized many religious institutions. Many still clove to the long-accepted assumption that religion's roles in public matters had declined and would continue to decline with modernization.

The dialogue process also brought home the doubts that prevailed within different religious institutions about the motivations and approach of global institutions, and especially the multilateral development and financial institutions. These included their perception that multinational corporations and powerful governments called the shots, concerns with effects of development like displacement of populations, the grip of economic theologies, and the fact that institutions seemed so enigmatic. A nagging distrust of governments generally and perception that they have been and remain chronically subject to corruption, color perceptions and relationships.[3] A general concern was the perception that ethics were largely invisible.

Wolfensohn persisted, though his faith initiative took a lower profile and smaller resource allocation than originally planned. The World Faiths Development Dialogue that was created to carry forward the initiative persists to this day. What the episode at the World Bank brought home most clearly, however, were the perils and the special sensitivities involved in engaging religion within a global institution. The very complexity of religious institutions and their complex ties to both political entities and to each other were seen as a source of potential distortion of international goals and institutional frameworks. The message then was clear: proceed with great caution.

In the past decade, global and religious institutions have gradually worked out a new set of relationships. The Millennium Development

Table 6.1 Issues that often feature in secular/faith dialogue

Gaps: Secular perceptions/questions about the work of faith-linked groups: (3 Ds and an E)

Concern	Issues	Examples	Response
Political and Divisive	Competition among groups makes cooperation impossible, proselytizing is the primary motivation, complexity, religion contributes to conflicts	Religious conflict, "sheep stealing", jealousies within faith communities, engagement with political parties, desire for power, Concerns about finance, which is often untransparent	Importance of religious communities and leaders in peacebuilding and conflict resolution, examples of cooperation, important contributions to social cohesion, trust that communities express for religious leaders and institutions
Dangerous to progress and modernization	Gender roles, reproductive health and women's health rights, association of religion and patriarchy, links to status quo	HIV and AIDS debates, lack of women in formal religious leadership and in community structures	Religious voices are often at forefront of social progress, represent prophetic voices calling for reform and social justice
Low priority, religion is essentially defunct in modern societies or relegated to private sphere	Assumption that religiousity declines with modernization	Many dismiss religion as a factor in development, "radar screen turned off"	Increasing evidence of staying power of religion in modern life, albeit often in new forms
Emotional and personal approach to religion	Experience of parallels in early and subsequent approaches to gender issues, limited evidence a roadblock, approaches to religion shaped by personal views of leaders	Institutional leaders and strategies in international bodies tend to reflect individual views rather than a well articulated approach.	Garner and present facts, need for a professional approach, thoughtful exploration of diverse roles

Table 6.1 (continued)

Gaps: Religious perceptions/questions about work of secular development institutions: (5 Es and a D)

Query/issue	Concern	Examples	Response
Development is about Empire	Power of US and wealthy countries, multinationals, seen as driving their approach and agendas	Agricultural subsidies, weight of power in international institutions	Slow progress is being made in shifting balance, focus on country-led processes, efforts at empowerment and voice
Institutions are often mute on ethics, or worse, seen as Godless and without values	Greed is the creed, development undermines cultures and traditions	Consumption and western style flaunted in the media, support for large land purchases, GMO promotion	Recognize and address contending ethical dimensions, purposeful dialogue
Effects of Development	Damage to communities, disruptions from change, undermining families	Dams, decline in traditions and families	Recognize complexity
Economics as theology	Mysterious and seemingly rigid	Push for privatization, free trade	Dialogue
The discipline and institutions are Enigmatic	Can't understand how financing works	Bewildering jargon	"grandmother economics": make sure concepts are clear and understandable
Development is simply Dangerous	Beware those who urge and profess it	Behaviour and attitudes of institutions and economists	Dialogue....

Figure 6.1 Religious minefields
Source: *Sunday Times*, 23 May 2010. © 2010–2012 Zapiro (All rights reserved).
Used with permission from www.zapiro.com. For more Zapiro cartoons visit
www.zapiro.com

Goals have proven to be an important impetus, as has the looming
awareness of the dangers of climate change. As active members of the
civil society bodies that play growing roles on virtually every global
issue, faith-inspired organizations are increasingly visible and they have
developed a growing and evolving set of relationships with virtually
every UN institution.

Notes

Introduction

1 Madeleine Albright, *The Mighty and the Almighty: Reflections on America, God, and World Affairs* (New York: Harper Perennial, 2007).
2 One exception is the monumental series resulting from the Fundamentalism Project: these include Marty E. Marty, R. Scott Appleby, John H. Garvery, and Timur Kuran, eds., *Fundamentalisms and the State: Remaking Polities, Economies, and Militance (The Fundamentalism Project)* (Chicago, IL: University of Chicago Press, 1996).
3 Samuel Huntington, "The Clash of Civilizations?" *Foreign Affairs* 72 (Summer 1993): 22–49.
4 John Micklethwait and Adrian Woolridge, *God is Back: How the Global Revival of Faith is Changing the World* (New York: Penguin, 2010); and Monica Duffy Toft, Daniel Philpott, and Timothy Samuel Shah, *God's Century: Resurgent Religion and Global Politics* (New York: W.W. Norton and Company, 2011).
5 R. Scott Appleby and Richard Cizik (Co-Chairs), *Engaging Religious Communities Abroad: A New Imperative for U.S. Foreign Policy* (Chicago, IL: The Chicago Council on Global Affairs, 23 February 2010), www.thechica gocouncil.org/UserFiles/File/Task%20Force%20Reports/2010%20Religion% 20Task%20Force_Full%20Report.pdf.

1 Religion: An institutional portrait

1 www.christianchronicler.com/history1/avignon_papacy.html.
2 Voltaire, "Letter to Frederic II, King of Prussia."
3 marxists.org/archive/marx/works/1843/critique-hpr/intro.htm.
4 www.un.org/en/documents/udhr.
5 John Witte, Jr and M. Christian Green, "Religious Freedom, Democracy, and International Human Rights," *Emory International Law Review* 23 (2009): 584–608, 590.
6 Ibid, 589.
7 For Department of State reports, see www.state.gov/j/drl/irf/rpt/index.htm.
8 Witte and Christian, "Religious Freedom, Democracy, and International Human Rights," 586.
9 Katherine Marshall, "Development, Religion, and Women's Roles in Contemporary Societies," *The Review of Faith & International Affairs* 8, no. 4 (2010): 33–40.

10 Samuel Huntington, "The Clash of Civilizations?" *Foreign Affairs* 72 (Summer 1993): 22–49, 22.
11 Ibid.
12 Comment at World Economic Forum Davos meeting 2005, panel with author.
13 See his argument laid out, for example, in Peter Berger and Anton Zijderveld, *In Praise of Doubt: How to Have Convictions Without Becoming a Fanatic* (New York: HarperOne, 2009).
14 Stephen Prothero, *Religious Illiteracy: What Every American Needs to Know— And Doesn't* (New York: HarperOne, 2008).
15 R. Scott Appleby and Richard Cizik (Co-Chairs), *Engaging Religious Communities Abroad: A New Imperative for U.S. Foreign Policy* (Chicago, IL: The Chicago Council on Global Affairs, 23 February 2010).
16 Ibid, 1.
17 Ibid.
18 This is a central message in Karen Armstrong, *The Battle for God* (New York: Ballantine Books, 2000), and is a thread running through her voluminous writings.
19 www.pluralism.org.
20 Douglas Johnston and Cynthia Sampson, eds., *Religion: The Missing Dimension of Statecraft* (New York: Oxford University Press, 1995).
21 See, for example, the author's summary of the 2011 Forum at www.huffingt onpost.com/katherine-marshall/sacred-music-sparks-dialo_b_872006.html.
22 This argument is made especially cogently in Philip Jenkins, *The Next Christendom: The Coming of Global Christianity*, third edition (New York: Oxford University Press, 2011).
23 Todd M. Johnson and Brian J. Grim, eds., *World Religion Database*, www. worldreligiondatabase.org, Leiden: Brill Online (6 July 2012).
24 Berger and Zijderveld, *In Praise of Doubt*, 3.
25 Ibid., 6.

2 Global religious bodies

1 Peter Willetts, *Non-Governmental Organizations in World Politics: The Construction of Global Governance* (New York: Routledge, 2011).
2 Comment at Millennium Summit, August 2000, New York (author's report).
3 A state religion (or official religion, established church or state church) is a religious body or creed officially endorsed by the state and government sanctioned. Such states are not secular but also not necessarily a theocracy. Christianity was historically the state church of the Roman Empire and the term is associated with Christianity. State religions are official, but the state need not be under the control of the church (as in a theocracy), nor is the state-sanctioned church necessarily under the control of the state. The first state-sponsored Christian church was the Armenian Apostolic Church, established in 301 AD.
4 An example is Jesuit Thomas Reese's excellent book, *Inside the Vatican: The Politics and Organization of the Catholic Church* (Cambridge, MA: Harvard University Press, 1996).
5 Vatican veteran journalist John Allen's book is appropriately titled *All the Pope's Men: The Inside Story of How the Vatican Really Thinks* (New York: Doubleday, 2004).
6 Cited in Allen, *All the Pope's Men*, 18–19.

7 The Vatican website is worth a look: www.vatican.va/phome_en.htm.
8 A treasure trove of data is available from CARA, the Center for Applied Research in the Apostolate. The source for these numbers is Bryan T. Froehle and Mary L. Gautier, *Global Catholicism: Portrait of a World Church* (Maryknoll, NY: Orbis Books, 2003).
9 For one source on Jesuit history, with many references, see www.newadvent. org/cathen/14081a.htm.
10 See a provocative publication reflecting new research by scholar Robert Woodberry, "The Missionary Roots of Liberal Democracy," *American Political Science Review* 106 (May 2012), which argues that missionary work had a major and positive impact on movement towards democracy.
11 www.worldea.org/whoweare/history.
12 Pew Forum on Religion and Public Life, *Spirit and Power: A 10-Country Survey of Pentecostals*, October 2006, www.pewforum.org/Christian/Evange lical-Protestant-Churches/Spirit-and-Power.aspx.
13 Account at www.saddleback.com/aboutsaddleback/. The Hartford Institution for Religion Research is an excellent source of information about trends: hirr.hartsem.edu.
14 For an account of this history, see interview with John Padwick, Organization of African Instituted Churches, at berkleycenter.georgetown.edu/interviews/ a-discussion-with-john-padwick-organization-of-african-instituted-churches.
15 See World Council of Churches, *Lead Us Not Into Temptation* (Geneva, Switzerland, 31 December 2001), www.oikoumene.org/fileadmin/files/wcc-main/ documents/p3/lead_us_not_into_temptation.pdf.; and Katherine Marshall and Marisa van Saanen, Chapter 16, in *Development and Faith: When Mind, Heart, and Soul Work Together* (Washington, DC: The World Bank, 2007), 195–208.
16 www.eni.ch/featured/article.php?id=4991.
17 Prominent among these was the joint WEF Georgetown University Report: *Islam and the West: Annual Report on the State of Dialogue*, 2008, berkley center.georgetown.edu/publications/islam-and-the-west-annual-report-on-the-state-of-dialogue.
18 www.acommonword.com.
19 www.oic-oci.org/home.asp.
20 www1.umn.edu/humanrts/instree/cairodeclaration.html.
21 This is a commentary cited in numerous sources, including, for example, forward.com/articles/7421/how-to-put-un-rights-council-back-on-track.
22 www.isdb.org/irj/portal/anonymous.
23 One of many books on the topic is Sulak Sivaraksa, *Conflict, Culture, Change: Engaged Buddhism in a Globalizing World* (Boston: Wisdom Publications, 2005).
24 www.jewishvirtuallibrary.org/jsource/Judaism/jewpop.html.
25 www.ajc.org/site/c.ijITI2PHKoG/b.789093/k.124/Who_We_Are.htm.

3 Religious movements in a globalized world

1 A large and growing body of scholarship and popular writings focus on new religions. Two useful guides to this broad category, focused on their religious dimensions, are James R. Lewis, *The Oxford Handbook of New Religious Movements* (New York: Oxford University Press, 2004); and the website of the Hartford Institute on Religion Research, hirr.hartsem.edu/ denom/new_religious_movements.html.

2 Catherine Ingram, *In the Footsteps of Gandhi: Conversations with Spiritual Social Activists* (Berkeley, CA: Parallax Press, 1990).
3 Cited in Katherine Marshall and Marisa Van Saanen, *Development and Faith: Where Mind, Heart, and Soul Work Together* (Washington, DC: The World Bank, 2007), 249.
4 Makarand Paranjape, ed., *Dharma and Development: The Future of Survival* (New Delhi: Samvad India Foundation, 2005) highlights several of the larger movements.
5 Some sources of general information include Paranjape, *Dharma in Development*; and Elizabeth Ferria, "Faith-based and Secular Humanitarian Organizations," *International Review of the Red Cross* 87 (June 2005): www.ikrk. org/eng/assets/files/other/irrc_858_ferris.pdf.
6 R.B. Williams, *A New Face of Hinduism: The Swaminarayan Religion* (Cambridge: Cambridge University Press,1984).
7 www.sathyasai.org/organize/content.htm.
8 An example of recent scholarship is Tulasi Srinivas, *Winged Faith: Rethinking Globalization and Religious Pluralism through the Sathya Sai Movement* (New York: Columbia University Press, 2010).
9 www.mahavidya.ca/wp-content/uploads/2010/08/Storoz-Kevin-Swaminarayan-Movement.pdf.
10 www.hinduwebsite.com/hinduism/sects/swaminarayana.asp.
11 www.vedantany.org/headquarters/http://www.belurmath.org/activities.htm.
12 www.artofliving.org/us-en/about-us/overview.
13 www.aolresearch.org/published_research.html.
14 www.newswiretoday.com/news/17261.
15 www.bkwsu.org.
16 forbesindia.com/article/third-anniversary-special/sadhguru-jaggi-vasudev-we-need-simple-and-direct-laws-that-limit-reliance-on-values-ethics/32926/1#ixzz1w0gC6UmZ.
17 www.ishafoundation.org/Health-Wellbeing/free-yoga-classes-mobile-medical-clinic-herbal-gardening-rural-rejuvenation.isa.
18 Ibid.
19 www.amritapuri.org/amma.
20 hinduism.about.com/cs/gurussaints/a/aa092803a.htm.
21 Marshall and Van Saanen, *Development and Faith*, 117–28.
22 www.sarvodaya.org.
23 articles.timesofindia.indiatimes.com/2011-04-01/india/29370168_1_mount-abu-ias-officer-haryana-police.
24 See, for example, Julia Day Howell, "Gender Role Experimentation in New Religious Movements: Clarification of the Brahma Kumari Case," *Journal for the Scientific Study of Religion* 37 (September 1998): 453–61.
25 www.dharmadrum.org.
26 See, for example, www.hrw.org/reports/2002/china.
27 Lorna Gold and Dimitrij Bregant, "Case Study: The Focolare Movement—Evangelization and Contemporary Culture," *International Review of Mission* 92 (January 2003): 27.
28 Donald W. Mitchell, "The Focolare Movement and a Buddhist-Christian Dialogue of 'Deeds and Collaboration'," *Buddhist-Christian Studies* (University of Hawai'i Press, 1985): 195.
29 Gold and Bregant, "Case Study: The Focolare Movement," 23.

30 Amelia J. Uelmen, "Caritas in Veritate and Chiara Lubich: Human Development from the Vantage Point of Unity," *Theological Studies* 71 (March 2010): 41.
31 www.nobelprize.org/nobel_prizes/peace/laureates/1979/teresa-bio.html/.
32 www.motherteresa.org/layout.html.
33 Mary Loudon, "The Missionary Position: Mother Teresa in Theory and Practice, Book Review," *BMJ* 312 (6 January 1996): 64–65.
34 www.bbc.co.uk/news/world-asia-15933481.
35 See, for example, the article published by the Guttmacher Institute: Jeremy Shiffman, *Political Management in the Indonesian Family Planning Program*, March 2004, www.guttmacher.org/pubs/journals/3002704.html.
36 Gulen Movement, "Education," www.gulenmovement.us/gulen-movement/education.
37 Edward Stourton, "What is Islam's Gulen Movement?" BBC, www.bbc.co.uk/news/world-13503361.
38 Gulen Movement, "Short Description of the Movement," www.gulenmovement.us/gulen-movement/short-description-of-the-movement.
39 Bulent Aras and Omer Caha, "Fethullah Gulen and his Liberal 'Turkish Islam' Movement," *Middle East Review of International Affairs* 4 (2000): 30.
40 Leslie Stahl, "US Charter Schools Tied to Powerful Turkish Imam," *60 Minutes*, 13 May 2012, www.cbsnews.com/video/watch/?id=7408418n&tag=contentBody;storyMediaBox.
41 Mohamed Nawab and Mohamed Osman, "Gulen Educational Philosophy: Striving for the Golden Generation of Muslims," 19 October 2010, www.fethullahgulen.org/conference-papers/323-gulen-conference-in-indonesia/3712-gulens-educational-philosophy-striving-for-the-golden-generation-of-muslims.
42 Aras and Caha, "Fethullah Gulen," 34.
43 "An Insider View to Success of Fethullah Gulen Inspired Schools: 'The Teacher Factor'," 2 July 2010, www.fethullah-gulen.net/gulen-schools/insider-view.
44 Council on Foreign Relations backgrounder, www.cfr.org/japan/aum-shinrikyo/p9238.
45 Victore Turner and Edith Turner, *Image and Pilgrimage in Christian Culture: Anthropological Perspectives* (New York: Columbia University Press, 1978), 6.
46 Walter Porges, "The Clergy, the Poor, and the Non-combatants on the First Crusade," *Speculum: A Journal of Mediaeval Studies* 21 (1946): 1.
47 James H. Foard, "The Boundaries of Compassion: Buddhism and National Tradition," *The Journal of Asian Studies* 41 (1982): 232.
48 Ibid., 231.
49 Agehananda Bharati, "Pilgrimage in the Indian Tradition," *History of Religions* 3 (1963): 161–62.
50 Ibid., 136.
51 Turner and Turner, *Image and Pilgrimage*, 38.
52 Basharat Peer, "Modern Mecca: The Transformation of a Holy City," *The New Yorker* (16 April 2012): 76.
53 C. Bawa Yamba, *Permanent Pilgrims: The Role of Pilgrimage in the Lives of West African Muslims in Sudan* (Washington, DC: Smithsonian Institution Press, 1995), 181.
54 Barbara Cooper, "The Strength in the Song: Muslim Personhood, Audible Capital, and Hausa Women's Performance of the Hajj," *Social Text* 60 (1999).

55 Malcolm X, and Alex Haley, *The Autobiography of Malcolm X* (New York: Ballantine, 1964), 348.
56 David Clingingsmith, Asim Ijaz Khwaja, and Michael Kremer, "Estimating the Impact of the Hajj: Religion and Tolerance in Islam's Global Gathering," *Quarterly Journal of Economics* (August 2009): 1133–70.
57 Peer, "Modern Mecca."
58 S. Coleman, "Do You Believe in Pilgrimage? Communitas, Contestation and Beyond," *Anthropological Theory* 2 (2002): 357; see also John Eade and Michael J. Sallnow, *Contesting the Sacred: The Anthropology of Christian Pilgrimage* (Champaign, IL: University of Illinois Press, 1991).

4 Interfaith encounters: Institutions, approaches, and questions

 1 Kung has stated this belief in many places and forms. This formulation is from a 2010 Telerama interview with Hans Küng, "An Idealist Without Illusions," www.parliamentofreligions.org/news/index.php/2010/08/hans-kung-an-idealist-without-illusions.
 2 Zoroastrians believe that all religions are equal, and that their religion is not superior to other religions; they do not accept converts. Zoroastrianism has encouraged interfaith action from the time of Cyrus the Great's speech in Babylon, permitting the population to follow their own religion and speak their own language. No state religion was enforced. Cyrus freed Jewish slaves from Babylon, earning him a place in the Jewish scriptures.
 3 Marcus Braybrooke, *Pilgrimage of Hope: One Hundred Years of Global Interfaith Dialogue* (New York: Crossroad, 1992), 1.
 4 Cited in Ibid., 13.
 5 Ibid., 29.
 6 Ibid., 79.
 7 See interview with former Pax Christi Secretary-General Etienne de Jonghe for a narrative of Pax Christi's history and the nature of its work, at berkley center.georgetown.edu/interviews/a-discussion-with-etienne-de-jonghe-former-secretary-general-pax-christi.
 8 Hans Küng has made the Global Ethic a centerpiece of his work. See *Global Responsibility: In Search of a New World Ethic* (Eugene: OR, Wipf and Stock Publishers, 2004).
 9 For a history by one of the founders, see Jack Homer, *WCRP: A History of the World Conference on Religion and Peace* (New York: World Conference on Religion and Peace, 1993).
10 See, for example, Religions for Peace, *Millennium Development Goals Toolkit for Religious Leaders*, religionsforpeace.org/resources/toolkits/faith-in-action.html.
11 www.vatican.va/holy_father/john_paul_ii/speeches/1986/october/documents/hf_jp-ii_spe_19861027_prayer-peace-assisi-final_en.html.
12 Successive events are detailed: www.santegidio.org/index.php?pageID=47&idLng=1064.
13 www.uri.org/about_uri.
14 www.imamsrabbisforpeace.org.
15 Braybrooke, *Pilgrimage of Hope*, 270–73.
16 Ibid.

17 Philip L. Berg, "Book Review: Science, Sin and Scholarship: The Politics of Reverend Moon and the Unification Church," *Journal for the Scientific Study of Religion* 18 (1979): 447.

18 Richard Bath, "Profile: Reverend Sun Myung Moon: Dark Side of the Moon," *Scotland on Sunday*, 18 October 2009.

19 Religion Counts produced a thoughtful analysis of religion at the UN in 2002: *Religion and Public Policy at the UN*. One of its areas of focus is the contentious political battles around reproductive health and rights and the effect these have had on attitudes towards religion within the UN system.

20 www.holyseemission.org.

21 Marie Juul Petersen, "International Religious NGOs at the United Nations: A Study of a Group of Religious Organizations," *Journal of Humanitarian Assistance* (November 2010), sites.tufts.edu/jha/archives/847#_ednref51.

22 www.earthcharterinaction.org/content.

23 A recent publication is *Exploring Synergies Between Faith Values and Education for Sustainable Development*, www.earthcharterinaction.org/invent/details.php?id=901.

24 See, for example, an interview with the author at berkleycenter.georgetown.edu/interviews/a-discussion-with-thoraya-obaid-executive-director-of-unfpa.

25 For more history about dialogue between world faiths and the World Bank, see Katherine Marshall and Lucy Keough, *Finding Global Balance: Common Ground Between the World of Development and Faith* (Washington, DC: World Bank, 2005); Katherine Marshall, "Development and Faith Institutions: Gulfs and Bridges," in *Religion and Development: Ways of Transforming the World*, ed. Gerrie Ter Haar (New York: Columbia University Press, 2011), 27–56; and Katherine Marshall, "Religion and Global Development: Intersecting Paths," in *Religious Pluralism, Globalization, and World Politics*, ed. Thomas Banchoff (New York: Oxford University Press, 2008).

26 Katherine Marshall and Richard Marsh, *Millennium Challenges for Development and Faith Institutions* (Washington, DC: The World Bank, 2003).

27 Katherine Marshall and Marisa van Saanen, Chapter 16, in *Development and Faith: When Mind, Heart, and Soul Work Together* (Washington, DC: The World Bank, 2007), 195–208.

5 Faith-inspired organizations at work

1 Personal communication to author.

2 The World Faiths Development Dialogue embarked on a review of faith-inspired work in Cambodia in 2007, expecting to find at least some information base and to complete the review in quite short order. Four years later it was clear that the task was far more complex than initially imagined. Organizations rarely share information with one another, much less the government and international organizations. Yet there is a wealth of knowledge and experience. See WFDD Cambodia portal, berkleycenter.georgetown.edu/wfdd/cambodia.

3 This chapter draws on the five-year, Henry R. Luce Foundation-funded religion and development project conducted by the Berkley Center for Religion, Peace, and World Affairs at Georgetown University. The full set of reports and interviews are available at berkleycenter.georgetown.edu/programs/religion-and-global-development.

4 See Barbara Ibrahim and Dina Sherif, eds., *From Charity to Social Change: Trends in Arab Philanthropy* (Cairo, Egypt: Gerhart Center for Philanthropy and Civic Engagement, American University of Cairo, 2009), www.aucegypt.edu/research/gerhart/rprogram/Pages/ReportsandPublications.aspx; also pertinent is Jon B. Alterman and Karin von Hippel, *Understanding Islamic Charities* (Washington, DC: CSIS, 2007).

5 See study commissioned for the UN Alliance of Civilizations (UNAOC) Thematic Platform on cooperation with and among faith-inspired actors in international humanitarian and development work, www.unaoc.org/wp-content/uploads/ThematicPlatformBridgingTheDividePB1.pdf, and www.unaoc.org/2012/02/report-on-a-survey-among-actors-in-the-field-of-humanitarianism-and-development.

6 Douglas Johnston and Cynthia Sampson, eds., *Religion: The Missing Dimension of Statecraft* (New York: Oxford University Press, 1995).

7 Samuel Huntington, "The Clash of Civilizations?" *Foreign Affairs* 72 (Summer 1993): 22–49.

8 The Berkley Center at Georgetown University and the United States Institute of Peace are engaged in a multi-year research program on this topic. See berkleycenter.georgetown.edu/projects/women-religion-and-peace-experience-perspectives-and-policy-implications.

6 Emerging issues and future directions

1 Jeffrey Harpham, "Human Rights in the Humanities," *The Chronicle of Higher Education* (23 July 2012), chronicle.com/article/Human-Rights-in-the-Humanities/132955.

2 Speech at the UN 4th World Conference on Women Plenary Session, Beijing, 5 September 1995, www.americanrhetoric.com/speeches/hillaryclintonbeijingspeech.htm.

3 While corruption is a common topic of sermons and prophetic critiques by leaders of many religious bodies, religious actors have played surprisingly limited roles in major transnational bodies fighting corruption. Reasons are many and include quite intimate association of some leaders with governmental and political bodies, concerns about honesty within faith institutions that can discourage full transparency, and limited engagement in defining and carrying out practical steps to combat corruption.

Select bibliography

There are libraries about religions, and an explosion of websites, electronic texts, databases, and other materials on which to draw. This list highlights texts and sources that are particularly pertinent to the global institutional dimensions of the vast world of religion.

Albright, Madeleine, *The Mighty and the Almighty: Reflections on America, God, and World Affairs* (New York: Harper, 2006). Former Secretary of State Madeleine Albright critiques the omission of religious factors in international affairs, arguing that this neglect has been and remains a critical impediment to effective policy making.

Armstrong, Karen, *The Battle for God* (New York: Ballantine Books, 2000). A bestseller post 9/11, this book explores the rise of modern religious fundamentalism. Armstrong explains the sources of Christian, Jewish, and Muslim fundamentalism, grounded above all in the tension between myth and reason, rooted as far back as the sixteenth century.

Barrett, David B., George T. Kurian, and Todd M. Johnson, *World Christian Encyclopedia: A Comparative Survey of Churches and Religions in the Modern World*, second edition (New York: Oxford University Press, 2001). See www.worldchristiandatabase.org. This monumental two-part encyclopedia covers contemporary Christianity worldwide in consideration of secularism; other faiths; and the social, economic, and political nature of diverse cultures. A scientific and theoretical work, heavy on statistics, it was prepared primarily by evangelical Christians, but is nonetheless recognized as one of the most authoritative sources of data on all religious traditions.

Berger, Peter, *The Desecularization of the World* (Grand Rapids, MI: Eerdmans Publishing, 1999). Once a prominent secularization theorist (see *The Sacred Canopy: Elements of a Sociological Theory of Knowledge*), Peter Berger argues for an appreciation of the resurgence of religion in this edited volume.

The Berkley Center for Religion, Peace, and World Affairs, berkleycenter.georgetown.edu (n.d.). The Berkley Center for Religion, Peace, and World Affairs at Georgetown University explores the intersection of religion and international affairs. The center's website and accompanying online database include the Center's research and a broad collection of resources regarding religion in the public sphere. These include some 200 interviews with (primarily) practitioners whose work is linked in various ways to religion.

Eck, Diana, *A New Religious America: How a Christian Country has become the World's Most Diverse Nation* (San Francisco, CA: Harper, 2002). This book describes the explosion of religious pluralism in the United States, with particular attention to Muslim, Hindu, and Buddhist populations. As the leader of the Pluralism Project at Harvard University, Diana Eck offers insight into the religious diversity of the United States, and the challenges and opportunities it presents through ethnographies across the country.

Huntington, Samuel, "The Clash of Civilizations?" *Foreign Affairs* 72 (Summer 1993): 22–49. In this widely cited, acclaimed, and criticized article, Huntington describes the future of international conflict as tension between the civilizations of the "Western" and "non-Western" worlds. He characterizes civilization as a composite of values and beliefs with regard to authority, liberty, rights, responsibilities, and God—citing the resurgence of religion as a critical element in the forthcoming clash. His book with a similar title, *The Clash of Civilizations and the Remaking of World Order* (1998), elaborates on the arguments.

Jenkins, Philip, *The Next Christendom: The Coming of Global Christianity* (New York: Oxford University Press, 2002). The first in a trilogy about contemporary Christianity, this seminal work describes the historical roots of Christianity in Africa, Asia, and Latin America and its rapid contemporary growth. It characterizes the unique nature of this "new" Christianity and the impact that it will have on global politics.

Johnston, Douglas, *Religion, Terror, and Error: U.S. Foreign Policy and the Challenge of Spiritual Engagement* (Santa Barbara, CA: Praeger, 2011). This work argues for the importance of cultural considerations in US foreign policy and provides prescriptions for how the country might face this challenge. It describes how the United States should approach the causes of religious extremism; includes a model of decision making that integrates "irrational" factors, including religion; and provides a new perspective for US leadership in the evolving multi-polar world.

Johnston, Douglas and Cynthia Sampson, eds., *Religion: The Missing Dimension of Statecraft* (New York: Oxford University Press, 1995). This edited volume argues for the consideration of religion in the construction of effective international diplomacy. Sponsored by the Center for Strategic and International Studies, it includes case studies that demonstrate the critical impact of analysis of the spiritual and religious dimension in conflict prevention and non-violent social change.

Juergensmeyer, Mark and Wade Clark Roof, eds., *Encyclopedia of Global Religion* (Los Angeles, CA: Sage Publications, 2012). This multi-volume encyclopedia covers the nature of religion in society historically and contemporarily in every country around the world. The work covers the diversity and dispersion of religious practices in conversation with a multicultural world.

Marshall, Katherine, "Religion and Global Development: Intersecting Paths," in *Religious Pluralism, Globalization, and World Politics*, ed. Thomas Banchoff (New York: Oxford University Press, 2008). This chapter explores the role of faith-inspired institutions in social development, with particular attention to the cases of the Catholic Caritas International, Protestant World Vision, and Islamic Relief. The piece describes trends of faith-based development initiatives of increasing breadth of international action and depth of development objectives—from health care to women's rights and human trafficking.

——"Development, Religion, and Women's Roles in Contemporary Societies," *The Review of Faith & International Affairs* 8, no. 4 (2010): 33–40. This article examines the intersection of religion and gender development describing tensions, overlap, and potential for collaboration regarding female genital cutting, domestic violence, preference for male offspring, family planning, child marriage, rape in war and conflict, sex trafficking, and HIV/AIDS.

Marshall, Katherine and Marisa Van Saanen, *Development and Faith: Where Mind, Heart, and Soul Work Together* (Washington, DC: The World Bank, 2007). This book explores the provision of social change and social services by faith actors. It explores the history and potential for collaboration between secular and faith-based development institutions with particular reference to the Millennium Development Goals as an agenda for action.

Micklethwait, John and Adrian Wooldridge, *God is Back: How the Global Revival of Faith is Changing the World* (New York: Penguin Books, 2009). This book is part of the growing set of publications that argue for the importance of the religious resurgence in society and international affairs. It highlights cases ranging from US "megachurches," to Islam in Nigeria, and growing Christianity in China, among others.

The Pew Forum on Religion & Public Life, www.pewforum.org. The Pew Forum on Religion & Public Life is an arm of the Pew Research Center which investigates religion and public affairs domestically and internationally. The Pew website includes the reports and data from their various studies providing surveys, demographic analyses, and other forms of social science research.

Toft, Monica Duffy, Daniel Philpott, and Timothy Samuel Shah, *God's Century: Resurgent Religion and Global Politics* (New York: W.W. Norton, 2011). This book offers an analysis of how and why religion's role in global politics has escalated and the challenges and the opportunities of this relationship. The authors explore the diverse impact of religion through theoretical analysis and case studies.

Willetts, Peter, *Non-Governmental Organizations in World Politics: The Construction of Global Governance* (New York: Routledge, 2011). This volume in the Routledge Global Institutions series describes the role of non-governmental organizations in global politics. The book details a number of NGOs, large and small, and their interaction with social movements, civil society, the United Nations, international law, and international policy making.

World Faiths Development Dialogue, berkleycenter.georgetown.edu/wfdd.

The World Faiths Development Dialogue (WFDD) is an independent policy research organization originally founded at the World Bank, which explores the intersection of religion and international development. WFDD's website makes available all of the organization's research, including practitioner interviews and publications, covering a range of topics: health, climate change, education, aid coordination, gender, and human rights. The site features a special focus section on Cambodia, where WFDD has been engaged in a multi-year country study to map the faith and development landscape.

Zelizer, Craig, *Integrated Peacebuilding: Innovative Approaches to Transforming Conflict* (New York: Westview Press, 2013). This volume includes a chapter on religious peacebuilding.

Index

Abdallah II, King of Jordan 111,
    149, 185
Abrahamic faiths see Christianity;
    Islam; Judaism
advocacy 6, 45; EAA 45; FBO 8;
    FIO 45, 154, 157, 158, 165, 167,
    174; religious movement 106, 115,
    122, 124
Afghanistan 21, 31, 32, 52
Africa 37, 70, 176; African
    independent churches 66, 72;
    demography 36, 37–38, 40, 41, 42;
    FIO 176; Hope for Africa's
    Children 139; IFAPA 136, 143;
    indigenous religious traditions 38;
    Prayer for Peace 140; religious/
    political authority relationship 10
Aga Khan 77, 78, 81, 158, 165;
    AKDN 81, 158, 165–66
    (development 165–66; education
    158, 165; volunteer 165)
AJWS (American Jewish World
    Service) 158, 164–65; advocacy
    165; development 164; poverty
    alleviation 164
Al Qaeda 7, 45, 75, 97, 117, 122
Allen, John 62
Anglican Communion/Church of
    England 45, 52, 66, 67, 77;
    colonial era 67; Episcopal Church
    66, 67; gender issues 68;
    governance 44–45, 67, 68
    (Anglican Consultative Council
    68; Lambeth Conferences 68);
    Henry VIII, King 67; HIV/AIDS
    68; interfaith dialogue 134, 144;

religion and state 52, 67 (state
    religion 52); transnational
    character 67–68; Trinity Wall
    Street Foundation 67; UK 12, 19,
    52, 67; UN 68; women 68; see also
    Anglican Communion,
    Archbishop of Canterbury;
    Protestantism
Anglican Communion, Archbishop
    of Canterbury 67, 68, 78, 134,
    144; Building Bridges Dialogue
    144; Carey, George 78, 151, 191;
    Runcie, Robert 134; see also
    Anglican Communion
apostasy 20
Armstrong, Karen 31, 32
Asia: Asia Indigenous People's Pact
    90; demography 36, 40, 41, 42, 83;
    FIO 176
assessment: FIO 173, 183; interfaith
    dialogue 132
atheism 33, 91, 94, 137; see also
    Humanism
authority 9; Islam 10, 11–12, 29, 78;
    religious/political authority
    relationship 10–12, 15–18, 29, 51,
    78; religious/secular authority
    distinction 9, 15; see also
    Archbishop of Canterbury under
    Anglican Communion, governance;
    Catholic Church, Pope

Bahá'í Faith 50, 84, 88–89, 131–32,
    143, 171; Bahá'u'lláh 88, 89;
    demography 41, 42, 88;
    governance 89; human rights 88;

interfaith dialogue 88, 131–32;
Israel 88–89; religious freedom 88;
UN 84, 88; Universal House of
Justice 89; women 84, 88
Berger, Peter 31, 47
blasphemy 20, 23
Boko Haram 45, 97
Bono (Paul David Hewson) 151
Brazil 21, 53, 56–58, 74; Catholicism
56, 57; Evangelical Church 57, 70;
pluralism 56; religion and state 21,
53, 57; religious freedom 57;
syncretism 56; tolerance 56
Brooks, David 31, 186
Buddhism 52, 82–84; Buddhist-
inspired movement 83, 94,
106–11; Buddhist Sangha 45;
Dalai Lama 55, 83, 137; Dharma
Drum Mountain 83, 109; Engaged
Buddhism 7, 45, 83, 108 (Nhat
Hahn, Thich 83); faith 4; FIO
176; global religious institution
50, 83–84; governance 50, 82–84
(decentralization 83); lay
movement 83; Mahayana
Buddhism 83, 107; peacebuilding
35; Sangha 83; Siddhartha
Gautama 83; state religion 52;
Theravada Buddhism 83;
transnational character 50, 83, 94;
WBSC 83–84; WFB 83; *see also*
Buddhism, countries
Buddhism, countries: Cambodia 20,
52; China 55; demography 37, 40,
83; India 53, 54, 83; Japan 83,
106–9; Sri Lanka 52, 83, 179;
Taiwan 83, 109–10; Thailand 26,
52, 83; US 83

Cambodia 19, 52, 109, 112, 154,
174; religion and state 20, 52;
WFDD 201
Caritas Internationalis 8, 156, 157,
158–60, 182; CAFOD 157, 158,
164; CRS 157, 158; governance
159; Misereor 157, 158; poverty
alleviation 158, 159–60; *see also*
Catholic Church
Catholic Church/Catholicism 59–60;
charity 169–70; the Crusades

28–29, 125; education 63, 64, 111,
112; human rights 28, 147, 190;
Inquisition 12, 18; interfaith
dialogue 113, 134, 135–36,
139–41; missionary purpose 66;
peacebuilding 35, 157; religion
and state 52, 57 (religious/political
authority relationship 10, 11, 12,
33; state religion 52); religious
institution 50, 65; Treaty of
Westphalia 16; women 28, 61, 64;
see also following Catholic
Church *entries*
Catholic Church, countries: Brazil
56, 57; demography 35, 40, 57, 60;
England 12, 67; Latin America
19–20; US 61, 111, 115
Catholic Church, governance 6, 50,
59–65; Canon law 62, 63; Eastern
Catholic Churches 64–65;
hierarchical structure 6, 44, 50, 60,
61–63; Holy See 50, 60, 111 (UN
147–48, 190); Pontifical Councils
63–64; Roman Curia/New Curia
623, 134; transnational character
6, 50; Vatican II Council 63, 140;
Vatican City 52, 60, 158, 159; *see
also* Catholic Church, Pope;
Catholic religious order
Catholic Church, movements/
organizations 111–16; Focolare
movement 7, 65, 111, 113–14
(Lubich, Chiara 113, 114); lay
movement 45, 65, 108, 111, 112,
113, 114, 115, 136, 140;
Liberation Theology movement
57, 94; Maryknoll organizations
111, 115; Missionaries of Charity
111, 114–15 (Mother Teresa
114–15); Opus Dei 45, 65, 73, 111,
115–16; Pax Christi 136, 180, 181;
see also Caritas Internationalis;
CRS; Jesuit Order; Prayer for
Peace; Sant' Egidio community
Catholic Church, Pope 29, 33,
61–63; Alexander VI 57; Benedict
XVI 76, 144; Clement XIV 112;
election 62–63; Innocent III 11;
Innocent X 16; John XXIII 113;
John Paul II 135, 139, 159–60;

Leo XIII 134; Paul VI 134; Pius VII 112; Urban II 125; *see also* Catholic Church, governance
Catholic religious order 60, 64, 94; Benedictines 64; Dominican Order 64; Franciscans 64; Knights of Malta 60–61; Missionaries of Charity 111, 114–15; Sisters of Charity 64; *see also* Jesuit Order
Charismatic church 6, 42, 56, 66, 70; Saddleback Church 70; transnational character 70; *see also* Protestantism
charity 160, 168–71; Charity Navigator 166; Christianity 169–70; Islam 81, 122, 155, 163, 170 (*zakat, sadaqah, waqf* 155, 164, 170); Judaism 169; Middle Ages 169; Missionaries of Charity 111, 114–15; Sisters of Charity 64; *see also* development; poverty
child: Brazil, Pastoral da Criança 57; ChildFund International 158, 166; Compassion International 158, 166–67; FIO 158, 160, 161, 162, 166, 167, 174 (orphan care 175–76); France 73; Hope for Africa's Children 139; Sarvodaya Movement 105; UNICEF 82, 138, 151, 190; World Vision 158, 160, 161, 162
ChildFund International/Christian Children's Fund 158, 166; Clarke, J. Calvitt 166
China 30; Buddhism 55; Christianity 55; Communism/Communist Party 55, 110, 111; Confucianism 55; Falun Gong/Falun Dafa 55, 110–11; indigenous religious traditions 55; Islam 55; NGO 55; Orthodox Church 55; proselytizing 55; religion and state 11, 53, 55–56; SARA 56; Taoism 55
Christian Green, M. 20, 27
Christianity 6; Bible 144, 160, 166, 169; charity 169–70; China 55; demography 37, 40, 55; FIO 168, 172; India 53–54; Middle Ages 11, 64, 124, 169; NGO 148, 179; pilgrimage 124–25; proselytizing

43, 111, 170; Roman Empire 11, 12, 13, 15, 196; shift of gravity beyond Europe and North America 6, 10, 37–38; state religion 196; *see also* Catholic Church; Orthodox Church; Protestantism
civil society 1, 148, 151, 182, 194; religious institution 44, 46; *see also* NGO
clash of civilizations: Chinese society 30; globalization 30, 39; Huntington, Samuel 2, 30–31, 39, 75–76; Islam 30, 75–76; religion 30, 181; UNAOC 148–49; "Western" vs. "non-Western" world 9–10, 30; *see also* conflict
colonial era 54, 99, 119, 178; exclusivism 12; Protestantism 66, 67, 69, 72
Communism 14, 18, 19, 104, 134, 185; China 55, 110, 111; *see also* Marxism
Compassion International 158, 166–67, 168; child support and advocacy group 158, 166–67; Swanson, Everett 167
conflict 33–34, 184, 186; conflict among religious traditions 7, 129, 130, 131, 139, 153; conflict and social/economic development 177, 178, 181; conflict prevention 177, 180, 183; conflict resolution 177, 180–81, 183; FIO 155, 176–81, 182, 183; Israel–Palestine conflict 29, 76, 81, 86, 124; Middle East 29, 78, 135, 186; Nigeria 34; religion as source of 1, 5, 8, 28, 33, 155, 177, 180, 183 (religious/political authority relationship 11, 15–16); religious actor 177, 178, 180–81 (ignored 180, 182, 183; excluded from negotiations 180); religious/political ambiguous nature of 28, 34, 54; religiously inspired violence 10, 29, 33–34; Sri Lanka 34, 178–79, 189; women 181; *see also* clash of civilizations; human security; Islam, conflict and tensions; peace; terrorism

Confucianism 41, 42, 55
conversion 11, 13, 22, 23, 25, 34, 39,
    43; *see also* proselytizing
corruption 105, 128, 163, 187, 191, 202
CRS (Catholic Relief Services) 44,
    49, 157, 172; Caritas
    Internationalis 157, 158;
    humanitarian relief 157;
    peacebuilding 157; US 157
cult/sect 70, 72–73, 77, 93, 111; Aum
    Shinrikyo 72, 97, 106, 123; France
    72–73; Jones, Jim 72; Order of the
    Solar Temple 72; Quiverfull 72

democracy 29, 53, 87, 96, 197;
    Gulen Movement 120; human
    rights 27; Indonesia 58, 120
Democratic Republic of the Congo
    22, 24, 154
demography 6, 10, 13, 35–44, 184;
    Africa 36, 37–38, 40, 41, 42; Asia
    36, 40, 41, 42, 83; Bahá'í Faith 41,
    42, 88; Buddhism 37, 40, 83;
    Catholic Church 35, 40, 57, 60;
    changing religious demography
    10, 38, 47; Christianity 37, 40, 55;
    Confucianism 41, 42; data on 6,
    35, 37; Europe 36, 37, 40, 41;
    growth rate 37, 38; Hinduism 37,
    40; Humanism 91; indigenous
    religious traditions 38, 89;
    institutional confidence 44; Islam
    35, 36, 37, 39, 40, 55, 58, 75;
    Judaism 13, 39, 41, 42, 86–87;
    major world religious
    communities 36, 37–38, 40;
    Orthodox Church 40;
    Protestantism 40, 65, 69, 70;
    religious adherence 37, 43, 55, 69,
    88; SBNR 33; shift of gravity
    beyond Europe and North
    America 6, 10, 37–38; smaller
    world religions 38, 41, 42; South
    America 36, 37, 40, 41, 42; US 33,
    36; World Values Surveys 35–36;
    Zoroastrianism 88
development: conflict and social/
    economic development 177, 178,
    181; FIO 45, 156, 158, 159, 163,
    164, 168, 172, 173, 176, 183;

interfaith dialogue 7, 151;
    proselytizing 189; role of religion
    5, 191; World Vision 158, 161; *see
    also* charity; poverty
disarmament 108, 180
discrimination 12, 21, 23, 24, 25, 46;
    nondiscrimination 28

Eck, Diana 33
economic issues 190; AKDN 166;
    donation 158, 160, 161, 164,
    188–89; financial flows 156, 187;
    funding 105, 135, 138, 167, 168,
    174; terrorism 187
ecumenical movement/organization
    45, 50, 74–75, 135–43, 152;
    Focolare movement 113;
    missionary purpose 74;
    proselytizing 74–75; World Vision
    161; *see also* interfaith dialogue
education 5, 154, 185; academic
    institutions 45–46; Catholic
    Church 63, 64, 111, 112; Dharma
    Drum Mountain 109; FIO 155,
    158, 175; higher education/
    university 55, 144, 180, 202; India
    54, 100; Islam 80 (AKDN 81;
    Al-Azhar University 46, 78;
    Gulen Movement 121; ISESCO
    79; Islamophobia 76;
    Muhammadiyah movement 118;
    NU 119); peace studies and
    religion 180; religious illiteracy 2,
    31, 152, 184, 185; Sarvodaya
    Movement 105; seminary 44, 45;
    Union Theological Seminary 46
Egypt 59, 121, 122; Al-Azhar
    University 46, 78; Khaled, Amr
    116–18; Muslim Brotherhood 94,
    116, 121–22; religion and state 18,
    22, 52
Enlightenment 16–17, 18, 27
environmental issues 62, 100, 101,
    104, 110; Alliance of Religions
    and Conservation 139; climate
    change 6, 130, 142, 143, 194;
    Dharma Drum Mountain 109;
    Earth Charter 131, 150; interfaith
    dialogue 130, 131, 139, 142, 143,
    150; URI 142

Ethiopia 22, 71–72, 139; Ethiopian
Orthodox Church 71; Ethiopian
Orthodox Tewahedo Church 71
Europe: demography 36, 37, 40, 41;
EU and religion/religious
institution 8, 185, 190; European
Humanist Federation 92; FIO 176;
religion and state 51; religious
freedom 51; "reverse missionary"
trend 70; secularism 2, 31
Evangelical Church 6, 32, 42, 48, 70;
Brazil 57, 70; human rights 28,
147, 190; Micah Challenge 70;
Morocco, inter-faith initiative 145;
NAE 161; National Evangelical
Alliance 145; proselytizing 145;
WEA 70; World Evangelical
Fellowship 70; *see also*
Protestantism; World Vision
exclusivism 2, 11, 12, 34
extremism 32, 123, 181; Aum
Shinrikyo 72, 97, 106, 123; causal
factors 39; a contemporary trend
6, 10, 32, 39, 184; Hezbollah 97,
123–24, 171; human rights 28;
violence 29, 39; *see also* Al Qaeda;
fundamentalism

faith 3, 4, 5; *see also* religion;
spirituality
FBO (faith-based organization) 5, 8,
34, 43, 45; advocacy 8; political
role 45; US 46; *see also* FIO; NGO
Finland 59; Evangelical Lutheran
Church 52, 59; Finnish Orthodox
Church 52, 59; religion and state
52, 53, 59
FIO (faith-inspired organization) 5,
45, 155–56, 175; Africa 176; Asia
176; assessment 173, 183;
categorization 154, 155–57;
Christianity 168, 172; conflict/
conflict resolution 155, 176–81,
182, 183; diversity 155–56, 157,
172, 173; Europe 176; "faith-
inspired" dimension 172–73, 174;
global institutions 155, 156,
157–74, 176, 182; Islam 168, 176;
Judaism 168; MDGs 156–57, 172,
183; NGO 156, 168, 179, 182,

189; peacebuilding 155, 157, 177,
180, 181, 183; proselytizing 172;
regional perspectives 176;
relationship with national/
community entities 155, 157, 172,
173, 176, 182; *see also following*
FIO *entries*; FBO; inter-/intra-faith
movement/organization; NGO;
religious movement
FIO, examples: ADRA 167, 168;
Habitat for Humanity 167, 168;
Pax Christi 136, 180, 181; Qatar
Foundation 171; Red Crescent
171; Salvation Army 167–68, 172;
Samaritan's Purse 168; *see also*
AJWS; AKDN *under* Aga Khan;
Caritas Internationalis;
ChildFund International;
Compassion International; CRS;
Islamic Relief; World Vision
FIO, major areas of action 153, 154,
172, 173–75, 181–82; advocacy 45,
154, 157, 158, 165, 167, 174; child
158, 160, 161, 162, 166, 167, 174
(orphan care 175–76); development
45, 156, 158, 159, 163, 164, 168,
172, 173, 176, 183; education 155,
158, 175; health 155, 163, 175;
HIV/AIDS 175; humanitarian
relief 45, 156, 157, 164, 171–72,
179, 182, 183; youth 175
France 73; 1905 Law 18; cult 72–73;
French Revolution 16–17, 18; *laïcité*
principle 18; Order of the Solar
Temple 72; Raffarin, Jean-Pierre
73; religion, role in society 18;
secular state 16, 18; *une foi, une
loi, un roi* 15
Francis of Assisi, St 139
fundamentalism 2, 39; causal factors
39, 184; a contemporary trend 6,
10, 32, 39, 184; globalization 2,
30, 39; religious identity 39;
transnational character 10; *see
also* extremism

G8/G20 129, 130
Gandhi, Mahatma 34, 94, 97, 105
gender issues 33, 181, 186; Anglican
Communion 68; gender equality

20, 28, 186–87; gender rights 28, 188; religious freedom 8; UN 28, 148 (UNFPA 149, 150); *see also* women

Germany 19, 96, 140, 157, 158

Glendon, Mary Anne 27

global religious institution 44–45, 48–92, 93, 184, 191; Bahá'í Faith 83; Buddhism 50, 83–84; Catholic Church 50, 59–65; church/state relationship 49–50; competition 92; complexity 49, 50, 92; ecumenical movement/ organization 45, 50, 74–75; FIO 155, 156, 157–74, 176, 182; governance 49, 50–51; Humanism 91–92; Islam 50, 77–82; Judaism 50, 84, 87–88; legitimacy 92; Orthodox Church 6, 50, 71–72; partnership 49; Protestantism 6, 50, 65–71, 74; Sikhism 84; transnational character 5, 6, 50, 84, 92; Zoroastrianism 84; *see also* governance; religion, global impact; religion and state; religious institution

globalization 10, 124; clash of civilizations 30, 39; fundamentalism 2, 30, 39; influence on religious institutions 48–49, 84, 184; migration/ diaspora 9, 13, 48, 54; missionary purpose of churches 66; pilgrimage 75, 98, 124, 125, 127; pluralism 184; religious institution 48–49, 84, 184; religious leader/ organization as globalizer 9, 54; religious responses to 2, 30, 39, 75, 114, 129–30

governance 49–51, 185; Bahá'í Faith 89; Buddhism 50, 82–84; complexity 49, 50; global governance 148, 152, 185, 189–94; Hinduism 50, 84; humanism 51, 91–92; indigenous religious community 50–51, 89–90; Judaism 14, 87; Orthodox Church 6, 50, 71–72; Paganism 51, 90–91; religious institution, overlapping 49; religious movement 94; *see*

also Catholic Church, governance; global religious institution; Islam, governance; MDGs; Protestantism, denominations and governance; religion and state; UN; World Bank; World Economic Forum

health 5, 154, 155, 169; BAPS 100; Christian hospital 169; FIO 155, 163, 175; Missionaries of Charity 114, 115; NU 119; Ramakrishna Mission 100; reproductive health 148, 149, 150, 154, 159, 175, 186 (and human rights 28, 147, 150, 165, 188, 190, 192, 201); TIMA 110; WCC 74; *see also* HIV/AIDS

Henry R. Luce Foundation 3

heresy 11, 16, 110

Hezbollah 97, 123–24, 171

Hinduism 53, 84, 98; Acharyas 84; Art of Living 45, 94; demography 37, 40; India 53, 54, 84; Nepal 52; new branches 50; organizations 50, 84; political party 84 (Bharatiya Janata Party 84); transnational character 50

HIV/AIDS 154, 175; African independent churches 72; Anglican Communion 68; Caritas Internationalis 159; EAA 45; FIO 175; Islam 154, 163; Missionaries of Charity 114; Religions for Peace 139; UNAIDS 151, 175; WCC 74; *see also* health

human rights 5, 27–28, 184, 188; Bahá'í Faith 88; Catholic Church 28, 147, 190; Evangelical Church 28, 147, 190; extremism 28; Falun Gong/Falun Dafa 110–11; "great awakening" of religion 27; "human rights imperialism" 30; human rights revolution 27–28; Islam 27, 28, 147, 190 (Cairo Declaration of Human Rights in Islam 79–80); law 20, 27; Maritain, Jacques 188; power struggle around 28, 30; religious freedom 8, 20, 27; reproductive health and human rights 28, 147,

150, 165, 188, 190, 192, 201; a source of religious/ethnic conflict 28; Universal Declaration of Human Rights 8, 9, 20, 27, 80, 147, 188; universality 30, 188; women's rights 5, 28, 81, 84, 88, 147, 188, 190; *see also* gender issues; religious freedom
human security: rebuilding 5, 34; reconciliation 5, 34, 139 (FIO 177, 178, 179, 180, 182; MRA 96); role of religion 5, 8, 10, 34; "shared security" 139; *see also* conflict; peace; peacebuilding/peacemaking
Humanism 51, 91–92, 94; CODESH 90; demography 91; European Humanist Federation 92; IHEU 91, 92; transnational character 91; Unitarian Universalist Association 92; US 91–92; *see also* atheism
humanitarian relief 5, 7; BAPS 100; FIO 45, 156, 157, 164, 171–72, 179, 182, 183; IAHV 102; Islamic Relief 163, 172; proselytizing 189; Soka Gokkai 108; Tzu Chi Foundation 110; World Mate 109; *see also* Knights of Malta
Huntington, Samuel, "clash of civilizations" 2, 30–31, 39, 75–76

identity *see* religious identity
IFAPA (Interfaith Action for Peace in Africa) 136, 143; Noko, Ishmael 143; Women's Desk 143; Youth Desk 143; *see also* interfaith dialogue; Protestantism
IMF (International Monetary Fund) 74; Camdessus, Michel 190; Koehler, Horst 190; WCC/World Bank/ IMF dialogue 74, 131, 152–53
India 2, 53–54; Buddhism 53, 54, 83; Christianity 53–54; education 54, 100; Hinduism 53, 54, 84; Islam 53, 54; Jainism 53, 54; law 54; leader/*sampradaya* 99, 101–2, 103–5; NGO 99, 101, 102; pilgrimage 125; pluralism 53; religion and state 53–54; religious freedom 54; religious identity 53;
secularism 53, 54; Sikhism 53, 54; tolerance 53, 54; UN 99, 101, 102, 103; Zoroastrianism 88; *see also* India, religious movements
India, religious movements 97–105; Amma, the "Hugging Saint" 99, 104–5; Brahma Kumaris 54, 99, 102–3, 106, 174 (Kripilani, Janki/ Dadi Janki 103); Hare Krishna movement 54; Ramakrishna Mission 99, 100, 106; Sadhguru Jaggi Vasudev 99, 103–4 (Isha Foundation 99, 104); Sathya Sai Baba 99; Svadhyay movement 99, 100–101 (Athavale, Pandurang Shasatri/Dada Ji 101); Swaminarayan movement 99–100 (BAPS 100); *see also* Sri Sri Ravi Shankar
indigenous religious traditions 89–90; Africa 38; Asia Indigenous People's Pact 90; China 55; demography 38, 89; governance 50–51, 89–90; Guatemala 42; interfaith dialogue 135, 137; polytheism 90; proselytizing 43, 50; UN 51, 90 (UN Permanent Forum on Indigenous Affairs 90); URI 142; World Council of Indigenous Peoples 89–90
Indonesia 52, 58, 120; Muhammadiyah 94, 116, 118–19, 172; NU 94, 116, 119–20; *Pancasila* 58, 120
interfaith dialogue 80, 129, 131–32, 133, 153; 2005 Alexandria Process 78; Anglican Communion 134, 144; assessment 132; Bahá'í Faith 88, 131–32; Braybrooke, Marcus 133; Catholic Church 113, 134, 135–36, 139–41; conflict among religious traditions 7, 129, 130, 131, 139, 153; indigenous religious traditions 135, 137; intra-faith reconciliation 133; Islam 35, 76–77, 81, 82, 117–18, 144–46; Judaism 135, 143, 145–46; Orthodox Church 74; pluralism 7, 133, 135, 138; Protestantism 74, 134, 136, 141–43, 145, 148,

152–53; rationale and issues
131–32; religious freedom 131,
145; religious unity 133, 138;
Risho Kossei-Kai 108, 138;
secular view 132, 149, 150–53; Sri
Lanka 178–79; Zoroastrianism
131–32, 200; *see also* inter-/
intra-faith movement/organization
inter-/intra-faith movement/
organization 7, 129–53;
"bilateral" dialogue and
cooperation 130, 143–46, 153;
competition 135; contemporary
interfaith 130, 134–43;
development 7, 151; diversity 130;
environmental issues 130, 131,
139, 142, 143, 150; faith-secular
engagement 130, 131, 133, 145,
149–53; global ecumenical bodies
45, 135–43, 153; global governance
148, 152; history 130, 132–34;
leader 129, 130, 132, 135, 139,
140, 142–43, 145–46; NGO 131;
overlapping 135, 153; peace 7, 34,
130, 131, 139–42, 143, 146, 153;
poverty 151, 152, 153; prizes and
honors 146; representativity 135,
138; UN 131, 149, 150–51, 153;
women 137, 138–39, 142, 143;
youth 7, 137, 138–39, 142, 143;
see also interfaith dialogue; inter-/
intra-faith movement/
organization, examples
inter-/intra-faith movement/
organization, examples: IARF
108, 134; Unification Church
146–47 (Moon, Sun Myung
146–47); Universal Peace
Foundation 146; World Congress
of Faiths 134; *see also* ecumenical
movement/organization; FIO;
IFAPA; interfaith dialogue;
Kazakhstan interreligious
dialogue; Parliament of the
World's Religions; Prayer for
Peace; Religions for Peace; URI;
WCC; WCRP; WFDD
international relations 3, 49;
Catholic Church 62; diplomacy 1,
31, 32, 76, 180; interfaith relations

and dialogue 30; neglect of
religion 1–2, 3, 31, 180; religion, a
central factor in modern
international relations 31–32, 35,
92; religious illiteracy 31, 184;
secularization 10, 31, 46; US 2, 32
IofC 94, 95–97; Alcoholics
Anonymous 94, 97; Buchman,
Frank N.D. 95; governance 96–97;
Oxford Movement/MRA 94, 95–97
Iran 154; 1979 Iranian Revolution 1,
75, 190; Hezbollah 124; religion
and state 20, 31, 34, 52, 58–59;
Shi'a Islam 58–59, 77; theocracy
52, 59
Iraq 31, 52, 77, 139
Islam 2, 21, 23, 28–29, 75–82;
charity 81, 122, 155, 163, 170
(*zakat, sadaqah, waqf* 155, 164,
170); contemporary geopolitics
75–77; democracy 29; education
46, 76, 78, 79, 80, 81, 118, 119,
121; five pillars of 122, 127, 155,
170; *Hajj* 75, 125–27; HIV/AIDS
154, 163; human rights 27, 28,
147, 190 (Cairo Declaration of
Human Rights in Islam 79–80);
Ismaili community 45, 77, 165;
Middle Ages 126, 169; Muslim
identity 29, 75, 176; Ottoman
Empire 12, 56, 77; peacebuilding
35, 81, 180; Prophet Mohammed
28, 77, 78, 125, 175; proselytizing
43 (*da'wa* 164); Qur'an 76, 119,
126, 144, 155, 170; religion and
state 20, 28, 51, 53, 58–59
(religious/political authority
relationship 10, 11–12, 29, 78;
state religion 52); Salafist Islam
45, 122; Sharia 58, 79–80, 122,
170; Shi'a Islam 12, 58–59, 77,
124; Sunni Islam 12, 77, 78, 118,
119; UN 79, 163 (UNAOC 76,
148–49); women 28, 78, 81, 82,
118, 119, 126; *see also following
Islam related entries*
Islam, conflict and tensions 29, 31,
76, 81, 121, 144; clash of
civilizations 30, 75–76; Danish
cartoon 76, 118, 131, 144;

Islamophobia 76; Muslim-Christian tensions 30, 76, 144, 189; Sunni/Shi'a schism 12, 77; terrorism 29, 75, 80–81, 187
Islam, countries: China 55; demography 35, 36, 37, 39, 40, 55, 58, 75; India 53, 54; Indonesia 58; Iran 58–59; Morocco 58; Pakistan 58; Saudi Arabia 20, 24, 35, 52, 58; shift of gravity from "north" to "south" 37–38; US 32, 121, 187
Islam, governance 6–7, 58–59; Al-Azhar University 46, 78 (Grand Sheikh of Al-Azhar 78); *fatwa* 78; global institution 50, 77–82; Muslim philanthropy 81–82 (Association of Muslim Philanthropists 78; WCMP 81–82); Muslim World League/ *Rabita* 80–81; WICS 81, 82; World Muslim Congress 78, 81, 181; World Prayer Call Society 78; *see also* OIC
Islam, interfaith dialogue 144–45; Common Word Initiative 35, 76–77, 143–44; Khaled, Amr 117–18; WICS 81, 82; World Congress of Imams and Rabbis for Peace 145–46; *see also* interfaith dialogue
Islam, movements/organizations 116–23; FIO 168, 176; Gulen Movement 94, 116, 120–21 (Gulen, Fethullah 120–21); Hezbollah 97, 123–24, 171; Khaled, Amr 116–18; Muhammadiyah movement 94, 116, 118–19, 172; Muslim Aid 168, 179; Muslim Brotherhood 94, 116, 121–22 (al-Banna, Hassan 121; Qutb, Sayyid 122); NGO 148; NU 94, 116, 119–20; political involvement 119–20, 121, 122, 123; Tijanniyah movement 116; *see also* AKDN *under* Aga Khan; Islamic Relief; Sufism
Islamic Relief 158, 162–63, 168, 172, 174; El Banna, Hany 158, 162, 163; *da'wa* 164; development 158, 163; HIV/AIDS 163;

humanitarian relief 163, 172; partnership 164; UN 163; *zakat, sadaqah, waqf* 164
Israel 85–87; Bahá'í Faith 88–89; Israel–Palestine conflict 29, 76, 81, 86, 124; religion and state 34, 52; State of Israel 7, 14, 85, 86, 87, 135; terrorism 81; *see also* Judaism; Zionism

Jainism 41, 42, 53, 54
Japan 171; Arigatou Foundation 107; Aum Shinrikyo 72, 97, 106, 123; Buddhism 83, 106–9; Happy Science 106; lay movement 94, 106, 107, 108, 138; Myochikai 107; new religions 106–9; peace 106–7, 108; pilgrimage 125; Religions for Peace 138; religious/ political authority relationship 11; Risho Kossei-Kai 83, 94, 106, 107, 108, 138; Soka Gokkai 83, 94, 106, 107–9 (SGI 107); World Mate 106, 108–9; World Peace Prayer Society 45, 106, 107, 109
Jesuit Order 46, 57, 64, 111–12; education 111, 112; Loyola, Ignatius 111; NGO 94, 111; *see also* Catholic Church
Johnston, Douglas 34
Judaism 7, 13–15, 84, 85–89; anti-Semitism 13; charity 169; demography 13, 39, 41, 42, 86–87; FIO 168; the Holocaust 13, 84, 85, 111, 134; interfaith dialogue 135 (Elijah Institute 143; World Congress of Imams and Rabbis for Peace 145–46); Jewish diaspora 12, 13–15, 85, 86; Jewish identity 14, 85, 86, 87; Jewish law 14, 87; Middle Ages 13, 14, 169; Orthodox Judaism 22, 39, 87; persecution 12, 85, 169; philanthropy/*tzedakah* 168, 169; politics 86, 87; proselytizing 13; state religion 52; sub-divisions 87; *tikkun olam* 155, 164, 169; transnational character 50, 84, 85, 87; US 86–88, 158, 164–65; *see also* AJWS; Israel; Judaism, governance; Zionism

Judaism, governance 14, 87; global
institution 50, 84, 87–88 (AJC 87;
B'nai B'rith 87–88; World Jewish
Congress 87)

Kaufmann, Eric 38–39
Kazakhstan interreligious dialogue
142–43; Congress of Leaders of
World and Traditional Religions
142–43; Nazarbayev, Nursultan
A. 142; *see also* interfaith dialogue
Kenya 22, 114, 138, 143
Keppel, Giles 30
King, Martin Luther, Jr. 34
Knights of Malta 60–61; *see also*
Catholic religious order
Kristof, Nicholas 186
Küng, Hans 34, 131, 190, 200

Latin/South America: Catholic
Church 19–20; demography 36,
37, 40, 41, 42
law 20, 21–26, 54; Catholic Church,
Canon law 62, 63; Finnish
Evangelical Lutheran Church 59;
Finnish Orthodox Church Act 52;
France (1905 Law 18; cult 72–73);
human rights 20, 27; India 54;
Islam, Sharia 58, 79–80, 122, 170;
Judaism 14, 87; proselytizing
74–75, 189; US (1998
International Religious Freedom
Act 27; Patriot Act 187)
lay movement: Buddhism 83;
Catholic Church 45, 65, 108, 111,
112, 113, 114, 115, 136, 140;
Japan 94, 106, 107, 108, 138
leader/leadership 130, 185–86;
Abdallah II, King of Jordan 111,
149, 185; Aga Khan 77, 78, 81,
158, 165; Albrigh, Madeleine 1,
31, 185; Blair, Tony 31, 185;
Camdessus, Michel 190; Dalai
Lama 55, 83, 137; G8/G20
summits 129, 130; Gandhi,
Mahatma 34, 94, 97, 105;
globalization 9, 54; Grand Sheikh
of Al-Azhar 78; Iglesias, Enrique
190; India 99, 101–2, 103–5;
interfaith dialogue 129, 130, 132,

135, 139, 140, 142–43, 145–46
(Kazakhstan interreligious
dialogue 142–43; World Congress
of Imams and Rabbis for Peace
145–46); Jones, Jim 72; Khaled,
Amr 116–18; Koehler, Horst 190;
Küng, Hans 34, 131, 190, 200;
Malcolm X 126; Mother Teresa
114–15; Orthodox Church 71;
religious leader and peace 34;
religious movement 98, 99, 101–2,
103, 116–18, 127, 128; secular
leadership and moral void 130;
training 44, 45; UN 190–91;
Wolfensohn, James D. 151, 152,
190–91; *see also* Archbishop of
Canterbury *under* Anglican
Communion, governance;
authority; Catholic Church, Pope
Libya 81, 82
Lutheran Church/Lutheranism 66;
Finland 52, 59; governance 68;
Lutheran World Federation 68,
181; state religion 52; *see also*
IFAPA; Protestantism

Maritain, Jacques 188
Marxism/Marx, Karl 16, 18, 104;
see also communism
Mauritania 20, 23, 52
MDGs (Millennium Development
Goals) 8, 148, 156–57, 185, 190,
194; 2000 Millennium General
Assembly 129; Evangelical Church,
Micah Challenge 70; FIO 156–57,
172, 183; partnership 139, 172, 185,
189; Religions for Peace 139, 148
Mennonites 35, 66, 181, 181;
Eastern Mennonite University
180; peacebuilding 35, 66, 180; *see
also* Protestantism
Methodist Church 66, 69; UMCOR
179; *see also* Protestantism
Micklethwait, John: *God is Back* 2
Middle Ages: charity 169;
Christianity 11, 64, 124, 169;
Islam 126, 169; Judaism 13, 14,
169; pilgrimage 124
Middle East: 2011 Arab uprisings
29, 59, 122; FIO 171, 172;

tensions in 29, 78, 135, 186; *see also* Egypt; Iran; Israel; Libya; Palestine; Saudi Arabia
migration/diaspora 10, 48, 56, 84, 92; globalization 9, 13, 48, 54; Jewish diaspora 12, 13–15, 85, 86; *see also* pilgrimage
missionary/religious mission 118, 170; Catholic Church 66; democracy 197; ecumenical movement 74; Europe, "reverse missionary" trend 70; Maryknoll organizations 115; Mormon missionary 66; Protestantism 66, 69
modernity 2, 48, 152, 184, 191, 192; contemporary trends/dynamics 6, 10, 31–33, 39, 42–43, 46 184 (Christianity, shift of gravity beyond Europe and North America 6, 10, 37–38; fundamentalism and extremism 6, 10, 32, 39, 184; growing number of charismatic, evangelical, pentecostal churches 6, 42, 70; interfaith dialogue 133, 153; pluralism 6, 10, 33, 47, 133, 184; religious movement 6, 7); need for sharper attention to religion 1–3, 31, 49, 180–81, 185–86; secularization 47, 152, 191
monotheism 88, 120; *see also* Christianity; Islam; Judaism
moral issues 47; ethical diversity 47; Falun Gong/Falun Dafa 110; Global Ethic 137; MRA 95–96 (moral capitalism 97); the Pope as moral authority 62; religious institution 6, 129; secular leadership and moral void 130
Morocco 35, 78, 138; Christian-Muslim relationship 145; Fes Festival of Global Sacred Music 35; religion and state 20, 23, 52, 58, 78
Mozambique 19, 23, 112, 113, 142, 173

the Netherlands 19, 150, 157
New Religions 41, 42, 73, 90, 93, 106–11, 135, 197; *see also* Japan; Paganism

NGO (non-governmental organization) 46; "brief-case"/ "cowboy" NGO 173, 179; China 55; Christianity 148, 179; FIO 156, 168, 179, 182, 189; India 99, 101, 102; interfaith dialogue 131; Islam 148; Jesuit Order 94, 111; Religions for Peace 138; religious movement 93, 94, 96, 101, 102, 106, 110, 111, 112; UN 148, 190; *see also* civil society; FBO; FIO
Nigeria 23, 34, 45, 68, 80, 114

OIC (Organization of Islamic Cooperation) 7, 27, 78, 79–80, 189; Cairo Declaration of Human Rights in Islam 79–80; IDB 79, 80; ISESCO 79; UN 79
Orthodox Church 71–72; Armenian Apostolic Church 71, 196; China 55; Coptic Orthodox Church of Alexandria 71, 72; demography 40; Eastern Catholic Churches 64; Eritrean Orthodox Tewahedo Church 71–72; Ethiopian Orthodox Church 71; Finland 52, 59; governance 6, 50, 71–72; interfaith dialogue 74; Malankara Orthodox Church of India 71; Oriental Orthodox Church 71; Patriarch/Metropolitan 71 (Cyril VI 72; Patriarch of Constantinople 71); state religion 52; Syriac Orthodox Church 71; WCC 74
Oxford Movement/MRA *see* IofC

Paganism 51, 90–91, 137; Neopaganism 90; polytheism 90; US 90–91; Wicca 51, 90–91
Pakistan 20, 77, 80, 142; religion and state 20, 23, 52, 58, 170; World Muslim Congress 82; *zakat* 170
Palestine 24; Hamas 7, 171; Israel–Palestine conflict 29, 76, 81, 86, 124
Parliament of the World's Religions 45, 135, 136–37, 138, 146, 148; 1893 World Parliament of Religions 7, 133–34, 136 (Bonney,

Charles 133); 1993 World
Parliament of Religions 134, 136;
Carus Prize 146; Global Ethic
137; governance 137; women 137;
youth 137; *see also* interfaith
dialogue
partnership 8, 87, 152, 167; aid
coordination 184–85, 188–89;
Earth Charter 150; Islamic Relief
164; MDGs 139, 172, 185, 189;
multi-religious partnership 138, 142,
172, 179; Religions for Peace 138,
139; URI 142; World Bank 151–52,
190–92; World Vision 161, 162
peace 34, 180; disarmament 108,
180; interfaith dialogue 7, 34, 130,
131, 139–42, 143, 146, 153; Japan
106–7, 108; Pax Christi 136, 180,
181; Pilgrimage for Peace 136,
140; religion as factor for 6, 8, 10,
34, 155, 178, 180, 183; religious
leader 34; religious movement 6,
102, 106–7, 108; Risho Kossei-Kai
108; Sant' Egidio community 108,
112–13, 180; World Peace Prayer
Society 106, 107, 109; *see also*
conflict; human security;
humanitarian relief; peacebuilding/
peacemaking; Prayer for Peace;
Religions for Peace
peacebuilding/peacemaking 5, 10,
33–35, 146; Buddhism 35;
Catholic Church 35, 157; FIO
155, 157, 177, 180, 181, 183;
IAHV 101; Islam 35, 81, 180;
Mennonites 35, 66, 180; Peace
Churches 35, 66, 180; Quakers 35,
66, 180; religious actor 180;
Sarvodaya Movement 105;
Seventh-day Adventists 66, 180;
WCC 74; *see also* conflict; human
security; peace
persecution 12, 50; of Bahá'ís 88; of
Jews 12, 85, 169 (the Holocaust
13, 84, 85, 111, 134)
philanthropy 109; charity 169, 170;
Islam 78, 81–82; Judaism 168, 169
Philpott, Daniel: *God's Century* 2
pilgrimage 61, 98, 124–27; Chaucer,
Geoffrey: *Canterbury Tales* 124;

Christianity 124–25; globalization
75, 98, 124, 125, 127; *Hajj* 75,
125–27; India 125; Japan 125;
Pilgrimage for Peace 136, 140
pluralism 6, 53, 56; constitutional
approach 27–28; a contemporary
trend 6, 10, 33, 47, 133, 184;
ethical diversity 46; globalization
184; interfaith dialogue 7, 133,
135, 138; Ottoman Empire 12, 56;
see also interfaith dialogue;
tolerance
politics 1, 10–12, 15–18, 32, 51; 1755
Lisbon earthquake 17–18;
extremism 32; FBO 45; French
Revolution 16–17, 18; global
politics 2, 32, 39, 80–81, 92, 94,
184, 185; Hinduism 84; Islam 28,
119–20, 121, 122, 123; Judaism
86, 87; Marxism 16, 18–19;
religion, neglected in international
relations 1–2, 3, 31, 180; religion,
political role 12, 18, 33, 51, 53;
religious movement 97, 119–20,
121, 122, 123; Soka Gokkai 108;
see also Communism; religion and
state; state; Zionism
polytheism 90; *see also* Paganism
poverty 156–57, 191; Amma, the
"Hugging Saint" 104–5; AJWS
164; Focolare movement 113, 114;
interfaith dialogue 151, 152, 153;
Islamic Relief 163; Jesuit Order
112; Make Poverty History 163;
Missionaries of Charity 114;
Religions for Peace 139; Sisters of
Charity 64; Tijaniyyah Order 123;
Tzu Chi Foundation 110–11;
WCC 74, 131, 152–53; *see also*
Caritas Internationalis; charity;
development
Prayer for Peace 135–36, 139–41;
John Paul II, Pope 135, 139;
Sant'Egidio community 136, 140;
see also Catholic Church;
interfaith dialogue
proselytizing/evangelizing 5, 43, 192;
2011 code of conduct: "Christian
Witness in a Multi-Religious
World" 75; China 55; Christianity

43, 111, 170; development 189; ecumenical movement/ organization 74–75; FIO 172; humanitarian relief 189; indigenous religious traditions 43, 50; Islam 43, 164; Judaism 13; law 74–75, 189; Protestantism 42–43, 66, 145; religious freedom 20, 74–75, 185, 189; World Vision 161; *see also* conversion

Protestantism: Africa 66; charity 170; colonial era 66, 67, 69, 72; contemporary expansion 6, 42, 70; demography 40, 65, 69, 70; interfaith dialogue 74, 134, 136, 141–43, 145, 148, 152–53; missionary purpose 66, 69; proselytizing 42–43, 66, 145; Protestant Reformation 11, 65, 67; transnational character 65, 66, 67, 68, 69–70; Treaty of Westphalia 16; US 65, 67; *see also* Protestantism, denominations and governance; World Vision

Protestantism, denominations and governance 6, 50, 65–71, 74; African independent churches 66, 72; Baptist Church 66, 68–69; Church of Latter-Day Saints 66, 69, 111, 174; decentralization 66; Episcopal Church 66, 67; Jehovah's Witnesses 73, 111; Methodist Church 66, 69; Peace Churches 35, 66, 180; Pentecostal Church 6, 42, 66, 70; Presbyterianism 66, 69; Quakers/Society of Friends 35, 66, 69, 180; Seventh-day Adventists 66, 69; *see also* Anglican Communion; Charismatic Church; Evangelical Church; Lutheran Church; Mennonites; Methodist Church; WCC

Red Cross movement 61, 109, 163; Red Crescent 163, 171

religion: Africa 37, 176; contemporary trends/dynamics 6, 10, 31–33, 39, 42–43, 46 184; criticism 19, 152, 191, 192; definition 3–4, 5; "great

awakening" of religion 27; need for sharper attention to 1–3, 31, 49, 180–81, 185–86; revival of religion 30, 31, 32–33; *see also following* religion *related entries*; faith; spirituality

religion and state 19–28, 34, 51–59, 185, 196; Anglican Communion 52, 67; Brazil 21, 53, 57; Buddhism 52; Cambodia 20, 52; Catholic Church 52, 57; China 53, 55–56; church/state relationship 49–50, 52, 53, 185; constitutional approaches 52 (religious freedom 20, 21–26, 27–28, 54, 55, 57; religious rights 27–28); corruption 191, 202; Egypt 18, 22, 52; Europe 51; Finland 52, 53, 59; France 15, 16–18 (*laïcité* principle 18); India 53–54; Iran 20, 31, 34, 52, 58–59; Islam 20, 28, 51, 52, 53, 58–59; Israel 34, 52; Morocco 20, 23, 52, 58, 78; Pakistan 20, 23, 52, 58, 170; religious/political authority relationship 10–12, 15–18, 29, 51, 78 (*Cuius regio, eius religio* 12; *une foi, une loi, un roi* 15); Saudi Arabia 20, 24, 52, 58, 170; Sri Lanka 25, 52; theocracy 51, 52, 59, 185, 196; Treaty of Westphalia 15–16, 51; US 51, 185; *see also* politics

religion, global impact 9, 186, 191, 194; Anglican Communion 67–68; Buddhism 50, 83, 94; Catholic Church 6, 50; fundamentalism 10; global religious institution 5, 6, 50, 84, 92; health 169; Hinduism 50; Humanism 91; Judaism 50, 84, 85, 87; Protestantism 65, 66, 67, 68, 69–70; religious movement 94, 97, 98–99, 114, 127–28; Sikhism 84; *see also* FIO; global religious institution; interfaith dialogue

Religions for Peace/WCRP (World Conference of Religions for Peace) 45, 108, 135, 137–39, 148, 180; governance 138; MDGs 139, 148; NGO 138; partnership 138, 139; peace 139, 180; "shared security" 139; UN 138; Vendley, William

139; women 138–39; youth
138–39; *see also* interfaith
dialogue
religious freedom 5, 9, 27, 185, 189;
apostasy 20; Bahá'í Faith 88;
blasphemy 20, 23; Brazil 57;
China 55; constitutional
approaches to 20, 21–26, 27–28,
54, 55, 57; Europe 51; freedom
from rule by religion 9; freedom
of belief 20; freedom to practice a
religion 9, 20; freedom to worship
20, 27, 54; human right 8, 20, 27;
India 54; interfaith dialogue 131,
145; proselytizing 20, 74–75, 185,
189; religious minorities 27;
Universal Declaration of Human
Rights 9, 20, 27; US 12, 27 (1998
International Religious Freedom
Act 27); Voltaire 17; *see also*
religious minorities
religious identity 1, 12, 32, 33, 180;
cultural assimilation 39;
fundamentalism 39; India 53;
Jewish identity 14, 85, 86, 87;
Muslim identity 29, 75, 176
religious illiteracy 2, 31, 152, 184, 185
religious institution 4, 44–46; civil
society 44, 46; globalization
48–49, 84, 184; governance,
overlapping 49; importance 92,
129; institutional confidence 44;
major categories 6, 44–46; moral
values 6, 129; national level
51–59; NGO 46; secular society 5,
129; technology 6; US 46;
volunteer 44
religious minorities 27, 87;
discrimination 12, 24, 27; France
73; India 53; persecution 12, 27,
50; *see also* religious freedom
religious movement 7, 93–128;
advocacy 106, 115, 122, 124;
Buddhism 83, 94, 106–11;
Christianity 111–16; cult/sect 93;
diversity 93–94, 98, 111, 127;
functions 94, 127; global impact
94, 97, 98–99, 114, 127–28;
governance 94; India 98–106;
Islam 116–23; leader 98, 99,

101–2, 103, 116–18, 127, 128;
New Religions 93, 106–11, 127;
NGO 93, 94, 96, 101, 102, 106,
110, 111, 112; peace 6, 102,
106–7, 108; pilgrimage 98,
124–27; political involvement 97,
119–20, 121, 122, 123; spiritual
nature 93, 94, 101; violence and
terrorism 123–24, 128; *see also* FIO
religious unity 133, 138; Buddhist
unity 83; Christian unity 11, 70,
75, 113; Muslim unity 81; *see also*
interfaith dialogue; pluralism
Rwanda 24, 70, 157

Sampson, Cynthia 34
Sant' Egidio community 7, 94, 111,
112–13; interfaith dialogue 113,
136, 140; lay movement 45, 65,
112, 136, 140; peace 108, 112–13,
180; *see also* Catholic Church
Saudi Arabia: *Hajj* 75, 125–27; IDB
80; Islam 20, 24, 35, 52, 58;
Muslim World League/*Rabita* 80;
OIC 78; religion and state 20, 24,
52, 58, 170; *zakat* 170
SBNR (spiritual but not religious) 33
schism 71; Islam, Sunni/Shi'a schism
12, 77; Protestantism 65, 66;
Reformation 65
Scientology 73, 97
sect *see* cult/sect
secular/secularism 2, 5, 9, 31, 39, 47,
152, 191; academic institutions 2;
definition 3, 4–5, 47; Europe 2, 31;
France 16–17, 18; India 53, 54;
interfaith dialogue 132, 149,
150–53 (faith-secular engagement
130, 131, 133, 145, 149–53);
international relations 10, 31, 46;
religious/secular actors
disconnection 181, 185, 186–89,
191–93; religious/secular authority
distinction 9, 15; secular
leadership and moral void 130;
secular state 16, 18; UN 148;
US 2, 31
Senegal 24, 122, 143
Seventh-day Adventist Church 66,
69; ADRA 167, 168

Shah, Timothy Samuel: *God's Century* 2
Shintoism 41, 42, 107, 108, 140, 143, 171
Sikhism 41, 42, 53, 54, 84, 171
social cohesion 10, 178, 192
Somalia 25, 31, 52
South Africa 25, 136, 163
South Sudan 34, 74, 163
Spinoza, Baruch 16
Spiritism 41, 42
spiritual movement 93, 94, 101, 142; Falun Gong/Falun Dafa 110; *see also* Sri Sri Ravi Shankar
spirituality 3, 4; *see also* faith; religion
Sri Lanka 34, 35, 115; Buddhism 52, 83, 179; religion and state 25, 52; religious tensions 34, 178–79, 189; Sarvodaya Movement 99, 105, 156 (Ariyaratne, A.T. 99, 105; SEEDS 105); WFB 83
Sri Sri Ravi Shankar 84, 99, 101–2; Art of Living 45, 94, 101, 102; IAHV 101, 102; SSRVM, VVKI, VVMVP 102; UN 101, 102; *see also* India
Stalin, Joseph 33, 62
state: fragile state 181; the Holy See 50, 60, 111, 147–48, 190; nation-state 9, 13, 15–16; secular norms, rise of 9; secular state 16, 18; state religion 52, 53, 196; Treaty of Westphalia 15–16, 51; *see also* authority; politics; religion and state
Sudan 20, 25, 34, 126, 170
Sufism 45, 77–78, 119, 122–23; peacebuilding 35; Rumi, Jalal ad-Din 78, 122; Tijaniyyah Order 122–23; *see also* Islam
Switzerland 52, 187
syncretism 56, 119

Taiwan 26; Buddhism 83, 109–10; Dharma Drum Mountain 83, 109; Tzu Chi Foundation 109–10 (TIMA 109)
Taoism/Daoism 41, 42, 55, 110, 143
technology 6, 10, 39, 105, 127; Islam 118, 126

Templeton Foundation 46; Templeton Prize 81, 101, 146
terrorism 1, 81, 123–24, 130, 144, 190; 9/11 attacks 1, 29, 75, 144, 145; Al Qaeda 75, 117; Aum Shinrikyo 123; financial flows 187; Hezbollah 124; Islam 29, 75, 80–81, 187; religion, role of 29, 31, 117, 181; religious movement 123–24, 128; *see also* conflict
Thailand 26, 52, 79, 83
theocracy 51, 52, 59, 185, 196
Toft, Monica Duffy: *God's Century* 2
tolerance 11, 12; Brazil 56; Gulen Movement 121; India 53, 54; Voltaire 17; *see also* pluralism
Treaty of Westphalia 15–16, 51
Turkey 18, 120; Gulen Movement 94, 116, 120–21
Tutu, Desmond 34

UK (United Kingdom) 3, 18; Alliance of Religions and Conservation 139; Anglican Communion 12, 19, 52, 67; Blair, Tony 31, 185; CAFOD 157, 158, 164; Catholic Church 12, 67; DfID 3; religious/political authority relationship 12; University of Bradford 180
UN (United Nations): 1994 Conference on Population and Development 28, 147, 190; 1995 Beijing Conference on Women 28, 147, 190; Annan, Kofi 76; communism 19; DESA 151; ECOSOC 96, 138; gender rights 28; India 99, 101, 102, 103; NGO 148, 190; OCHA 171; secular principles 148; UN Charter 147; UN Convention against Corruption 163; UNAIDS 151, 175; UNAOC 76, 148–49, 151; UNDP 139; UNESCO 82, 102, 138, 146, 149, 151, 189–90; UNICEF 82, 138, 151, 190; Universal Declaration of Human Rights 8, 9, 20, 27, 80, 147, 188; women 147, 148, 201; *see also* UN, religion/ religious institution; UNFPA

UN, religion/religious institution
2–3, 8, 130, 131, 147–49, 150–51,
153, 185, 189–93; Anglican
Communion 68; Bahá'í Faith 84,
88; Holy See 147–48, 190;
indigenous religious traditions 51,
90; interfaith dialogue 131, 149,
150–51, 153; Islam 76, 79, 148–49,
163; Knights of Malta 61;
Religions for Peace 138; "spiritual
council" 130; Sri Sri Ravi Shankar
101, 102; URI 136, 141, 148
UNFPA (UN Population Fund)
149, 190; interfaith dialogue 131,
150–51; Obaid, Thoraya 149, 150;
reproductive health and human
rights 149, 150
URI (United Religions Initiative)
136, 141–42, 148; CCs 142;
environmental issues 142;
partnership 142; Swing, William
141; UN 136, 141, 148; women
142; youth 142; *see also* interfaith
dialogue; Protestantism
US (United States of America):
Albrigh, Madeleine 31, 185; (*The
Mighty and the Almighty* 1);
Chicago Council on Global
Affairs 2, 32; Clinton, Hillary 190;
Clinton, William J. 31; colonial
era 12; Constitution 12; Obama,
Barack 2, 32; religion and state
51, 185; religion, importance in
foreign policy 2, 32; religious
freedom 12, 27 (1998
International Religious Freedom
Act 27); SBNF 33; secularism 2,
31; US-Moroccan relationship
145; Vendley, William 139;
university (Georgetown University
180, 202; Notre Dame University
180; Yale University 144); *see also*
US, religion/religious institution
US, religion/religious institution 51,
185; Branch Davidians 45, 72;
Brookings Institution 144;
Buddhism 83; Catholic Church
61, 111, 115; demography 33, 36;
Episcopal Church 67; FBO 46;
Humanism 91–92; Islam 32

(Gulen Movement 121; Patriot
Act 187); Judaism 86–88, 158,
164–65; Paganism 90–91;
Parliament of the World's Religions
135, 136–37; Protestantism 65, 67;
World Vision 161, 162

vegetarianism 54, 94, 103, 174
Voltaire16, 17–18
volunteer 100, 104–5, 109, 110, 111,
112, 156, 183; AKDN 165;
religious institution 44

WCC (World Council of Churches)
7, 45, 134, 181; ecumenical
organization 74; *Lead Us Not Into
Temptation* 152; Orthodox Church
74; poverty relief 74, 131, 152–53;
Protestantism 74, 134; WCC/World
Bank/IMF dialogue 74, 131,
152–53; *see also* interfaith dialogue
WFDD (World Faiths Development
Dialogue) 145, 191; Cambodia
201; Wolfensohn, James D.
151–52; World Bank 151–52; *see
also* interfaith dialogue
WHO (World Health Organization)
74, 151
Witte, John 20, 27
women: 1994 Conference on
Population and Development 28,
147, 190; 1995 Beijing Conference
on Women 28, 147, 190; Anglican
Communion 68; Bahá'í Faith 84,
88; Brahma Kumaris 102; Catholic
Church 28, 61, 64; conflict, role in
181; gender equality 28, 186–87;
IFAPA 143; interfaith dialogue 137,
138–39, 142, 143; Islam 28, 78
(*Hajj* 126; Muhammadiyah
movement 118, 119; Sisters in
Islam 81; WICS 82); Parliament of
the World's Religions 137; Religions
for Peace 138–39; religious
movement 94; rights 5, 28, 81, 84,
88, 147, 188, 190 (reproductive
health and human rights 28, 147,
150, 165, 188, 190, 192, 201); role
in family and society 184, 186–87;
Tzu Chi Foundation 110; URI

142; "Western feminism" 186–87; *see also* gender issues; UNFPA
Wooldridge, Adrian: *God is Back* 2
World Bank 8, 74, 151; interfaith dialogue 131, 145, 151–53; partnership 151–52, 190–92; WCC/World Bank/IMF dialogue 131, 152–53; WFDD 151–52, 191; Wolfensohn, James D. 151–52, 190–91
World Economic Forum 8, 185; Council of One Hundred 76, 144
World Vision 8, 45, 156, 157–58, 160–62, 172, 182; child sponsorship 158, 160, 161, 162; development 158, 161; ecumenism 161; governance 161–62; Pierce, Bob 160; proselytizing 161; staff 157; Stearns, Richard 161; US 161, 162; WVI 161–62; *see also* Evangelical Church

World War II 14, 74, 85, 86, 96, 107, 113, 134

yoga 54, 99, 104
youth 7; FIO 175; IAHV 101; IFAPA 143; interfaith dialogue 7, 137, 138–39, 142, 143; Khaled, Amr 116–18; Muhammadiyah movement 118, 119; Parliament of the World's Religions 137; Religions for Peace 138–39; Sarvodaya Movement 105; URI 142

Zionism 13–14, 29, 85–86, 169; 1897 Zionist Congress 14, 86; Herzl, Theodore 86; *see also* Judaism
Zoroastrianism 41, 42, 50, 54, 84, 88, 200; demography 88; interfaith dialogue 131–32, 200; religious/ political authority relationship 11; Zarathushtra 88

Routledge Global Institutions Series

75 Global Institutions of Religion (2013)
Ancient movers, modern shakers
by Katherine Marshall (Georgetown University)

74 Crisis of Global Sustainability (2013)
by Tapio Kanninen

73 The Group of Twenty (G20) (2013)
by Andrew F. Cooper (University of Waterloo) and Ramesh Thakur (Australian National University)

72 Peacebuilding (2013)
From concept to commission
by Rob Jenkins (Hunter College, CUNY)

71 Human Rights and Humanitarian Norms, Strategic Framing, and Intervention (2013)
Lessons for the Responsibility to Protect
by Melissa Labonte (Fordham University)

70 Feminist Strategies in International Governance (2013)
edited by Gülay Caglar (Humboldt University, Berlin), Elisabeth Prügl (the Graduate Institute of International and Development Studies, Geneva), and Susanne Zwingel (the State University of New York, Potsdam)

69 The Migration Industry and the Commercialization of International Migration (2013)
edited by Thomas Gammeltoft-Hansen (Danish Institute for International Studies) and Ninna Nyberg Sørensen (Danish Institute for International Studies)

68 Integrating Africa (2013)
Decolonization's legacies, sovereignty, and the African Union
by Martin Welz (University of Konstanz)

67 **Trade, Poverty, Development (2013)**
Getting beyond the WTO's Doha deadlock
edited by Rorden Wilkinson (University of Manchester) and James Scott (University of Manchester)

66 **The United Nations Industrial Development Organization (UNIDO) (2012)**
by Stephen Browne (FUNDS Project)

65 **The Millennium Development Goals and Beyond (2012)**
Global development after 2015
edited by Rorden Wilkinson (University of Manchester) and David Hulme (University of Manchester)

64 **International Organizations as Self-Directed Actors (2012)**
A framework for analysis
edited by Joel E. Oestreich (Drexel University)

63 **Maritime Piracy (2012)**
by Robert Haywood (One Earth Future Foundation) and Roberta Spivak (One Earth Future Foundation)

62 **United Nations High Commissioner for Refugees (UNHCR) (2nd edition, 2012)**
by Gil Loescher (University of Oxford), Alexander Betts (University of Oxford), and James Milner (University of Toronto)

61 **International Law, International Relations, and Global Governance (2012)**
by Charlotte Ku (University of Illinois)

60 **Global Health Governance (2012)**
by Sophie Harman (City University, London)

59 **The Council of Europe (2012)**
by Martyn Bond (University of London)

58 **The Security Governance of Regional Organizations (2011)**
edited by Emil J. Kirchner (University of Essex) and Roberto Domínguez (Suffolk University)

57 **The United Nations Development Programme and System (2011)**
by Stephen Browne (FUNDS Project)

56 The South Asian Association for Regional Cooperation (2011)
An emerging collaboration architecture
by Lawrence Sáez (University of London)

55 The UN Human Rights Council (2011)
by Bertrand G. Ramcharan (Geneva Graduate Institute of International and Development Studies)

54 The Responsibility to Protect (2011)
Cultural perspectives in the Global South
edited by Rama Mani (University of Oxford) and Thomas G. Weiss (The CUNY Graduate Center)

53 The International Trade Centre (2011)
Promoting exports for development
by Stephen Browne (FUNDS Project) and Sam Laird (University of Nottingham)

52 The Idea of World Government (2011)
From ancient times to the twenty-first century
by James A. Yunker (Western Illinois University)

51 Humanitarianism Contested (2011)
Where angels fear to tread
by Michael Barnett (George Washington University) and Thomas G. Weiss (The CUNY Graduate Center)

50 The Organization of American States (2011)
Global governance away from the media
by Monica Herz (Catholic University, Rio de Janeiro)

49 Non-Governmental Organizations in World Politics (2011)
The construction of global governance
by Peter Willetts (City University, London)

48 The Forum on China-Africa Cooperation (FOCAC) (2011)
by Ian Taylor (University of St. Andrews)

47 Global Think Tanks (2011)
Policy networks and governance
by James G. McGann (University of Pennsylvania) with Richard Sabatini

46 United Nations Educational, Scientific and Cultural Organization (UNESCO) (2011)
Creating norms for a complex world
by J.P. Singh (Georgetown University)

45 The International Labour Organization (2011)
Coming in from the cold
by Steve Hughes (Newcastle University) and Nigel Haworth (University of Auckland)

44 Global Poverty (2010)
How global governance is failing the poor
by David Hulme (University of Manchester)

43 Global Governance, Poverty, and Inequality (2010)
edited by Jennifer Clapp (University of Waterloo) and Rorden Wilkinson (University of Manchester)

42 Multilateral Counter-Terrorism (2010)
The global politics of cooperation and contestation
by Peter Romaniuk (John Jay College of Criminal Justice, CUNY)

41 Governing Climate Change (2010)
by Peter Newell (University of East Anglia) and Harriet A. Bulkeley (Durham University)

40 The UN Secretary-General and Secretariat (2nd edition, 2010)
by Leon Gordenker (Princeton University)

39 Preventive Human Rights Strategies (2010)
by Bertrand G. Ramcharan (Geneva Graduate Institute of International and Development Studies)

38 African Economic Institutions (2010)
by Kwame Akonor (Seton Hall University)

37 Global Institutions and the HIV/AIDS Epidemic (2010)
Responding to an international crisis
by Franklyn Lisk (University of Warwick)

36 Regional Security (2010)
The capacity of international organizations
by Rodrigo Tavares (United Nations University)

35 The Organisation for Economic Co-operation and Development (2009)
by Richard Woodward (University of Hull)

34 Transnational Organized Crime (2009)
by Frank Madsen (University of Cambridge)

33 The United Nations and Human Rights (2nd edition, 2009)
A guide for a new era
by Julie A. Mertus (American University)

32 The International Organization for Standardization (2009)
Global governance through voluntary consensus
by Craig N. Murphy (Wellesley College) and JoAnne Yates (Massachusetts Institute of Technology)

31 Shaping the Humanitarian World (2009)
by Peter Walker (Tufts University) and Daniel G. Maxwell (Tufts University)

30 Global Food and Agricultural Institutions (2009)
by John Shaw

29 Institutions of the Global South (2009)
by Jacqueline Anne Braveboy-Wagner (City College of New York, CUNY)

28 International Judicial Institutions (2009)
The architecture of international justice at home and abroad
by Richard J. Goldstone (Retired Justice of the Constitutional Court of South Africa) and Adam M. Smith (Harvard University)

27 The International Olympic Committee (2009)
The governance of the Olympic system
by Jean-Loup Chappelet (IDHEAP Swiss Graduate School of Public Administration) and Brenda Kübler-Mabbott

26 The World Health Organization (2009)
by Kelley Lee (London School of Hygiene and Tropical Medicine)

25 Internet Governance (2009)
The new frontier of global institutions
by John Mathiason (Syracuse University)

24 Institutions of the Asia-Pacific (2009)
ASEAN, APEC, and beyond
by Mark Beeson (University of Birmingham)

23 United Nations High Commissioner for Refugees (UNHCR) (2008)
The politics and practice of refugee protection into the twenty-first century
by Gil Loescher (University of Oxford), Alexander Betts (University of Oxford), and James Milner (University of Toronto)

22 Contemporary Human Rights Ideas (2008)
by Bertrand G. Ramcharan (Geneva Graduate Institute of International and Development Studies)

21 The World Bank (2008)
From reconstruction to development to equity
by Katherine Marshall (Georgetown University)

20 The European Union (2008)
by Clive Archer (Manchester Metropolitan University)

19 The African Union (2008)
Challenges of globalization, security, and governance
by Samuel M. Makinda (Murdoch University) and F. Wafula Okumu (McMaster University)

18 Commonwealth (2008)
Inter- and non-state contributions to global governance
by Timothy M. Shaw (Royal Roads University)

17 The World Trade Organization (2007)
Law, economics, and politics
by Bernard M. Hoekman (World Bank) and Petros C. Mavroidis (Columbia University)

16 A Crisis of Global Institutions? (2007)
Multilateralism and international security
by Edward Newman (University of Birmingham)

15 UN Conference on Trade and Development (2007)
by Ian Taylor (University of St. Andrews) and Karen Smith (University of Stellenbosch)

14 The Organization for Security and Co-operation in Europe (2007)
by David J. Galbreath (University of Aberdeen)

13 The International Committee of the Red Cross (2007)
A neutral humanitarian actor
by David P. Forsythe (University of Nebraska) and Barbara Ann Rieffer-Flanagan (Central Washington University)

12 The World Economic Forum (2007)
A multi-stakeholder approach to global governance
by Geoffrey Allen Pigman (Bennington College)

11 The Group of 7/8 (2007)
by Hugo Dobson (University of Sheffield)

10 The International Monetary Fund (2007)
Politics of conditional lending
by James Raymond Vreeland (Georgetown University)

9 The North Atlantic Treaty Organization (2007)
The enduring alliance
by Julian Lindley-French (Center for Applied Policy, University of Munich)

8 The World Intellectual Property Organization (2006)
Resurgence and the development agenda
by Chris May (University of the West of England)

7 The UN Security Council (2006)
Practice and promise
by Edward C. Luck (Columbia University)

6 Global Environmental Institutions (2006)
by Elizabeth R. DeSombre (Wellesley College)

5 Internal Displacement (2006)
Conceptualization and its consequences
by Thomas G. Weiss (The CUNY Graduate Center) and David A. Korn

4 The UN General Assembly (2005)
by M.J. Peterson (University of Massachusetts, Amherst)

3 United Nations Global Conferences (2005)
by Michael G. Schechter (Michigan State University)

2 The UN Secretary-General and Secretariat (2005)
by Leon Gordenker (Princeton University)

1 The United Nations and Human Rights (2005)
A guide for a new era
by Julie A. Mertus (American University)

Books currently under contract include:

The Regional Development Banks
Lending with a regional flavor
by Jonathan R. Strand (University of Nevada)

Millennium Development Goals (MDGs)
For a people-centered development agenda?
by Sakiko Fukada-Parr (The New School)

UNICEF
by Richard Jolly (University of Sussex)

The Bank for International Settlements
The politics of global financial supervision in the age of high finance
by Kevin Ozgercin (SUNY College at Old Westbury)

International Migration
by Khalid Koser (Geneva Centre for Security Policy)

Human Development
by Richard Ponzio

The International Monetary Fund (2nd edition)
Politics of conditional lending
by James Raymond Vreeland (Georgetown University)

The UN Global Compact
by Catia Gregoratti (Lund University)

Institutions for Women's Rights
by Charlotte Patton (York College, CUNY) and Carolyn Stephenson (University of Hawaii)

International Aid
by Paul Mosley (University of Sheffield)

Global Consumer Policy
by Karsten Ronit (University of Copenhagen)

The Changing Political Map of Global Governance
by Anthony Payne (University of Sheffield) and Stephen Robert Buzdugan (Manchester Metropolitan University)

Coping with Nuclear Weapons
by W. Pal Sidhu

Private Foundations and Development Partnerships
by Michael Moran (Swinburne University of Technology)

The International Politics of Human Rights
edited by Monica Serrano (Colegio de Mexico) and Thomas G. Weiss (The CUNY Graduate Center)

Twenty-First-Century Democracy Promotion in the Americas
by Jorge Heine (The Centre for International Governance Innovation) and Brigitte Weiffen (University of Konstanz)

EU Environmental Policy and Climate Change
by Henrik Selin (Boston University) and Stacy VanDeveer (University of New Hampshire)

Making Global Institutions Work
Power, accountability and change
edited by Kate Brennan

The Society for Worldwide Interbank Financial Telecommunication (SWIFT)
by Susan Scott (London School of Economics and Political Science) and Markos Zachariadis (University of Cambridge)

Global Governance and China
The dragon's learning curve
edited by Scott Kennedy (Indiana University)

Rules, Politics and the International Criminal Court
Committing to the court
by Yvonne Marie Dutton (Indiana University)

The Politics of Global Economic Surveillance
by Martin S. Edwards (Seton Hall University)

Mercy and Mercenaries
Humanitarian Agencies and Private Security Companies
by Peter Hoffman

Regional Organizations in the Middle East
James Worrall (University of Leeds)

Reforming the UN Development System
The Politics of Incrementalism
by Silke Weinlich (Duisburg-Essen University)

Corporate Social Responsibility
by Oliver Williams (University of Notre Dame)

For further information regarding the series, please contact:
Craig Fowlie, Publisher, Politics & International Studies
Taylor & Francis
2 Park Square, Milton Park, Abingdon
Oxford OX14 4RN, UK
+44 (0)207 842 2057 Tel
+44 (0)207 842 2302 Fax
Craig.Fowlie@tandf.co.uk
www.routledge.com